Grant Morrison and the
Superhero Renaissance

Grant Morrison and the Superhero Renaissance

Critical Essays

Edited by
DARRAGH GREENE
and KATE RODDY

McFarland & Company, Inc., Publishers
Jefferson, North Carolina

LIBRARY OF CONGRESS CATALOGUING-IN-PUBLICATION DATA

Grant Morrison and the superhero renaissance : critical essays / edited by Darragh Greene and Kate Roddy.
    p.   cm.
Includes bibliographical references and index.

ISBN 978-0-7864-7810-1 (softcover : acid free paper) ∞
ISBN 978-1-4766-2233-0 (ebook)

1. Morrison, Grant—Criticism and interpretation. 2. Superheroes in literature. 3. Comic books, strips, etc.—History and criticism. 4. Graphic novels—History and criticism. I. Greene, Darragh, editor. II. Roddy, Kate, editor.

PN6737.M67Z64 2015
741.5'9411—dc23
                                                  2015024433

BRITISH LIBRARY CATALOGUING DATA ARE AVAILABLE

© 2015 Darragh Greene and Kate Roddy. All rights reserved

No part of this book may be reproduced or transmitted in any form or by any means, electronic or mechanical, including photocopying or recording, or by any information storage and retrieval system, without permission in writing from the publisher.

On the cover: Colored illustration of woodcut from *Isagogae breues et exactissimae in anatomia humani corporis* by Jacopo Berengario da Carpi, 1523 (National Library of Medicine)

Printed in the United States of America

McFarland & Company, Inc., Publishers
  Box 611, Jefferson, North Carolina 28640
    www.mcfarlandpub.com

Acknowledgments

The initial versions of many of the essays contained in this volume were first presented at the conference *Grant Morrison and the Superhero Renaissance* in 2012 at Trinity College Dublin. We would therefore like to express our gratitude to the Long Room Hub, the School of English, and, in particular, Prof. Darryl Jones, for their financial and organizational support of the event.

We would also like to thank Dr. Dara Downey, Dr. Graham Price, Dr. Edel Semple, Triona Kirby, John Dillon, and Hector "Rafael" Guerra for their invaluable comments and suggestions on earlier drafts of this collection.

Table of Contents

Acknowledgments v

Introduction
    Darragh Greene *and* Kate Roddy 1

Part I: Formal Analysis

"And so we return and begin again": The Immersive/
    Recursive Strategies of Morrison's Puzzle Narratives
    Chris Murray 17

"Screw symbolism and let's go *home*": Morrison and Bathos
    Kate Roddy 43

The Writer and "the Writer": The Death of the
    Author in *Suicide Squad* #58
    Roy T. Cook 64

"Let me slip into someone more comfortable":
    The Imaginary Adolescence of the Superhero
    Keith Scott 82

Parasitic Signifiers: The Invasiveness of Language in
    Grant Morrison's Comics
    Clare Pitkethly 100

Part II: Thematic Analysis

From Shame into Glory in *The Filth*
    David Coughlan 115

"The Jungian Stuff": Symbols of Transformation
    in *All-Star Superman*
    Darragh Greene 131

The Dark Knight and the Devil: Demons and Demonology
   in *Batman*, 2005–2013
      SCHEDEL LUITJEN   150

"Our Father, Who Art in Gotham": The Life, Death
   and Rebirth of Batman
      NICHOLAS GALANTE   166

Fallout Boys: Paranoia, Power and Control in Morrison's
   Cold War Superheroes
      MUIREANN O'SULLIVAN   183

"Morrison Inc." and Themes of Benevolent Capitalism
      EMMET O'CUANA   205

Bibliography   223

About the Contributors   235

Index   237

Introduction

Darragh Greene *and* Kate Roddy

Who Is Grant Morrison?

If you have picked up this volume, then you probably do not need to be told who Grant Morrison is. His powers as a self-publicist are second only to those as a creator of mind-bending, genre-reconfiguring comics; he is quite simply the most successful writer working in comics today. Since the 1980s, Morrison's serialized superhero comics have defined and radically redefined the superhero archetype for our culture. His distinctive yet diverse work addresses both topical and universal themes in science, spirituality, politics, and art, and his stylistic innovations serve to produce comics of tremendous depth, power, and brilliance.

Within the field of comics, Morrison has spearheaded a more than reactionary movement away from the "grim and gritty" antiheroes of the mid-to-late 1980s (defined, above all, in the works of Alan Moore and Frank Miller), by effectively engineering the reconfiguration of the core values of the superhero. In his works, he asks readers to consider the superhero's transformation from cheap-print ephemera of lowbrow entertainment to enduring, vibrant, and ever-meaningful cultural object. Moreover, he has worked to transform and reinvent the idea of the superhero and imbue it again with hope and meaning, by using it to combat the particular fears of the present cultural moment.

One of the greatest strengths of Morrison's work lies in his incredible mastery of over seventy-five years of comics history, a knowledge that encompasses all but forgotten characters and titles that he revives in his own works. Yet Morrison is more than a comics antiquary: as we will see, he views himself not only in relation to a venerable, vanished past of comics production, but as an architect of a new age.

A Superhero "Renaissance"

Traditional historiographers of superhero comics divide the genre into series of ages or developmental stages labeled to mirror those which Hesiod in *Works and Days,* and later Ovid in *Metamorphoses,* ascribed to the history of mankind. The Golden Age begins in 1938 with the first appearance of Superman in *Action Comics* #1 and lasts until the cataclysm of Fredric Wertham's *Seduction of the Innocent* (1954), the book that launched a McCarthy-style witch-hunt against comics as a medium that promoted juvenile delinquency and sexual perversion. Almost immediately, the major comics publishers responded by clubbing together and creating the Comics Code Authority, which was designed to stave off any further attacks that might injure the industry. Superheroes were considered a safe alternative to the crime and horror comics that had especially drawn Wertham's ire, and so with the first appearance of Barry Allen as the new Flash in *Showcase* #4 (October 1956), the Silver Age began and lasted from the late 1950s through the late 1960s. At DC Comics, the industry giant, the requirement to keep interesting the monthly adventures of god-like superheroes was marked by increasing zaniness and a preoccupation with the possibilities of science. In parallel to this, at Marvel Comics, the industry upstart, Stan Lee, Jack Kirby, and Steve Ditko reinvented the superhero by giving him real-world problems. These new superheroes took the shape of the nerdy, cash-strapped Spider-Man; the ever-bickering family of the Fantastic Four; the competition and in-fighting of the Avengers; and the emotional torments of the weird and outcast mutant teenagers of the X-Men. By bringing the superheroes down to Earth, Lee, Kirby, and Ditko increased their appeal to teen- and college-aged readers who in the past would have outgrown the simplistic and repetitive adventures of Superman and his peers.

Next, the Bronze Age, spanning the 1970s and early 1980s, marked a more ponderous, serious turn, which witnessed superheroes engaging with controversial social issues such as racism, feminism, drug addiction, and environmental pollution. The first non–Code-approved superhero comics arrived with *Amazing Spider-Man* #96–98 (May-July 1971), issues in which Peter Parker's friend Harry Osborn is revealed to be a drug addict. Following the publication of these comics, editors at DC and Marvel met and rewrote the Comics Code to allow for treatment of socially relevant topics, such as drug abuse. These revisions to the code resulted in scope for the depiction of more complex moral issues generally, and saw the recrudescence of horror comics, such as *Tomb of Dracula, Ghost Rider,* and *Swamp Thing*, which became unlikely vehicles for asking existential questions concerning the meaning and value of human life. This period also saw the rise of anti-hero protagonists who killed, such as the Punisher (in *Amazing Spider-Man* #129) and Wolverine (in *Incredible Hulk* #181).

The Dark Age, beginning in the mid–1980s with Frank Miller's *The Dark Knight Returns* (1986) and Alan Moore and Dave Gibbons's *Watchmen* (1986–87), took the new seriousness and "realism" a step further, sparking a trend for superficial imitations that reveled in the depiction of extreme violence and "deconstructed" heroes, who were increasingly portrayed as sociopathic and dysfunctional. In retrospect, those real-world problems that Lee and his collaborators had given their heroes to humanize them now were repurposed to shrink and diminish them. The sunny, god-like superheroes of the early Silver Age were dragged from the skies and beaten into the streets or sent to the insane asylums of the corrupted, modern city.

The very names of these ages betray the fear of comics readers—a readership particularly given to nostalgia—that the genre is going inevitably and irreversibly downhill, and they also raise the question of what age comes next. Morrison's answer, as given in his memoir-cum-manifesto, *Supergods* (2011), is "renaissance," and he writes of how these "new comics would be populated by relaxed, unashamed, confident superheroes, purged of Dark Age neuroses."[1] In this way, Morrison envisions the future of the superhero to be a rebirth of what made the idea great in its classic periods, but with differences that speak to the present.

The editors of this volume are, respectively, a medievalist and a Renaissance scholar, and to us, Morrison's choice of phrase sparks a number of deeper associations. His hopeful vision of the superhero in the present cultural moment—as mythically resonant and resistant to the depressing mass media narratives of war, famine, disease, and looming environmental disaster—reflects and parallels key features of the move from the medieval, so-called "Dark Ages" to the Renaissance in the art and culture of fifteenth- and sixteenth-century Europe.

Our motivating idea in assembling this volume was to draw on and expand these associations, moving beyond a view of comics as a uniquely "modern" phenomenon to consider their ideological resonance with much older literary, artistic, and philosophical discourses. In the section that follows, we detail therefore a number of suggestive ways in which the preoccupations of Morrison's writing recall those of the earlier Renaissance.

Morrison as Renaissance Man

Renaissance humanists called for *ad fontes* reading, by which they meant a return to the Greek and Roman sources of Western literary and artistic genius. By clearing away what they considered medieval detritus and thereby allowing the Greek and Roman classics to speak for themselves, they hoped these works would speak anew to the post-medieval present, so that their readers could draw fresh learning and inspiration from them. Morrison's own principle of *ad fontes* reading is revealed in his persistent return to, and mining of, Silver Age comics—not just for characters and ideas, but significantly for their mood of optimism, creative ingenuity, and fascination with technology, science, and exploration. In similar fashion, Morrison draws on old superhero continuity to transform and reinvigorate it, making it speak to the concerns of the present. This was seen most recently in his reclamation of Superman's 1930s Depression era socialist roots, rewritten in *Action Comics* (2011–13) to be relevant to the socio-economic conditions and problems of the post–2008 global recession. Furthermore, Morrison recreates and so defines continuity, much like Shakespeare does when he draws on the historical material of Raphael Holinshed's *Chronicles* in his history plays. Just as anyone writing a biography of Henry V or Richard III today has to contend with the cultural impact of the larger-than-life characters conceived by Shakespeare, so it is with Morrison's re-conception of DC characters: his version of Animal Man, his version of the Doom Patrol, his versions of Batman and Superman, have all become iconic representations, such that all subsequent writers have found themselves either reproducing his characterizations or struggling—arguably unsuccessfully—to redefine them anew. Morrison's relationship to his sources is discussed in further detail by two of the contributors to this volume: in his essay, Nicholas Galante analyzes the evolving characterization of Batman, while Muireann O'Sullivan considers the author's representations of Superman.

In the humanist re-reading of classical literature, Neoplatonist texts took pride of place. Indeed, Neoplatonism was *the* major philosophy behind the Italian Renaissance, informing the arts of architecture, sculpture, painting, and poetry. In effect, Neoplatonism heralded a return to a proud conviction in the power and promise of human imagination. Marsilio Ficino, Pico della Mirandola, and Giordano Bruno, among others, in developing their own philosophies of human genius and achievement, drew on the newly discovered Platonic Dialogues, which had been almost all lost during the Middle Ages. These men were profoundly impressed by Plato's vision, expressed in a series of allegories and myths in works such as *Symposium*, *Phaedo*, and, above all, *Republic*, of an ideal realm of Ideas—Beauty, Truth and the Good—which only the human mind could grasp because it was, as Plato showed in the *Phaedo*, an immortal soul, a luminous, inextinguishable spark of eternal divinity. There are many key ideas of Neoplatonism paralleled in Morrison's work: most particularly and repeatedly, that the world is authored and moreover a plagiarized or inferior copy of a higher reality. Thus, Morrison's Animal Man discovers, to his horror, that his life is merely entertainment for the people watching from beyond the fourth wall, while in *All-Star Superman* our "real" world is Superman's own artificial creation, just as Superman himself is a fictional construct in ours. In this volume, Chris Murray unfolds the structural and architectural elements of Morrison's recursive multiple worlds, while Schedel Luitjen explores the Neoplatonic background to the author's conception of the Batman mythos.

Morrison, like the Erasmus of *De Copia Rerum et Verborum* (1512) and other humanists, shares a common interest in language; in particular, how words are central to human being and imagination. Renaissance humanists, from Petrarch (1304–74) onward, were profoundly influenced by the Roman rhetorician Quintilian's vision of the *vir bonus, dicendi peritus* or the good man speaking well.[2] What they emphasized was the centrality of language to a full and distinctly human life. If one was to live well, one had to speak well. In the Renaissance, thinkers such as Machiavelli in *The Prince* (1513) and Castiglione in *The Book of the Courtier* (1528) identified—if they did not extol—persuasion, the ability to sway opinion, as more important, politically speaking, than truth. And the humanist courtier, adventurer and gentleman poet Philip Sidney, in the late sixteenth century, affirmed how the poet could in his eloquence make a better world: "[Nature's] world is brazen, the poets only deliver a golden."[3] If one had the art, if one knew how, one could speak one's desires into being. In a similar way, Morrison's works continually stress the magical and creative powers of words: in *Flex Mentallo* his puzzle "SHA_A_" prompts the reader to think both of the magic word that will turn the powerless child Billy Batson into his adult, heroic counterpart Captain Marvel (shazam!) and the word "shaman," while in both *The Invisibles* and *Vimanarama!* the heroes are disconcerted by words that take literal or physical form. For Morrison, indeed, the alphabet is both a spell and a prison; thus, within her essay in this volume, Clare Pitkethly explores Morrison's conviction that language is potent but also potentially sinister because of its power to control people and worlds.

Magic is not merely metaphorical for Morrison, but a practical way of making one's influence felt in the universe. His brand of magic is, as he describes it himself, "punk" or "chaos magic," and he claims to eschew any backwards-looking or obfuscatory mysticism ("all this wearying symbolic misdirection that's being dragged up from the Victorian Age ... bullshitting around with Qabalah and Thelema...").[4] Yet despite these protestations about magic's ahistoricity, we might point out that there is a distinctly Renaissance flavor to the way Morrison evokes magic and its relationship to the natural world.

Our contemporary understanding of Renaissance alchemy is "part primitive science, part impossible magic."[5] The alchemist's quest to discover the Philosopher's Stone—the substance that would turn all base metals to gold—is now seen as ludicrous and supremely avaricious, yet for "true" alchemists such as Giordano Bruno, George Ripley, and John Dee, the work was philosophical rather than acquisitive. The legendary stone's power was not, after all, to apply the Midas touch, but to *perfect* all matter, including the self. Alchemy was a holistic scheme: not science tainted by magic, but a harmonious marriage between the two; its promise was not of gold, but that the hidden forces of nature are discoverable, and workable, by virtuous human beings.

Morrison's characters share this holistic view, as they perform "magic in hotel rooms,"[6] combining the occult with the everyday (or rather, seeing both as part of the same continuum). Like the alchemist, Morrison describes his endeavors in writing as a form of magical self-creation; of his early major work, he writes: "*The Invisibles* was a six-year long sigil in the form of an occult adventure story which consumed and recreated my life during the period of its composition and execution."[7] In his essay, Keith Scott further explores the aims and methods of Morrisonian magic, and in particular its relationship to youthful idealism and the creative power of language.

Morrison's obsession with altering and remaking worlds applies not only to that which is external, but also to the self. His work shows a continuing fascination with what Stephen Greenblatt famously terms "self-fashioning": an awareness of the malleability of identity that begins to flourish in the Renaissance with increasing social mobility, developing notions of interiority and selfhood, and the humanistic belief in mankind's limitless potential. Giovanni Pico della Mirandola's seminal Renaissance text *Oration on the Dignity of Man* (1486) described mankind as more fortunate, and more heroic, than angels because man was granted the unique gift of transformation. He imagines God telling Adam:

> Once defined, the nature of all other beings is constrained within the laws We have prescribed for them. But you, constrained by no limits, may determine your nature for yourself, according to your own free will.... We have made you neither of heaven nor of earth, neither mortal nor immortal, so that you may, as the free and extraordinary shaper of yourself, *fashion yourself* in whatever form you prefer.[8]

"Self-fashioning" is certainly a term fit to describe Morrison's superhero in terms of its protean and relentlessly self-perfecting nature, whether through his Bruce Wayne's quest to cultivate optimum humanity in his ordeal of death and rebirth at Nanda Parbat in *Batman #673* and collaborative project to "build a better Batman," in *Batman, Incorporated,* or through the complex humanism of his Kal-El in *All-Star Superman*, striving not only to perform ever-more heroic feats, but to create a world which is itself valorized to the point that Superman is no longer required as its savior. In his essay on the latter text, Darragh Greene explores the Jungian archetypes and theory of individuation underpinning and driving Superman's self-actualization.

Yet, self-fashioning refers to more than a character's changeability. As Greenblatt states, the idea is fundamentally metatextual: "it functions without regard for a sharp distinction between literature and social life. It invariably crosses the boundaries between the creation of literary characters, the shaping of one's own identity, the experience of being molded by forces outside one's control, the attempt to fashion other selves."[9] In this vein, Emmet O'Cuana examines the connections between Morrison's own self-development and the uses he makes of superheroes who strive to change society.

As many of the essays in this volume observe, few—if any—writers are as relentlessly metatextual as Morrison, or cultivate such strong links between themselves and their creations; "their" world and "ours." Key to Morrison's world (or, more properly, multiversal) view is Jorge Luis Borges' observation: "If the characters in a fictional work can be readers or spectators we, its readers or spectators, can be fictitious."[10]

Thus, universal boundaries are always porous in Morrison's comics: his characters traverse the alternate realties of the DC multiverse, find themselves (as in *Animal Man*) shaking hands with their strange creator (who comes, he admits, from a world more washed-out and depressing than their own), or looking out at the reader-voyeur who gazes down at them from the comfort of another dimension, a reader who is perhaps no more (nor less) "real" than they are. For Morrison, writing is literally self-fashioning: through the many author-avatars, beginning with Zenith and (perhaps most notably) King Mob, he creates and recreates himself in the image of his works, and vice-versa. Developing these themes within this volume, Kate Roddy explores Morrison's subversion of conventional notions of authorship, while Roy T. Cook questions the limits and paradoxes of the author's self-fictionalization.

The Renaissance inaugurated a wave of scientific discovery that pushed forward the boundaries of human knowledge of not only the physical world but of the body too. The sixteenth and seventeenth centuries saw the rise of the study of anatomy in the universities, leading to the advent of works such as Vesalius' *De Humani Corpis Fabrica* (on the composition of the human body, 1543) and William Harvey's revelation of the circulatory system *De Motu Cordis* (on the movement of the heart, 1628). Yet the dissected body in medical textbooks was not depicted as static or passive: Vesalius' excoriated men and women sit, stand, even dance while drawn against a backdrop of bucolic landscapes or classical Attic ruins. They represent, simultaneously, human frailty and endurance as well as the inscription of pain on the human body and transcendence of it. The convention of drawing superheroes so that the entire body is displayed to the reader's curious gaze mirrors the representation of bodies in the Renaissance anatomy books. Superhero bodies are clad in skin-tight uniforms or costumes that highlight every physical contour; such bodies can be plastic and warped into physically impossible contortions, inflicted again and again with mortal injuries like a twentieth-century Wound Man. Like Vesalius' figures, they are representative of multiple and even paradoxical values, provoking in the viewer sensations of wonder, admiration, envy, and desire—but also fear and disgust. Morrison's works continually highlight the visibility of the superhero, and the cultural inscribability of its body: his Flex Mentallo, for instance, evoking the Charles Atlas bodybuilding advertisements of the 1950s as a figure of both masculine admiration and homoerotic panic, his Superman moving from iconic pencil drawing to the soaring, primary-colored symbol of hope. David Coughlan's essay thus takes as its focus this tension in Morrison's work between the superheroic body as an ideal self, or a profoundly abject one.

The "Renaissance" in the title of this volume therefore does not simply apply to superhero comics historiography; rather, as we have shown above, it captures how Morrison himself is a Renaissance man, not only in how he melds genres in his comics, but in how he uses superhero comics to explore difficult and complex ideas concerning the nature of humankind and reality. The essays that follow illuminate Morrison's humanism, artistry, ambition, and, above all, magic.

Relation to Existing State of Art

At this point in an introduction to the study of superheroes, it has become traditional to discuss the perennial question/problem of the appropriateness of the genre as worthy of "serious study." This has been debated at length elsewhere,[11] and beginning in this fashion often seems to betray more anxiety than confidence that the genre is worthy of such study. By contrast, we take it as a given that the best superhero comics do offer serious contributions to culture and art.

The field of comics studies has already generated a growing body of seminal critical works, and scholarship is ever growing and expanding. In addition, academic journals, such as the *Journal of Popular Culture*, have published scholarly articles on the works of Grant Morrison and other comics creators, and moreover, new journals devoted exclusively to comics criticism and analysis have been founded, such as the *International Journal of Comic Art* (since 1999), *ImageTexT* (since 2004), *Studies in Comics* (since 2010), and *The Journal of Graphic Novels and Comics* (since 2010).[12] Scholarship is growing in terms of not only theory and praxis, but also critical studies of Morrison's work in particular, such as Marc Singer's *Grant Morrison: Combining the Worlds of Contemporary Comics* (2011). Our intention is to build on this existing scholarship and so contribute to the further development of an exciting new field of academic discipline.

While studies of Morrison have invaluably opened an important area of discussion, their scope has so far been limited primarily to cataloguing and reviewing the writer's body of work, typically in chronological fashion. Our inaugural volume will firmly establish Morrison's comics oeuvre as a subject of scholarship, by developing and emphasizing analyses that draw more widely on the approaches, methods, and tools of cultural, media, and literary studies. To this end, we have divided the essays in our collection into two categories: formal and thematic. Those essays that come under the heading of "formal analysis" investigate Morrison's style and techniques, while those under "thematic analysis" consider his ideas, recurring themes, and literary influences.

That this collection focuses on a single creator introduces another key element of debate within comic book studies: that of authorship. While Morrison originally began his career in comics in the late 1970s as a writer-artist, in the 1980s he turned exclusively to writing comics for other artists to realize visually. This raises the question of just who *authors* comics produced in collaborations (and who should therefore receive the most credit for the finished product).

Much of the discussion on this topic so far has centered on the problem of what matters most in a comic, namely, image or text? There is remarkably little consensus on the degree of influence that these elements exert on the comic viewer/reader, or even how the term "comic" itself should be defined. There are those, such as Will Eisner, who deem that it is the "sequential art" of the "arrangement of pictures or images and words to narrate a story or dramatize an idea" that fundamentally make a comic.[13] Others, however, such as Scott McCloud, assert the primacy of the image by defining comics as "juxtaposed pictorial and other images in deliberate sequence, intended to convey information and/or to produce an aesthetic response in the viewer."[14] Our own contributor Roy T. Cook has recently argued elsewhere that it is possible to conceive of a comic without images, that what defines a "comic" is to do with reader expectation and the conditions of its serialized publication, in addition to these former touchstones of sequentiality and images.[15] It is also worth noting that although there are many famous examples of "silent" comics (which would seem to support McCloud's thesis regarding the primacy of the image),[16] most comics are made up not only of the text letterers assign to dialogue boxes, speech balloons, and the like, but shaped by a hidden textual structure: the writer's script.

It is not the intention of the editors of this volume to take a partisan position on the "image versus text" debate; rather, it is our opinion that comics are a multimodal art form with complicated intersections of text and image. Comics studies has largely grown out of other disciplines (such as literature, art history, and film studies) and currently lacks a common methodological apparatus that would equip critics to analyze and evaluate the complex notions of authorship which are unique to this art form. Although the issue is beyond the scope of this present volume dedicated to a single author, we expect that it will be a key topic of further comics studies in the near future.

While this collection of essays focuses on Morrison as a comics architect and visionary, it also acknowledges the collaborative nature of his achievements in the genre; the more-than-supporting role of pencilers, inkers, letterers and, indeed, editors and other "behind-the-scenes" creative staff, in bringing his vision to the published comics page. Over the years, however, certain collaborators have distinguished themselves as Morrison's favorites, most notably and consistently Frank Quitely whose distinctive style brings both delicacy and emotive power to Morrison's imaginings. Indeed, Morrison himself says, "Frank Quitely was the artist I wished I could be."[17] Other important artists he collaborates with include

Cameron Stewart (*Batman and Robin, Seven Soldiers* and *Seaguy*), Chris Burnham (*Batman and Robin, Batman, Incorporated*), Frazer Irving (*Seven Soldiers, Batman and Robin, The Return of Bruce Wayne* and *Batman, Incorporated*), and Steve Yeowell (*Zenith, The Invisibles, Sebastian O*). Collaborators who worked on major projects with Morrison across a number of years include Richard Case (*Doom Patrol*), Chaz Truog (*Animal Man*), Phil Jimenez (*The Invisibles*), Howard Porter (*JLA*)—and many others too numerous to list here. Our desire to acknowledge the input of these creators is reflected in our method of citation and the fuller credits given in the bibliography (see "Note on Referencing" below).

Volume Overview

The contributors to this book form an international network of scholars, diverse in academic disciplines and theoretical approaches, yet each of their essays variously informs and touches on the volume's unifying idea of "Renaissance." The first part of the book, which is devoted to formal analysis, collects essays that interrogate Morrison's use of semiotics, language, and literary tropes. In the opening essay, Chris Murray reveals the underpinning structure of Morrison's works through his use of recursion, arguing that this concept has linguistic, philosophical, and political significance for the writer. Kate Roddy traces the development of the writer's craft, arguing that the movement away from the cynicism, post-modern trickery and "downbeat" endings of the early works shows Morrison's increasing structural experimentalism and questioning of notions of authorship. Next Roy T. Cook considers the limits, logical fallacies and paradoxes of self-creation and fictionalization in his study of Morrison as a character in his own works. Keith Scott considers Morrison's writing as "adolescent," valorizing this term to evoke ideas of flexibility, imagination, and magical possibility. In the final essay of this section, Clare Pitkethly demonstrates another side to Morrison's linguistic playfulness, by showing how his treatment of words reveals they can be signifiers of darkness and alienation in comics.

The second part of the volume, thematic analysis, presents studies of Morrison's major ideas, motifs, and values. In the opening essay, David Coughlan deconstructs Morrison's *The Filth* in terms of its dialectical process of perversion and policing that is proposed to underpin the superhero's role in redeeming male shame. Next Darragh Greene interprets and analyzes the Jungian framework and symbolism of Morrison's master narrative of self-creation and transformation, *All-Star Superman*. Schedel Luitjen uncovers Morrison's appropriation of and affinity with Neoplatonic mythopoeic metaphysics and reveals both the reification and tenability of the idea of the superhero to conquer Nothingness. Nicholas Galante shows the development of Morrison's constructions of Batman across three decades, by discovering the occult and religious symbolism that marks and informs continuing cycles of the character's birth, death and rebirth. Following this, Muireann O'Sullivan considers Morrison to be a product of British Cold War politics; she explores his critique of authoritarianism through examining his uses and reconfigurations of such cultural and moral icons as Batman and Superman. Finally, Emmet O'Cuana explores the ostensibly left-wing Morrison's recurring theme of benevolent capitalism in the context of the utopian potential of the superhero, by critiquing his synthesis of socially conscious values and the benevolent corporate entity as a bulwark against societal nihilism.

With this thematically and methodologically diverse collection of essays we offer a variety of new ways to read and engage with Morrison's works, and it is our hope that this volume will open avenues for further scholarship on superhero comics and their creators. Today, superheroes, once marginalized, faintly ridiculous figures of a niche culture, have taken their place in the mainstream of popular culture and consciousness. Morrison himself eloquently asserts that these stories "tell us where we've been, what we feared, and what we desired, and today they are more popular, more all-pervasive than ever because they still speak to us about what we really want to be. Once again, the comics were right all along."[18]

If Morrison is right in his vision of superheroes, and their especial value for our self-analysis and exploration, then comics studies has much to offer the future of humanities research.

Note on Conventions of Referencing Comics

It is notoriously difficult to produce a consistent referencing system for comics. This is largely to do with the nature of how such works are published—anything from monthly floppies, traditionally seen as a publishing ephemera (at least in the early days of the industry), to trade paperback reproductions of material originally published in serial form, to hardbound, slip-cased *objets d'art* for display on a coffee table or personal library shelf. None of these items are produced with a view to satisfying academic analysis, and basic details such as page numbers are often missing. Furthermore, as many comics are line-produced, involving a large number of artistic collaborators (writers, pencilers, inkers, letterers, and editors), to produce a citation that provides full credit to everyone who worked on the title would involve swelling the footnote or endnote to an unwieldy size.

The system of citation we employ in this volume, therefore, is a hybrid form which tries (but perhaps does not always succeed) in trying to contain the variety of comics within the structure of *The Chicago Manual of Style*, the latest edition of which offers little guidance on the subject of how to cite these materials. In creating our own system for comics citation we have aimed to present information in a fashion that is legible and, above all, concise. As we envision the writer and primary penciler as together comprising the main "author" of a comic, the individual citations utilize the short form of "[writer] and [penciler]" where there are multiple contributors, while the bibliography provides fuller creator credits. We have treated trade paperbacks as volumes of a single work. Thus, for ease of citation, "Say You Want a Revolution" becomes simply volume 1 of the trade paperback edition of *The Invisibles*. For example, a reference to page 23 of this item is cited as "Grant Morrison *et al.*, *The Invisibles* (New York: DC/Vertigo, 1999–2002) 1.23." Where printed page numbers are absent (for example, in floppies), we have counted the pages of the comic proper (omitting paratext such as covers and advertising material from our numbering). This approach has allowed our contributors to make use of a full and diverse range of sources—floppies, trade paperbacks, and deluxe hardcovers—as their own research necessitated.

Notes

1. Grant Morrison, *Supergods: What Masked Vigilantes, Miraculous Mutants, and a Sun God from Smallville Can Teach Us About Being Human* (New York: Spiegel & Grau, 2011), 288.
2. See Quintilian, *Institutio Oratoria*, 12.1.1.
3. Sir Philip Sidney, *The Defence of Poesy*, in *The Major Works*, ed. Katherine Duncan-Jones (Oxford: Oxford University Press, 2002), 216.
4. Grant Morrison, interview by Jonathan Ellis, in "Grant Morrison: Master and Commander" (part 4), *Popimage*, accessed February 11, 2014, http://www.popimage.com/content/grant20044.html.
5. Charles Nicholl, *The Chemical Theatre* (London: Routledge & Kegan Paul, 1980), 2.
6. Grant Morrison *et al.*, *The Invisibles* (New York: DC/Vertigo, 1999–2002), 7.209.
7. Grant Morrison, "Pop Magic," in *Book of Lies: The Disinformation Guide to Magic and the Occult*, ed. Richard Metzger (New York: Disinformation, 2003), 21.
8. Giovanni Pico della Mirandola, *Oration on the Dignity of Man*, ed. and trans. Francesco Borghesi, Michael Papio, and Massimo Riva (Cambridge: Cambridge University Press, 2012), 117; emphasis ours.

9. Stephen Greenblatt, *Renaissance Self-Fashioning from More to Shakespeare* (Chicago: University of Chicago Press, 1980), 3.

10. Jorge Luis Borges, "Partial Magic in the Quixote," trans. James E. Irby, in *Labyrinths: Selected Stories and Other Writings*, ed. Donald A. Yates and James E. Irby (New York: New Directions, 1964), 196.

11. For an up-to-date discussion of this topic, see the Introduction to *The Superhero Reader*, ed. Charles Hatfield, Jeet Heer and Kent Worcester (Jackson: University Press of Mississippi, 2013).

12. In 2015, an issue of *ImageTexT* will be devoted to the analysis of Morrison's work.

13. Will Eisner, *Comics and Sequential Art* (Tamarac, FL: Poorhouse Press, 1985), 5.

14. Scott McCloud, *Understanding Comics* (New York: Kitchen Sink, 1993), 9.

15. Roy T. Cook, "Do Comics Require Pictures? Or Why *Batman* #663 Is a Comic," *The Journal of Aesthetics and Art Criticism* 69, no. 3 (2011): 285–96.

16. See, for example, Larry Hama and Ron Wagner's "Hush Job," *G.I. Joe Yearbook* #3 (New York: Marvel Comics, 1987); Frank Miller's *Sin City* one-shot *Silent Night* (Milwaukie, OR: Dark Horse Comics, 1995); and Grant Morrison and Frank Quitely's *New X-Men* #121 (New York: Marvel Comics, 2002).

17. Morrison, *Supergods*, 268.

18. Ibid., 415.

Part I
Formal Analysis

"And so we return and begin again"

The Immersive/Recursive Strategies of Morrison's Puzzle Narratives

Chris Murray

> What draws me to comics is the freedom. There is something magical about that comics space. It's on two dimensions but you can represent these stories, and with drawn figures made of ink you can make people laugh or cry, or change the reader's life. I find that fascinating. There is something very primal about the physicality of comics, and the fact that you as a reader are actually controlling the process through the story. You can look at a panel, or a page as a whole, and you can go backwards, and move around in the continuum of a comic. There's something very magical about that. That seems much more in touch with the roots of creativity. Comics allow you to go further, and faster and wider and wilder.—Grant Morrison, "More Space Combat!"[1]

Grant Morrison's work is marked by a fascination with memory, time, illusion, and shifting perspectives, and the model he most often applies is that of the game or puzzle. His narratives exploit what he calls the magical freedom of the comics space, twisting and turning, continually driving towards complexity, ambiguity and sometimes, incoherence, with the reader having to unravel the enigma. There are two main strategies at work: firstly, the immersion of the reader within the narrative (usually alongside a figure who represents the author and who acts as a mentor); and secondly, an emphasis on repetition and cyclical structures. The fact that Morrison's stories often bring the reader and author together in the same space looking for a solution means that his comics frequently resemble a maze or labyrinth and have a recursive structure with some kind of riddle at their heart. Moreover, the characters are often caught up in the same kinds of interpretative traps set for the reader. Many of his stories are therefore overt metaphors for the reading process, with characters leaping into or out of fictional worlds, or being consumed by the comics page, with the immersive strategies employed offering the same kind of entanglement for the reader.

These two strategies of immersion and recursion are aimed at exploiting the potential of comics as a narrative form, involving the reader in a complex game of intertextuality and interpretation. This also has implications for narrative structure, and Morrison's stories often take a form analogous to what cognitive scientist Douglas Hofstadter refers to as "strange loops" or "tangled hierarchies,"[2] structures that Morrison uses to undermine narrative logic, embed contradictions and play with expectations. His unique approach to the comics medium and the superhero genre has been instrumental in bringing about the recent "renaissance" of the superhero, a figure that Morrison sees as an emblem of liberation and empowerment.[3] Whereas other influential comics creators, such as Alan Moore, Frank Miller, Warren Ellis, Garth Ennis, and Mark Millar, have deconstructed the superhero over the last three decades, revealing the flaws, limitations, moral bankruptcy and political conservatism of the superhero, Morrison has held onto the notion that the superhero is a redemptive figure, and that the iconography of the genre still has resonance. While for some the resurgence of interest in superheroes is related to the rise in patriotism and militarism in America post–9/11, and the superhero films that have come to dominate cinema screens in this time are the continuation of the War on Terror by other means, this is certainly not the case in Morrison's comics. Contrary to the propaganda seen in many mainstream superhero comics, or, on the other hand, cynicism about the genre, Morrison seeks to recapture the wonder of the superhero and to immerse the reader in this fantasy world so as to imagine new possibilities and tap into the liberating potential of this mythic figure. The refinement of what this essay will refer to as the "immersive/recursive complex" is one way in which Morrison pursues this.

"The universe is a holodeck and we are being played": Narrative Immersion

To say that a narrative is immersive carries with it several connotations. In Kendall L. Walton's *Mimesis as Make-Believe* (1988) the point is made that in many fictions and artworks there is a strong element of immersion:

> Participation in games of make-believe [and readers/viewers] not only recognize and comply with prescriptions to imagine but also themselves serve as reflexive props, generating by their actions and thoughts and feelings fictional truths about themselves, and imagining accordingly. They [can be, but are not necessarily] carried away by the pretence, caught up in the story.[4]

With their emphasis on secret identities and fantasies of empowerment superhero narratives certainly encourage identification with the hero and immersion in the story world, but this does not mean that they are written or received uncritically. Indeed, the issue of narrative immersion is not purely a matter of an absorbing experience generated by a popular text designed as throwaway entertainment, even if that implicit criticism of popular culture were to be accepted (which it is not). Rather, an immersive experience is fundamental to how most narratives work, be they literary or visual representations, or in the case of comics, both. However, for the purposes of this discussion immersion will not be primarily conceived as the participation in the "make-believe" of the story, but the effect created by narrative and visual strategies that place the perspective of the reader within the point of view of the characters, a technique that Morrison favors in many of his works.

There is a long tradition of this. The application of the rules of perspective to painting in the fifteenth century during the Italian Renaissance served to draw the spectator into a physical and perceptual relationship with the two-dimensional plane of representation, just as the narrative techniques, conventions and the numerous literary effects developed by novelists in the fifteenth and sixteenth centuries created the illusion of the transparency of prose, and powerful effects of immersion, giving the reader access to the private thoughts and feelings of the narrator and characters. Likewise, visual media like film and comics have achieved similar effects by employing embodied perspectives, presenting a particular point of view, usually that of a character. As Gérard Genette notes, the main concern of narratology is to address "who is speaking" and "who sees."[5] This is something that is also a concern of visual narratives. However, contemporary theory has developed far beyond the idea that readers are simply drawn into the stories, instead stressing that they are active in *constructing* the narrative. As Marie-Laure Ryan points out in *Narrative as Virtual Reality: Immersion and Interactivity in Literature and Electronic Media* (2001):

> The history of Western art has seen the rise and fall of immersive ideals, and their displacement, in the twentieth century, by an aesthetics of play and self-reflexivity that eventually produced the ideal of an active participation of the appreciator—reader, spectator, user—in the production of the text.[6]

But being a "playful" reader in the postmodern sense does not preclude immersion in the narrative. Indeed, in some respects it implies it. In much comics scholarship the idea that the reader is actively engaged in producing meaning is key, and Scott McCloud's oft-cited *Understanding Comics* (1993) stresses the importance of the reader performing an act of "closure" in order to imaginatively fill in the gaps between panels.[7] Added to this, comics combine words and images, potentially doubling the opportunity for narrative immersion with both embodied perspectives and literary techniques at their disposal. As Thierry Groensteen points out in "The Monstrator, the Recitant and the Shadow of the Narrator" (2010):

> The difficulty of a narratology of comics lies in its polysemiotic nature. It combines text and image in varying proportions. I postulate that both are fully engaged in narration. It is not a question of having, on one hand, a text that recounts (and therefore would be *diegetic*) and, on the other, images that display (therefore solely *mimetic*). In *Système de la bande dessinée* [*The System of Comics*] my aim was precisely to demonstrate that a substantial part of the narration occurs in and through the images and their different levels of articulation.[8]

Morrison is keenly aware of these aspects of the comics medium, and exploits them both formally and thematically in his work, and the immersive effects that he achieves in collaboration with his artists are not simply of the kind that emerge from a story being absorbing and entertaining, rather narrative and visual techniques are employed to entangle the reader not just in plot and character but in the spatial and temporal framework of the comic. This is closely linked to the use of repeating patterns and repetitions, recursions which hint at greater significance, encouraging the reader to follow the clues and unravel the enigma.

Push, Pop, Stack—The Jargon of Recursive Sequence

A recursion is a kind of loop in which self-similar base units (usually numbers or images) exist in a relationship to one another defined by repetition. Sometimes this can be a simple repetition, or else it can be one which extends to infinity. One of the most famous examples of a recursion in visual terms is a *mise en abyme*, in which identical images repeat within each other to a theoretically infinite degree (although this term has come to have a much wider application, referring to conventions such as the play within a play, and other recursive structures within artworks). In terms of a visual image *mise en abyme* is similar to the effect of holding two mirrors parallel to one another and creating an infinite regression of images. Such repetitions are seen frequently in Morrison's comics, notably in *Flex Mentallo* (1996), where the protagonist is seen as a child creating this effect by positioning himself between two bathroom mirrors (Fig. 1.1), and in *Doom Patrol* (1989–93) in which the characters become trapped in a painting within a painting within a painting, and so on (Fig. 1.2). Indeed, Kevin Colden's cover for Timothy Callahan's book *Grant Morrison: The Early Years* (2007) acknowledges Morrison's preoccupation with such repeating structures, showing Morrison caught up in an example of a *mise en abyme*, looking over his shoulder, out at the reader, mirroring the well-known image from *Animal Man* #19 (1990), where the title character, realizing he is a fictional character in a comic, looks out at the reader, announcing, "I can see you!" just as Morrison does on this cover. This image is "nested," which is to say repeated (potentially to infinity) in a series of images that recur on Morrison's computer screen (the same computer seen in *Animal Man* #26 which has the character meet Morrison, the writer, and witness him writing his adventures on this computer).

Morrison's interest in recursive structures partially came from popular culture at the time,

Fig. 1.1 Mise en abyme. Morrison and Quitely. From "Flex Mentallo" #2 © DC Comics. Used with permission.

Fig. 1.2 The Brotherhood of Dada and the Painting That Ate Paris. Morrison and Case. From "Doom Patrol" #27 © DC Comics. Used with permission.

especially dance music culture of the late 1980s and early 1990s, which embraced fractals and Mandelbrot patterns (identical non–Euclidean self-repeating shapes within shapes). This is certainly part of the frame of reference for *The Invisibles* (1994–2000) with its psychedelic overtones and use of recursive linguistic, narrative and visual techniques to create a sense of being drawn in and entangled in the narrative. Yet there is a deeper meaning. The mathematics of fractal patterns described by Benoît Mandelbrot showed that the seeming chaos in nature was part of a much larger pattern of non–Euclidean objects (examples being clouds, mountains, coastlines) that are infinitely variable but shaped by mathematically determined (though infinitely complex) patterns.[9] Like Alan Moore in *Big Num-*

bers (1990), Morrison was intrigued by the possibilities of such theories for comics. The collapse of the supposed boundaries between order and chaos, fiction and reality, with each being bound up in the other, became a theme that occupied Morrison at the end of his run on *Animal Man*, and during his work on the surreal *Doom Patrol*. In one *Doom Patrol* story arc the Brotherhood of Dada unleash the power of "The Painting That Ate Paris," which Rebis describes as "an infinite recursive structure" presented as a classic example of a *mise en abyme*, and which is said to be "hungry," drawing people, and whole cities, into itself, into fictional worlds (see Fig. 1.2 above).[10] One of the inspirations for this was the work of Douglas Hofstadter. As Morrison notes in the afterword in *Doom Patrol* #20 (1989):

> Douglas Hofstadter's brilliant book *Godel, Escher, Bach*, which is an immensely readable voyage into the twilight world of logic and abstract mathematics, was another useful springboard for me ... and some of that material will doubtless find its way into upcoming adventures.[11]

Hofstadter's book, subtitled "An Eternal Golden Braid," is an exploration of the non-hierarchical nature of cognition. In this and other works he explores the idea of "strange loops," in which apparently hierarchical relationships are actually closed systems that are involved in feedback loops or "tangled hierarchies." This idea offers some fascinating possibilities for comics, and in many ways corresponds to Groensteen's concept of the braid, where the act of reading a comic establishes loops and sets all the time, regardless of whether there are repetitions within the actual page.

The influence of Hofstadter on *Doom Patrol* is overt. One of the characters, Rebis, ponders the recursive nature of the "virtual universe," using Russian dolls as a metaphor for its structure. S/he even uses "the jargon of recursive sequence ... push, pop, stack,"[12] which readers of Hofstadter would recognize from Chapter V of *Gödel, Escher, Bach*, "Recursive Structures and Processes," which opens with a discussion of Russian dolls, and which has a section called "Pushing, Popping and Stacks." These were terms that were applied to IPL (Information Processing Language), one of the first computer languages, developed in the mid–1950s at the RAND Corporation and the Carnegie Institute of Technology. The phrase "push, pop, stack" came from how trays were stacked in cafés and referred to how information was stored and organized by this programming language, which managed lists (stacks) by operating a last-in first-out data structure, from which data is inserted (pushed) or removed (popped). The "virtual universe" Rebis (and through him, Morrison) is pondering is the world of the comic itself (for which the painting is a metaphor). This raises the question of whether in the reading of comics the data (images, words, panels) is assembled in a way that is analogous to IPL, or nested Russian dolls, with the page (or comic as a whole) being the stack, and the images, words and panels being "pushed" or "popped" in the process of being read. While the limitations of IPL ultimately make it a rather basic and unhelpful metaphor for the reading process it is intriguing that Morrison was thinking about the structure and grammar of comics in this way, and exploring these ideas through his comics. This interest in the uncanny power of repetition taps also into one of his central concerns—language.[13]

Linguistic play and riddles are an important part of many of Morrison's stories. Riddles and games rely on repetition, recognition of patterns, and creative insight, forming unique responses to such stimuli. This is also a description of language use. In Morrison's work the power of language is frequently presented in the form of games which can challenge preconceptions, and indeed, break down established order. Language can reshape identity, and even reality. This is seen in *Animal Man*, where the writer bends "reality" to his will by typing, or in *Flex Mentallo*, in which a magic word transforms reality, or in *The Invisibles*, where Key 17, the word drug, transforms words into perceptions. In all these examples the immersive nature of language, and its ability to (re)make the world, or alter perceptions, is linked to recursive, circular narrative structures, riddles and play. These are stories about stories that turn inwards upon themselves and twist back around to their beginnings. Intriguingly, noted linguist Noam Chomsky has argued from the mid–1950s that recursion is the defining aspect of human communication and that grammar is hard-wired into the human brain. His thoughts on the idea of Universal Grammar hold that the key component of the faculty of language is its ability to create recursive grammatical structures, embedding (nesting) one clause within another, allowing humans to make "infinite use of finite means" (a phrase Chomsky borrows from Prussian philosopher and linguist, Wilhelm von Humboldt (1767–1835), who was one of the first to appreciate that language was a system of rules).[14] The idea of recursion in language is that there are only so many words in use at any time but they can be infinitely recombined and arranged (merged) in a recursive structure to endlessly modify meaning. An example is seen on the first page of *The Invisibles*. The first panel contains the enigmatic phrase "And so we return and begin again," and in the second panel Elfayed, speaking to King Mob, says, "Khephra, the sacred beetle, goes down into darkness and rises again, bearing the sun in his mandibles."[15] This recursive sentence can be unpicked, producing several separate sentences: "Khephra is a sacred beetle"; "Khephra goes down into darkness," this being modified by the addition of "and rises again"; and "Khephra bears the sun in his mandibles." The process can potentially extend to infinity, with the addition of more clauses and descriptions. Each addition merges imagery, symbolism, adding to the idea being communicated in a way that is self-referential and recursive. One of the ways humans express their individuality is through how they speak, how they present their own world through their own words. This is part of a shared language, but the expression of that language is an individual creative act, made possible by the recursive power of language to refer to itself, and to embed idea within idea, allowing for complexity and creativity within the tangled hierarchies of meaning that emerge in language use. Along with Marc D. Hauser and W. Tecumseh Fitch, Chomsky has argued that such a faculty is a relatively recent trait, found in humans, but not in other animals.[16] Language is what sets us apart. The idea that language has a close link to evolution and biology is of interest to Morrison, whose stories often equate linguistic play with radical shifts in perspective and evolutionary change (as in the examples cited above).

Morrison's comics, exploiting the intersection of words and images at play in the medium, conflate the two forms of recursion: one a function of linguistics (following Chomsky's argument), the other expressed in visual representations (as noted above with the recurring use of *mise en abyme* and fractal geometry in his work). Comics provide a unique opportunity to nest these different forms of recursion within one another, to merge them, producing a complex pattern of recursive structures at the level of text, narrative and picture, immersing recursions within recursions. In this sense the relationship between recursion and immersive strategies is a very close one in Morrison's work, arguably because linking them is a strategy employed by him to achieve a hypnotic, slightly dizzying effect of dislocation in an attempt to have his comics mimic the effect of a drug. One of the ways in which Morrison's comics achieve this trippy immersive effect is through the complex layering of meaning and significance and shifts in perspective, and through the exploration of altered states of consciousness. In *The Invisibles* and *Flex Mentallo* the nesting of images and ideas within one another across the structure of the story leaves the reader with the sense that some images are loaded with meaning, and that deeper connotations emerge over the course of reading, only becoming explicit much later. This is seen most clearly in *The Invisibles* with the repeating image of Barbelith, and the idea that the whole comic forms a "hypersigil" (a magical symbol extended across a whole narrative).

Just as the idea of immersion has close links to McCloud's theory of comics, recursion has come to be important to current debates in comics theory due to its central position within Groensteen's *The System of Comics* (1999/2009), which argues that comics should be thought of as a "multiframe," extending the idea that comics panels have complicated temporal/spatial relations across all the panels in the story, not just on the page.[17] Groensteen theorizes that there are non-linear points of contact between all the panels, which he refers to as a "braid" (or a weave). This is his metaphor for how the reading of comics operates, and it relies on the reader making connections by remembering parts of the discourse that they have encountered earlier, or if reading for the second time, projecting ahead to what is known to be coming. Groensteen's notion of the multiframe posits a kind of heterarchy—a recursive loop, in which images, ideas, themes, and forms establish patterns that are not hierarchical but rather formed by overlaps, repetitions, and multiple and divergent relations. This is a kind of nesting and merging of words and images that produces an assemblage that generates potentially infinite meanings from the ways that the clauses (combinations of signifying units, be they panels, groups of panels, or pages) are embedded within each other in ways that produce a variety of meanings, depending on the reader to weave them together. This draws the reader into the stories as an active agent, solving a puzzle, and relies on their faculty for recursive reading, understanding the relationship between elements in a non-linear, non-hierarchical way, making links and returning to earlier points to explore those connections. Therefore, Groensteen's theory brings immersive strategies together with recursive ones. As well as being an influential theory of how the reading of comics works generally this is a particularly good description of the effects found in many of Morrison's comics, precisely because Morrison, as a writer who thinks deeply about his work, anticipates some of what McCloud and Groensteen would later come to argue about the medium. Works like *Zenith, Doom Patrol, Arkham Asylum, Flex Mentallo, The Invisibles,* and *The Filth* make especially good use of this immersive/recursive complex.

The Immersive/Recursive Complex in Morrison's Puzzle Narratives

The potential for the narrative and formal properties of comics to create a disjunction between diegesis and mimesis, ensnaring the reader in repeating puzzle narratives, is exploited even in Morrison's earliest works, and is something that recurs throughout his career. In "Time Is a

Four Letter Word," which appeared in *Near Myths* #2 (1978), there is an odd sense of dislocation at work. Morrison provides both the script and the artwork for this story, and everything, including the art, dialogue, and composition, is pushed to the periphery, straining at the edges. This has the effect of drawing the reader in, delivering minimal information in strangely constructed panels, which are often too small and with too many words. While the result is not always successful, these early comics show a keen awareness of the potential of comics to produce unnerving dream-like and hallucinatory effects, and the ways in which Morrison draws the reader in are ingenious. In *Near Myths* #4 (1979) Gideon Stargrave fights a being with "cosmic powers" (Fig. 1.3). The use of perspective lines draws the reader's view to the center of the page, but also encourages the reader to look beyond the central figure to the arcs of energy she wields. Following the path of these two curving bolts of energy the reader finds that these lines converge in a panel underneath this central image, and a bit further along in the story to where the antagonist's hand glows with energy as she prepares to strike. This manipulation of the composition reflects the idea that the villain is "tear[ing] reality apart."[18] The pacing and composition are remarkable for such early work, and show Morrison's awareness of how to manipulate temporal and spatial relations on the comic page.

Another early work was *Abraxas* (1987), a collaboration with Glasgow artist Tony O'Donnell which was intended to be a graphic novel in the European album style (a design-led publication with high production values), about, as Morrison puts it "aliens, gnosticism, Celtic mythology, the End of the Universe, and girls in leather underwear."[19] This never appeared, apart from a couple of prologues which were eventually published in the short-lived *Sunrise* (Harrier Comics). Even in this early work there is a simple recursion at work on the first and last page for the first prologue to *Abraxas*, with the last image mirroring the first. However, the unpublished pages of *Abraxas* show even greater formal play of the sort that would later be familiar to readers of *The Invisibles* (Fig. 1.4). In a sequence introducing Black Alice, the aforementioned "girl in leather underwear," Morrison and O'Donnell fracture time and space so that the composition works against the expected reading order. The unlettered page has aliens bursting into a room, ambushing Black Alice, who is assisted by her companion. The panels are skewed, leaning against the direction of the expected reading order, and the gun flies out of the last panel. This interrupts the flow of the narrative, creating the sense that time and space are being manipulated in unusual ways. The effect is further complicated by the fact that in the background, as the action unfolds, there is a large tel-

Fig. 1.3 Tearing reality apart. Morrison. *Near Myths* #4. Used with kind permission of author.

"And so we return and begin again" (Murray)

Fig. 1.4 Black Alice. Morrison and O'Donnell. Unpublished page of *Abraxas*. Used with kind permission of author and artist.

evision screen showing the character Black Alice (who is also involved in the fight in "real time") placing the muzzle of her gun in the mouth of what appears to be an angel. This bizarre and sexually charged imagery creates an odd tension between foreground and background, past and present, and slows down the pace of reading of what should otherwise be a very quick action sequence, as there are now two very different timeframes at work in some of the panels. This requires the reader to pay more attention, and to read in a non-linear fashion, reading one line of action, then repeating to follow the other line, all the while negotiating the shifts in perspective, which push Black Alice into the "off-panel" space. If, as Groensteen says, all the elements of the comic constitute a weave, connected in unusual and unpredictable ways, then Morrison and O'Donnell, even in this early work, are adept at exploiting this, and exaggerating it, putting obstacles in the way, compelling the reader to look twice, and to work harder to decipher what is being presented. Again, the immersive strategies (creating two planes of action, shifting perspective) lead to a circular pattern. The first panel starts with a close-up of Black Alice looking towards the door where the aliens will enter, and the reverse view in the next panel offers her point of view, an embodied perspective. The final panel on the page shows another shift in perspective as the gun is thrown out of the panel (presumably) towards Black Alice, putting the reader in the dislocated, off-panel point of view position of Black Alice, as she reaches to catch the gun in order to kill her assailant. These shifts in perspective in the main action are echoed in the background action, as seen in the fifth panel, where the direction the angel is facing seems to have reversed. Again, immersive and recursive strategies are intrinsically linked.

By the time Morrison came to write *Zenith* (1987–1993), the deconstructive superhero story he created with artist Steve Yeowell for the British science fiction weekly *2000AD*, he had perfected the technique of luring the reader in with an overload of information and playing with perspective. The first panel of *Zenith* Phase One shows the light from a film projector illuminating a screen in a dark cinema, with the unmistakable dialogue of a newsreel presenter introducing what we are about to see. The point of view is slightly elevated, giving the reader the impression that they are in that darkness, watching the newsreel about the World War II British superhero Maximan flicker to life. The next few pages deftly play around with perspective and angles, as the reader is wrenched out of the propaganda newsreel and back into "reality," with Maximan being beaten by the Nazi superhuman, Masterman (Fig. 1.5–7). The art by Yeowell, with its decompression of time and space, has been referred to by Morrison as

Fig. 1.5 The Big One. Morrison and Yeowell. Zenith Phase I © 1987, 2014 Rebellion A/S. All rights reserved. Zenith Copyright © 2014 Rebellion A/S. All rights reserved. Pages reproduced by kind permission of the publisher.

Fig. 1.6 "Darkness is coming, and..." Morrison and Yeowell. Zenith Phase I © 1987, 2014 Rebellion A/S. All rights reserved. Zenith Copyright © 2014 Rebellion A/S. All rights reserved. Pages reproduced by kind permission of the publisher.

"high contrast Western Manga,"[20] and it certainly captures the sense of immediacy that Japanese comics are renowned for. As Groensteen observes, citing Paul Gravett, "the narrative techniques specific to mangas produce a feeling of immersion in the action, which Western comics cannot attain."[21] This is because traditionally Western comics have been much faster paced than Japanese ones. Mangas, having much higher page counts, can decompress the action, slowing everything down and allowing the reader to dwell on specific moments, inhabiting them. In *Zenith* Morrison and Yeowell were trying to replicate the immersive effects of manga by slowing down the action through use of repetition, long panels, heightening emotional tension, and deepening characterization. The panels in the cockpit of the bomber demonstrate this slow pacing, with careful use of what McCloud would term "moment-to-moment" transitions.[22] The release of the atom bomb and its fall towards Berlin, which is shown in three repeating panels, is a good example of this. The measured building of suspense concludes a page later with the off-panel detonation of the bomb which occupies the space of the reader, with the characters staring right out of the panel at the reader/approaching blast. They are reduced to smudges on the last panel of the page, and that panel has no borders.

Similar tricks of perspective are seen in the first few panels of the second installment of Phase One, which show London from above, from what the reader quickly becomes aware is Zenith's perspective as he drunkenly flies home after a night out. This sequence is intercut with another person's point of view, that of Zenith's manager, Eddie, who is watching the television, which is showing a pre-recorded interview with Zenith and another superhuman, Ruby Fox (Voltage). The repeating close-ups on London/Zenith's home are matched by close-ups on the television, moving closer each time, building tension as the effect of zooming towards the window/television culminates in Zenith crashing through the window and landing on the table in the kitchen, blocking Eddie's view of the television. The parallel action, and its coming together is an effective technique for driving the action forward, and the introduction of Ruby Fox, and some exposition about the history of superheroes in this world. As is common with Morrison's page transitions in *Zenith* there is some ironic word play. The interviewer asks Fox if she feels that the author of a history book about the superhero team Cloud 9, of which she was a part, "came down too hard" on them. The page turn then has Zenith crashing through the kitchen window. The inclusion of a book (Robert Ludlum's 1971 novel *The Scarlatti Inheritance*, with a prominent swastika on the cover) near the middle of the page is a reminder of the previous installment, set During World War

Fig. 1.7 Flying High. Morrison and Yeowell. Zenith Phase I © 1987, 2014 Rebellion A/S. All rights reserved. Zenith Copyright © 2014 Rebellion A/S. All rights reserved. Pages reproduced by kind permission of the publisher.

II, and foreshadows the return of Masterman, or to be more precise, his twin, whose body is inhabited by an inter-dimensional entity known as Iok Sotot.

At a later point in *Zenith*, when Zenith, Ruby Fox and Siadwel Rhys (The Red Dragon) combine forces to tackle the resurrected Maximan, Morrison employs different immersive techniques, shifting the narration into the mode of memoir, providing excerpts from Ruby's diary to narrate events in the first person. The change in narration is signaled visually as well as linguistically, with the caption boxes resembling pages torn from her diary, and the typography representing her handwriting. Later, Morrison switches to a cinematic "voiceover" effect, with dialogue in captions juxtaposed against images showing events transpiring in a different place. This is seen in the sequence where Ruby and Siadwell build a cloud using their rekindled powers, which is another example of the decompressed storytelling Morrison and Yeowell were experimenting with. Little happens, apart from a lightning strike, but the slow move towards the close-up creates tension, and the pace is further slowed by the narration. This rather downbeat tone is maintained in the battle between Masterman and Siadwell Rhys, which is abrupt. The fight is practically over before it begins, but it leads to a recursion, with the sequence in which Maximan and Masterman are killed by the atomic blast in 1944 being echoed, with almost identical images and dialogue, but this time it is not an atomic blast that appears, but the superhuman Peter St. John (Mandala), who joins the battle against Masterman. This plays with the expectations of the reader by exploiting their memory of the previous sequence. This is another example of Groensteen's braiding effect at work. Indeed, the array of techniques that Morrison and Yeowell employ to draw the reader into the text is remarkable, and these continue throughout the series. What is most interesting in *Zenith* though, in terms of narratology at least, is the way that these techniques of narrative immersion are set against metafictional strategies, where irony, parody, and allusion draw the reader out of the experience of the text, positioning them as critics and self-aware consumers of superhero narratives, able to appreciate Morrison and Yeowel's play with the genre and its conventions. This is partly why Morrison referred to *Zenith* as a "hip-hop" comic, "representing old material as new material"[23] in a complex weave of associations, a maze—or perhaps more correctly, a labyrinth, encouraging the reader to navigate the tangled intersecting patterns of the narrative.

The oscillation between immersive and metafictional strategies in *Zenith* is playful in many senses, and as noted, at several points the action is resolved, somewhat anti-climactically, by wordplay or trickery. In Phase One Masterman is defeated by a post-hypnotic suggestion, planted earlier in his mind, and triggered by the words "Tyger, Tyger," another repetition, and taken from William Blake's 1794 poem "The Tyger," which itself has a circular structure. In Phase Two, the nuclear missiles targeted on London are stopped when Zenith's ally, Peter St. John, provides him with the answer to a riddle by Lewis Carroll, unlocking the control center and allowing Zenith to force the villain to disarm the missiles. In the last part of *Zenith*, Phase Four, the immersion within the narrative takes a stranger turn, as much of the story occurs within a miniature universe within a universe, called Chimera (another *mise en abyme*), in which the villains have been trapped without their knowledge. This is the culmination of the immersive/recursive strategies employed in *Zenith*. At the end of the story the narrative returns to an earlier point, revealing that most of the action has been an elaborate trick on both the villains and the reader, who are immersed within this fiction. Inside this fake universe Dr. Payne narrates his memoir as he ages in reverse, eventually losing his language skills and his ability to comprehend what he has written. This artificial universe, which takes the form of a crystal pyramid, is held by Peter St. John (as one would hold a book) while he quotes Blake's "Auguries of Innocence" (c.1803):

> To see a World in a Grain of Sand
> And a Heaven in a Wild Flower,
> Hold Infinity in the palm of your hand
> And Eternity in an hour.[24]

This signals Morrison's observation that the story world of a fiction is like a parallel universe, one that we can enter and leave at will, much like the reader enters and leaves the world of the story. This collapses the distinction between the "fictional" and the "real" in the narrative, and potentially, beyond it.

Literary allusions are hidden throughout the series, giving the reader a barrage of clues to the wider plot. These aspects of *Zenith*, with the recursive structure and narrative decompression were very much ahead of their time, putting it on the same level as other innovative works of the mid–1980s, such as Alan Moore and Dave Gibbons' *Watchmen*, and Frank Miller's *The Dark Knight Returns* (both 1986), but what Morrison does that these creators do not is enter the worlds of his fictions. He uses avatars to enter the story, and this is yet another immersive technique, establishing the story-world as a space where reader, author and characters meet.

Avatars and Fiction Suits

In *Zenith* there are several characters who represent the author. Firstly there is Zenith himself, who is a brash character obsessed with fame, who by Morrison's own admission is very much modeled on himself at the time, and the persona he crafted to make his way in the comics industry.[25] However, it is too simple to say that Morrison is Zenith, as it is clear that the central opposition throughout much of *Zenith* is between youth and age, mirroring the schema of Blake's *The Four Zoas*, with its opposition between Orc and Urizen. If Zenith is Orc (the spirit of youthful transgression) then the villain, Dr. Payne, creator of the superhumans, and who looks somewhat like an older version of Morrison, is Urizen ("your reason," restriction, and rationality), but in Blake's cosmology Orc becomes Urizen, rebellion becomes conformity, and then back again in an endless cycle, or what might be termed a strange loop.[26]

This kind of self-conscious metafictional play with avatars is also seen in *Flex Mentallo*, in which Wally Sage, a troubled young man with a drug problem, discovers that characters he created as a child in homemade comics are, in fact, real. Lord Limbo, a character Wally read in a comic as a child, tells him that "we made comics because we knew. Somehow we knew something was missing and we tried to fill the gap with stories about gods and superheroes… comics are just crude attempts to remember the truth about reality."[27] At the end Wally, an avatar for both Morrison and Frank Quitely, the artist, completes a crossword puzzle (another example of a game or riddle as a plot device), and the "magic word" he utters is not "SHAZAM" (as those familiar with Captain Marvel comics might expect) but "SHAMAN," triggering the collapse of the imaginary world into the "real" world. Whether this is a signal of Wally's insanity or his transcendence remains unclear. To complicate matters there is another avatar for Morrison in the text. This is the Hoaxer, an amalgamation of the Batman villain the Riddler and the Flash (one of Morrison's favorite superheroes as a child).[28] The former plays linguistic and semantic games and the latter is a modern version of Hermes, the messenger of the gods who is associated with language.[29] Given his fascination with language it is no surprise one of the avatars Morrison adopts in *Flex Mentallo* is steeped in linguistic power.

When reality and imagination start to collide, a recurring image appears: Wally's hand, which at times becomes Flex Mentallo's hand, seen from the same embodied perspective, situates the reader in the position of both Wally and Flex (Fig. 1.8). This repeating image of a character star-

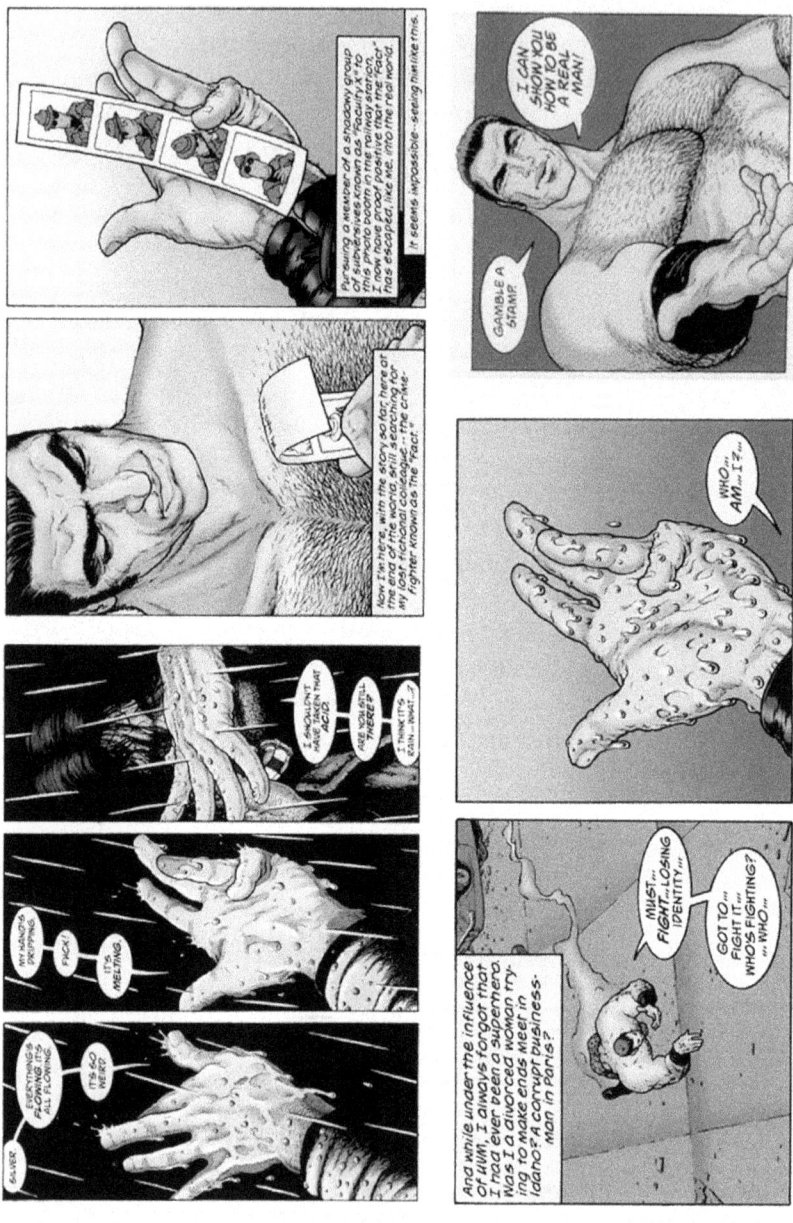

Fig. 1.8 "Time for all the works and days of hands." Morrison and Quitely. From "Flex Mentallo" #2 © DC Comics. Used with permission.

ing at their own hand also appears in *The Filth* at a key point, signaling the crossover between supposed "reality" and an elaborate fantasy world. A similar shift comes at the end of *Flex Mentallo*, with the integration of the world of imagination with the "real world." Taking Flex's hand Wally breaks down, saying, "I made the world to end," confessing that the fantasy world he has created is a product of his neurosis, but also making him a symbol for creativity. At this point an unknown narrator's voice intervenes, and text appears in strangely slanted caption boxes. It is unclear who speaks, but this voice talks of the narrative as if it is an experiment or computer game. It says, "Welcome, you have been inhabiting the first ultra-post-futurist comic: characters are allowed full synchointeraction with readers at this level."[30] The last page, which shows all the fictional superheroes bursting through into reality, is again, from an embedded point of view, but it is not clear whose. Perhaps it is Wally's, perhaps the reader's.

Such play with words, images, and narration is also seen in *The Invisibles*, perhaps Morrison's signature work, containing his most overt intrusion into his own comics (with the possible exception of *Animal Man*) in the character of King Mob. King Mob is another Morrison look-alike, but this time he takes it further. Treating the comic as a magical ritual Morrison claims to have affected his own life by writing King Mob into situations that would later manifest in reality, such as when King Mob is tortured by having flesh-eating bacteria put on his face. Morrison was later admitted to hospital with an infection on his face.[31] Whether this was the result of fiction altering reality or synchronicity, the main thing is the mythos that came to surround this performance of himself in the narrative, and the way that this becomes the key to the narrative puzzle, with readers being encouraged to see themselves as characters, to liberate themselves through similar performances, using the comic as a stage, a world in which to conjure new, better selves. *The Invisibles* is about the fluidity of identity, with characters adopting different roles and personalities, and who are caught up in a kind of elaborate game. Indeed, there is the theme of playing chess with the devil, a reference to Ingmar Bergman's film *The Seventh Seal* (1957). Also, the image of the various characters as pieces on the chessboard was a common trope in 1960s comics.

In a further metafictional twist the story of *The Invisibles* is revealed to be the product of a time travel experiment in which a girl from the future (Ragged Robin) reads a book called *The Invisibles* and comes back in time to make it happen. Do the events produce the book, or does the book produce the events? This is an example of a strange loop at work, and one of the key elements of this is Barbelith, an inherently recursive symbol (two circles, one within the other, and two parallel lines). In one of its first appearances it is literally a strange loop—a Möbius Strip, much like an Escher drawing, bending back upon itself, creating a paradox. This is mirrored in the conclusion of the story, where the revolutionary struggle towards enlightenment that has made up the story is re-produced as an immersive experience, a virtual reality game in an aerosol can which users/players can use to enter and re-experience the narrative of *The Invisibles* itself. As with *Zenith*, *Animal Man*, and *Flex Mentallo*, it is unclear whether the final pages of the story are actually happening or whether they take place in a parallel world. But then, the answer is obvious—both yes and no, as the world portrayed in the story is not real, and these different levels of fiction all have the same status within the tangled hierarchies that Morrison creates, but these puzzlebox narratives unfold to reveal a profound truth—that in a very real sense we make the world through our imagination. This is very much the case in *The Invisibles*. In a story called "And We're All Policemen," Gideon Stargrave (a version of Michael Moorcock's Jerry Cornelius character who appeared in Morrison's early *Near Myths* stories, and another avatar for Morrison) announces the arrival of the new millennium as he enters the Supercontext (the apocalypse re-conceived as immersion in a fictional universe) while disembodied narration offers an oblique commentary:

> And Jesus said, "Hands up who's seen *Star Trek: The Next Generation* 'The Holodeck'...?" Whereupon Thomas, called The Doubter, spake, saying, "Jesus! The goddamn thing is on TV every five minutes! What's the point?" Saith the Lord, "The point is this: We're on the Holodeck! The universe is a holodeck and we are being played..." The disciples shook their heads and tried in vain to interpret what they took, mistakenly, to be symbolically [sic] language.[32]

Here it is unclear who speaks, but this sums up the central idea of *The Invisibles*—that we are all immersed in language, and this creates our sense of reality, which is analogous to experiencing a virtual reality simulation, or playing a game and forgetting that you are outside of the game, mistaking its rules for universal natural laws. Little wonder then that the Wachowskis, creators of the film *The Matrix* (1999), which is about immersion in a computer simulation that has replaced the real world, were so influenced by *The Invisibles*.[33] Morrison's desire to equate *The Invisibles* with a computer game is made clear in an interview published in *Anarchy for the Masses: The Disinformation Guide to the Invisibles* where he says that it "was designed to be involving [and] immersive. The sooner I can actually translate it into a game, the better."[34]

The series concludes with an example of the power of symbols and signs, with King Mob using a pop gun to destroy the Archon of the Outer Church, the King of all Tears. At the same time Barbelith explodes following contact with humanity, signaling the end of the world as we know it, but the apocalypse (or Supercontext) is not the end: it is a recursion, a revelation that tangles hierarchies and dualisms, resets things, allowing new patterns to emerge. The series ends with this contact with the unrepresentable, but here too there is a recursion to a nascent state. The last "image" of *The Invisibles* is nothingness—a blank white space, which could signify the blank sheet of paper onto which the script or drawings will be inscribed. This return to the point before the comic was created suggests a return to the start, and in the first panel of the first page of the first issue of *The Invisibles* the caption reads "And so we return and begin again."[35] If one considers Hofstadter's description of strange loops, the significance is all the greater:

> What I mean by "strange loop" is ... not a physical circuit but an abstract loop in which, in the series of stages that constitute the cycling-around, there is a shift from one level of abstraction (or structure) to another, which feels like an upwards movement in a hierarchy, and yet somehow the successive "upward" shifts turn out to give rise to a closed cycle. That is, despite one's sense of departing ever further from one's origin, one winds up, to one's shock, exactly where one had started out. In short, a strange loop is a paradoxical level-crossing feedback loop.[36]

This could serve as a description of the entire narrative structure of *The Invisibles*, moving towards enlightenment, then folding back upon itself. The whole story is a strange loop, and characters and readers move through it in a non-linear way, making great use of the immersive/recursive complex that Morrison has been refining throughout his career. Clearly Morrison's experiments in comics form, and the superhero genre, blending immersive and recursive structures, are far from over.

Notes

1. Grant Morrison, in Chris Murray, "More Space Combat! An Interview with Grant Morrison," *Studies in Comics* 4, no. 2 (2013): 232.
2. Douglas Hofstadter, *Gödel, Escher, Bach: An Eternal Golden Braid* (London: Penguin, 1979), 684–719.
3. Chris Murray, "Invisible Symmetries: Superheroes, Grant Morrison and Isaiah Berlin's Two Concepts of Liberty," *Studies in Comics* 4, no. 2 (2013): 299.
4. Kendall L. Walton, *Mimesis as Make-Believe: On the Foundations of the Representational Arts* (Cambridge: Harvard University Press, 1990), 274.
5. Gérard Genette, *Narrative Discourse: An Essay in Method* (Ithaca: Cornell University Press, 1972).

6. Marie-Laure Ryan, *Narrative as Virtual Reality: Immersion and Interactivity in Literature and Electronic Media* (Baltimore: Johns Hopkins University Press, 2001), 19.

7. Scott McCloud, *Understanding Comics: The Invisible Art* (New York: HarperPerennial, 1994), 60–93.

8. Thierry Groensteen, "The Monstrator, the Recitant and the Shadow of the Narrator," *European Comic Art* 3, no. 1 (2010): 1–2.

9. Benoît Mandelbrot, *The Fractal Geometry of Nature* (New York: Freeman, 1982).

10. Grant Morrison and Richard Case, *Doom Patrol* #27 (New York: DC Comics, 1989), 37.

11. Grant Morrison, "Afterword," in Grant Morrison and Richard Case, *Doom Patrol* #20 (New York: DC Comics, 1989).

12. Morrison and Case, *Doom Patrol* #27, 37.

13. Marc Singer, *Grant Morrison: Combining the Worlds of Contemporary Comics* (Jackson: University Press of Mississippi, 2012), 118–126.

14. Noam Chomsky, *Aspects of the Theory of Syntax* (Cambridge: MIT Press, 1965).

15. Grant Morrison and Steve Yeowell, *The Invisibles* 1 #1 (New York: DC Comics, 1994), 1.

16. Marc D. Hauser, Noam Chomsky and W. Tecumseh Fitch, "The Faculty of Language: What Is It, Who Has It, and How Did It Evolve?" *Science* 298, no. 5598 (2002): 1569–1579.

17. Thierry Groensteen, *The System of Comics*, trans. Bart Beaty and Nick Nguyen (Jackson: University Press of Mississippi, 2009), 144–158.

18. Grant Morrison, in *Near Myths* #4 (Edinburgh: Galaxy Media, 1979), 52.

19. Grant Morrison, "The Wilderness Years," introduction to *Abraxas*, in *Sunrise* #2 (Northwood, Middlesex: Harrie, 1987), 25.

20. Grant Morrison, *Supergods: Our World in the Age of the Superhero* (London: Jonathan Cape, 2011), 212.

21. Groensteen, *The System of Comics*, 5.

22. Scott McCloud, *Understanding Comics: The Invisible Art* (New York: HarperPerennial, 1994), 70.

23. Grant Morrison, in *Halfway to Paradise—Grant Morrison*, dir. Jim Gillespie (Glasgow: Big Star in a Wee Picture, 1988).

24. William Blake, "Auguries of Innocence," in *Blake: The Complete Poems*, ed. W.H. Stevenson (Harlow: Pearson Education, 2007), 612.

25. Morrison, *Supergods*, 211–213.

26. For more on this see Chris Murray, "Subverting the Sublime: Romantic Ideology in the Comics of Grant Morrison," in *Sub/versions: Genre, Cultural Status and Critique*, ed. Pauline MacPherson, *et al.*, (Newcastle: Cambridge Scholars, 2008), 34–51.

27. Grant Morrison and Frank Quitely, *Flex Mentallo* (New York: DC Comics, 1996), 4, 11.

28. Morrison, *Supergods*, 83.

29. Ibid., 30.

30. Morrison and Quitely, *Flex Mentallo*, 22.

31. Morrison, *Supergods*, 281.

32. Grant Morrison *et al.*, *The Invisibles* (New York: DC/Vertigo, 1999–2002), 5.239.

33. Morrison, *Supergods*, 315.

34. Grant Morrison, in Patrick Neighly and Kereth Cowe-Spigai, *Anarchy for the Masses: The Disinfomation Guide to the Invisibles* (New York: Mad Yak Press, 2003), 258.

35. Morrison and Yeowell, *The Invisibles* 1 #1, 1.

36. Douglas Hofstadter, *I Am a Strange Loop* (New York: Basic Books, 2007), 101–102.

"Screw symbolism and let's go *home*"

Morrison and Bathos

KATE RODDY

> REBIS. In fact, the whole *tower* indicates a symbolic wish to *transcend* duality and achieve some kind of *union* with a fundamental state of pure consciousness. Cliff?
>
> CLIFF. Yeah. Screw symbolism and let's go *home*.
>
> —Grant Morrison and Richard Case,
> *Doom Patrol* #41[1]

Introduction: The Art of Sinking in Superhero Comics

As Timothy Callahan observes in one of the earliest works of scholarship on the writer: "anti-climax is typical of Morrison's work."[2] However, as yet there has been no in-depth analysis of the uses and effects of this device within Morrison's superhero narratives. In this essay I consider what Callahan terms "anti-climax" in its more literary guise, "bathos." Taking examples of bathetic moments in Morrison's writing I examine how and in what ways he achieves the effect, and, most importantly, what his use of bathos reveals about his attitudes to storytelling and authorship.

Any discussion of bathos immediately runs up against the problem of definition. In an essay devoted to the topic, the poet and critic Keston Sutherland admits "I think it is very difficult to say satisfactorily what bathos is."[3] Dictionary definitions lack precision, describing the word variously as a narrative feature ("anticlimax")[4] or one of broken style ("the sudden appearance of the commonplace in otherwise elevated matter of style").[5] Bathos can be accidental, the result of a lack of writerly skill (especially in an attempt to elicit pathos which becomes "excessive or insincere,"⁶ and thus, deflates); or, as in this essay's opening quotation from Morrison's *Doom Patrol*, deliberate—a device that creates humor out of sudden and unexpected juxtapositions.

The slipperiness and multiplicity of the term have much to do with the fact it is not so much a word as a "complex, satirical invention."[7] "Bathos" entered the English lexicon through the poet and essayist Alexander Pope's 1727 work *Peri Bathous, or, The Art of Sinking in Poetry*. Bathos, Pope explains, is the Greek word for "profound," by which he means depth or nadir.[8] His purpose in writing is "to lead [the reader] by the hand and, step by step, the gentle downhill way to the bathos—the bottom, the end, the central point, the *non plus ultra* of true modern poesy,"[9] and the essay offers a guide to the composition of criminally bad verse, well supported by examples from the works of his contemporaries.

Pope's bathos already encompasses many of the ideas the term has come to represent in popular culture: it is a destination, the sinkhole of all talent; it is also a series of rhetorical tics—mixed metaphors, opaque syntax, linguistic vulgarity—which serve to transform mediocre poetry into that which is execrable. Here bathos is always accidental, the result of a lack of education, good taste, and skill in a writer for whom poetry is a "morbid secretion from the brain" and composition an "evacuation" (i.e., a kind of mental enema).[10] This is because, to Pope, the purpose of literature is to capture the Sublime, defined by the ancient Greek rhetorician Longinus (c.100 CE) as "a certain loftiness and excellence of language … [which] illumines an entire subject with the vividness of a lightning-flash, and exhibits the whole power of the orator in a moment of time."[11] It is therefore beyond Pope and his Augustan contemporaries that any writer would be bad *on purpose*. Yet artifice, vulgarity, and broken style have been deliberate features of many movements post–1900, often serving to lampoon notions of "high" art, challenge the limitations of genre, or to stress the irredeemable baseness of the human condition. Although the title of Pope's work was tongue-in-cheek, he foreshadowed this himself: there is, after all, an *art* to sinking. I would therefore argue that there are two discernible traditions of bathos: the eighteenth-century, Popean one which describes a failure to achieve sublimity (anticlimactic); and the twentieth-century or "modern" tradition, which is concerned with the subversion of established artistic conventions (iconoclastic). In this essay I show that Morrison's work makes use of both anticlimactic and iconoclastic bathos, and that both are used (albeit in different ways) to challenge and reinvent the superhero narrative.

"All you had to do was switch it off": Anticlimactic Bathos

Morrison's earliest comics for DC are dogged by unsatisfactory endings, and nowhere is this more evident than in his run on *Animal Man* (1988–90). Not once, but twice, the eponymous hero is confronted with a doomsday bomb only for the story to end with the revelation "all you had to do was switch it off."[12] Within a Popean scheme, such narrative anticlimaxes signal a failure to achieve the Sublime, yet the self-consciousness and deliberateness with which Morrison orchestrates these events precludes us from understanding them as the result of a lack of writerly care or skill. As I will make evident below, the persistence of anticlimactic bathos in *Animal Man* provides opportunities for Morrison to engage with complex ideas concerning metatextuality, deterministic narrative structure, and the role of the author within comics.

Anticlimactic bathos emerges in *Animal Man* in the seminal issue "The Coyote Gospel" (#5). In this story, Buddy Baker (Animal Man) encounters a tortured, lupine being in Death Valley, California, named Crafty Coyote (an analogue for the Loony Tunes character Wile E. Coyote). Crafty gives to Buddy his "gospel," which tells the story of how he was banished from his own world by its shadowy, paintbrush-wielding Jehovah for daring to "challenge the futile brutality of existence."[13] While the reader is granted insight into the pathos of Crafty's position as eternal scapegoat, Buddy merely squints at the scroll he has been given, revealed through his eyes to be a series of hieroglyphic squiggles: "I'm sorry...," he tells Crafty, "I... I can't *read* it."[14] Animal Man fails to aid or even empathize with Crafty, and the comic ends with the latter's death at the hands of a grief-stricken trucker who believes the innocent Crafty to be the Devil.

As well as marking the first instance of metatextuality in the comic (a feature which becomes more and more prominent as Buddy gains awareness of his own rewritten origin story and role as entertainment for an omniscient audience), the issue serves as a capsule narrative for the whole *Animal Man* series: Buddy, too, comes from a world where endless violence and repetitive conflict are the norm (the DC Comics universe) and also serves the whims of a demiurgic creator, whom he will eventually meet and petition.

Following the death of Animal Man's family at the hands of an enemy assassin, the final bathetic moment of Morrison's run on the series is Buddy actually coming face to face with a sepia-toned simulacrum of Grant Morrison to demand an answer for all the suffering he has been made to endure.

> ANIMAL MAN. Why did you *do* this? You killed my *family*. You ruined *everything*. Do you know what you've *done* to me? ...
>
> GRANT MORRISON. It added *drama*. All stories need drama and it's easy to get a cheap emotional shock by killing popular characters.[15]

Morrison is here placed in the position of the villain who has lured the hero to his lair. Yet, instead of revealing the endgame of his elaborate and dastardly plot over the past twenty-five issues, 2D–Morrison merely admits to folding under the pressure of reader expectation, to falling back on clichéd plot devices when invention failed him. It seems that the writer, just as much as Animal Man, is apt to fall beneath the trundling wheels of narrative determinism. The link between creator and his flawed creation is highlighted once more when Animal Man chastizes Morrison for his inconsistent plotting:

> ANIMAL MAN. You haven't been much *good* at writing my life, have you? I've just wandered through a series of unconnected events with people telling me that *everything* is connected.
>
> GRANT MORRISON. Yeah. Well, that's the *trouble* with my stories—they always seem to build up to something that never actually *happens*. That's the trouble with my *life* too.[16]

Buddy is increasingly frustrated with Morrison for his failure to compose a narrative suitable for the world he, as Animal Man, lives in (i.e., the DC Comics universe): "Listen, where *I* come from, we expect *real* stories. I'm getting *sick* of these pseudo-existential narratives!"[17] Apparently taking his creation's criticisms about his genre-fiction improprieties to heart, Morrison begins to toy with alternative endings: should he have been less preachy about animal rights? Should he have taken up his readers' suggestions to have Animal Man fight other animal-themed characters, or given him a nemesis who "thrives on burgers"?[18] "I'm out of space," he complains, "out of time, and I haven't said anything worthwhile. ... Go home, Buddy. Forget we ever met."[19] With this dismissal, Buddy finds himself at home on his couch. Outside the sun is shining and his miraculously resurrected wife and children are waiting on the porch: in other words, Morrison's final gift to him is to press a narrative reset button, to make it so that Buddy Baker's world is exactly what it was before a fit of ill-intentioned writing tore it apart. While this denouement may be read as a happy ending for Buddy, it is also constitutes a rejection by Morrison of his responsibility to craft a suitable ending for the arc: "Nothing's wrong," Morrison's avatar says, repeating Buddy's last words in the comic as he sits before his computer in a monochromatic rendering of his Glasgow flat. "Nothing's wrong. Is that it? Is that the best you can do? Nothing."[20]

More than simply an authorial cop-out, the non-ending of *Animal Man* is a reflection of the tension in Morrison's early works between what Marc Singer terms revisionism and nostalgia. Revisionism refers to the movement in comics (typified by the mid-'80s works of Alan Moore and Frank Miller) which popularized "stories that attempted to represent superheroes realistically, cynically, or with mature artistic sensibility,"[21] while nostalgia is, "a retro movement that rejected the innovations of the revisionists" in favor of the tropes and conventions of the classic superhero comics of the Golden and Silver Ages.[22] On the one hand, Morrison frequently critiques the post–Millerian suggestion of a direct correlation between realism and violence. As 2D–Morrison tells Buddy: "we thought that by making your world more violent, we would make it more 'realistic,' more 'adult.' God help us if that's what it means."[23] Elsewhere, Morrison derides the very idea that an escapist genre such as superhero comics should aspire to something so tawdry as "realism." Of the 1980s revisionists, he says:

> I didn't think it was right for superheroes to be burdened with real world problems. I was more interested in going into their world—I wanted to find out what it was like in there—where the sky was always blue, where everything was primary-colored. ... I felt that Moore was about bringing ... bringing the grit and the grime into superheroes' lives and hurting them and kind of messing them up—and exposing their futility and their frailty. To me it's like, I don't want to expose the futility and the frailty of one of the last great ideas that we have.[24]

Yet although Morrison rejects the violent, grim "realism" of the revisionists, he also evinces discomfort with the overly-simplistic conflicts and inherently static nature of the classic superhero narrative. The conventions of Golden and Silver Age storytelling involve the creation of what Umberto Eco termed an "oneiric climate" where "what has happened before [the story] and what happens after appears extremely hazy. The narrator picks up the thread of the event again and again as if he had forgotten to say something and wanted to add details to what had already been said."[25] The traditional superhero narrative is episodic, with the passage of time between each adventure remaining undefined. These conventions ensure that the characters always return to the status quo, the narrative essentially resetting at the beginning of each issue. As 2D–Morrison explains it to Buddy:

> See, your world is so much *simpler* than ours. It can be invaded by aliens, or suffer catastrophes and nothing *matters*. It all just comes back, good as new. There's no problem that can't be solved by *some* idiot in tights.[26]

The anticlimactic bathos of Animal Man's conclusion is revealed to be not (as 2D-Morrison self-deprecatingly suggests) a result of poor or unimaginative writing, but of a seemingly irresolvable tension between an ending that is devastating, but final, and one which is uplifting but merely reinstates the status quo.

Yet bathos is present in *Animal Man* not simply in the overall shape of the narrative and its ending, but in more minute and subtle ways too. It can be seen as a fundamental part of the hero's psychological makeup: Buddy Baker is so anxious about the morality of his own actions as a self-professed "superhero," and so doubtful about his ability to effect positive change, that he often ends up doing nothing at all. An early issue culminates in a fight with the character B'wana Beast, a former superhero who has been unhinged by the abduction and death of his chimpanzee companion, Djuba. Where we might reasonably expect our hero to glory in his victory over a deranged and dangerous foe, Animal Man simply leaves the conquered B'wana Beast unconscious and propped against a wall. "I guess I should have been pleased," Buddy reflects, "but I felt nothing too much had happened. ... Well, what was I supposed to do? Take him to jail like a good superhero?"[27]

Animal Man continues to be deeply ambivalent about his right to apprehend those identified as villains, who—as in the case of the aging, suicidal Red Mask and hysterical, grieving Time Commander—often turn out to be deeply pitiable figures. He tells the latter in issue #16, "just because I wear a costume doesn't mean that I enjoy fighting,"[28] and throughout the series Animal Man continues to search for a mode of heroism that does not involve the kind of violent, neurotic methodology Morrison attributes to Batman: "[his] obsessive, impossible quest to punch crime into extinction, one bastard at a time."[29]

In the process, Buddy often ends up not acting at all, resigning himself to his own inefficacy. We might consider these tendencies in Animal Man as a character to be micro-expressions of bathos peppered throughout the work, prefiguring the series' ultimate non-ending. Buddy's anguished vacillation also provides a fundamental link between creator and created: as Animal Man hesitates to unleash the violent, decisive action expected of him as a character in a comic, so Morrison resists the generic pressures to script it. As we will see in the following section, these bathetic associations between plot, character and writer are further strengthened in Morrison's next series, *Doom Patrol* (1989–92), and here given an added dimension through the stress laid upon the heroes' physical atypicality.

Bathetic Bodies

While Animal Man's personality sets him apart from his superhero peers, he is, in purely physical terms, fairly typical. 2D–Morrison even goes so far as to call him "a generic comic book hero with blond hair and good teeth. One of *hundreds*."[30] In *Doom Patrol*, by contrast, the protagonists are deliberately set apart from their peers, advertising themselves as "the world's strangest heroes." Their ranks include Crazy Jane, a woman whose superhero powers manifest as multiple-personality disorder; Rebis, a hermaphroditic entity fused with a "negative spirit"; Cliff Steele, the human brain of a former race-car driver implanted in a robot body; and Danny the Street, a sentient, transvestite street that latterly serves as both a team member and as their base of operations. In discussing his motivations for taking on the rebooted Silver Age title, Morrison writes that the team's atypical make-up was simultaneously repulsive and darkly attractive to his younger self:

> When I was a kid, I hardly *ever* read DOOM PATROL; that comic frightened me, and the only reason I read any of the stories at all was that there was a certain dark and not-altogether-healthy glamour about those four characters. ... Back in the '60s, when DC super-heroes still sported right-angled jawlines and Boy Scout principles, the Doom Patrol slouched into town like a pack of junkyard dogs with a grudge against mankind.[31]

In his own run on the comic, Morrison both foregrounds and valorizes the team's counter-culture identity by having their leader, Professor Caulder, state:

> The world needs Doom Patrol ... needs *us* more than ever. Don't you see? There are areas in which only *we* are qualified to operate. When the rational world breaks down, we can *cope* ... because we've *been* there ourselves.[32]

This speech seems to promise that when far-out crises present themselves, the Doom Patrol will be just the men (and women and transvestite streets) for the job. Yet, like Animal Man, the Doom Patrol frequently discover that their efforts have little or no bearing on the events that unfold. In issue #34, for example, Cliff's brain is imprisoned in a jar while his robot body is commandeered by Brotherhood of Evil members the Brain and his super-intelligent gorilla sidekick Monsieur Mallah. While the comic's drama of Cartesian debate and inter-species homoerotic romance unfolds, Cliff (the supposed "hero" of the narrative) is confined to the background, rendered not only helpless, but also blind and insensate: "Oh, God. Can someone please tell me what's going *on* out there?"[33] In the longer story arc between issues #37 and 41, Doom Patrol find themselves caught up in the war between the Orthodoxy of the Insect Mesh and their mortal enemies the Hussite Ultraquist Geomancers (a grandly incomprehensible sci-fi rendition of the Reformation). In this multi-issue plotline Cliff, Jane and Rebis are little more than puzzled bystanders, decentered within their own narrative.

Like Animal Man in the interview with his writer, Cliff frequently expresses annoyance at the fact that the team's adventures never follow conventionally superheroic plotlines. Discussing Danny the Street's defeat of Mr. Jones and the Men from N.O.W.H.E.R.E. (an episode where drag cabaret saves the day), he grouses: "sometimes it might be nice to just stop a bank robbery or foil a criminal mastermind. You know, like regular super-guys."[34] Reflecting on the unfolding of the Orthodoxy-Ultraquist conflict, he sarcastically comments: "Looks like the end of another two-fisted adventure for the Doom Patrol, eh?"[35] Cliff's chorus-like commentary serves a number of paradoxical functions in the narrative, simultaneously offering a sort of glib closure to the story, while highlighting the generic violations that create this lack of closure in the first place. As a would-be two-fisted hero, he draws attention to the ways in which the composition of Doom Patrol (as both a text and a team) renders it incapable of fitting into the typical episodic, "oneiric" superhero narrative.

In both *Animal Man* and *Doom Patrol*, much of this atypicality pertains not only to what the characters do or say, but to the very make-up of their bodies. Morrison's heroes are frequently placed in opposition to more normative heroes through their gender identities. In the former title, this play is more subtle. On the surface, Buddy Baker is the very model of American male heteronormativity; yet, despite his family-man status and typically superheroic good looks, Animal Man is made to seem a less impressive, less forcefully masculine figure than his peers. In the second issue of Morrison's run, Buddy has a surprise run-in with a smiling, self-confident Superman. Buddy's inner monologue expresses his mingled sense of wonder and painful consciousness of his own inadequacy at this encounter with the original superhero: "He shakes my hand and makes me feel like I'm made of *glass*."[36]

Superman's primary-colored costume stands out on the page next to Animal Man's more muted tones; he strikes stiff, iconically heroic poses in contrast to Buddy's more unassuming, casual stance. Superman is physically bigger than Buddy—bulkier, ripped with muscle, and he occupies the foreground of every panel in which he appears. His purpose is, ostensibly, to encourage Buddy and welcome him to the superhero community, but he forgets Buddy's identity and has to be reminded ("Animal Man! Of course. I like the costume, the big 'A.'"),[37] and leaves as abruptly as he arrived:

> SUPERMAN. You *hear* that? Sorry. Of course you don't.
>
> ANIMAL MAN. Hear what?
>
> SUPERMAN. Light aircraft in trouble over *Port Townsend*. Have a nice day.[38]

While it is not the well-meaning Superman's intention to patronize Buddy, or cruelly mock his comparatively modest superpowers, it is a sharp reminder to Buddy (and the reader) that Animal Man's story is not going to play out like that of the JLA superstars. Buddy is no lantern-jawed hulk, no man of steel, and thus his narrative is predisposed towards the bathos of its ultimate ending.

The surreal characters and situations of *Doom Patrol* give Morrison room to deconstruct notions of heroic masculinity more comprehensively. The Doom Patrol's core members are all, in different ways, androgynous. Some of Crazy Jane's personalities have masculine names and characteristics ("Merry Andrew ... Sun Daddy ... Driller Bill").[39] Cliff Steele is a man's brain transplanted into a robot body, and his demonstrable lack of male genitalia is what enables him to gain entry to the feminine sanctuary of Jane's subconscious: he appeals to her misandrist persona Black Annis by figuring his loss of body as a castration: "I'm not a man. Not anymore. ... It was all burned or ripped away or amputated."[40] Rebis is an alchemical forced marriage of a man, Larry Trainor, and a woman, Eleanor Poole, yoked together by an inhuman "negative spirit." Danny is a transvestite street, his mixed identity symbolized by the presence of traditionally masculine stores ("Army-Navy ... Gun Shoppe ... Hardware")[41] decorated with frills, tinsel, fairy lights and chintz, as well as his communication in Polari, an early twentieth-century gay slang.

The team's counter-culture identity as the "junkyard dogs" of the superhero community is underlined in an encounter with Justice League Europe. The opening of *Doom Patrol* #28 discovers JLE members Booster Gold, Blue Beetle and Animal Man standing in front of "The Painting that Ate Paris" (a "hungry" artwork that seeks to devour the whole world), debating how to pursue the villains the Brotherhood of Dada into the seemingly impermeable canvas. As Crazy Jane, Cliff Steele and Rebis stride into view, Booster Gold quips: "Hey, speaking of nut-cases, here comes the *Doom Patrol*."[42] Identical in stature, and all sporting brightly-colored spandex costumes to show off their armor-like abs, the JLE represent the masculine power fantasy of the "hard body," which is defined by Susan Jeffords as "indefatigable, muscular and invincible."[43] The Doom Patrol, by contrast, come in markedly different shapes and sizes, and wear altered civilian garb set off with bulky coats.

As a team of officially-recognized and authorized superheroes, the JLE believe themselves to be rightfully in charge of the situation, yet their left-brained approach to problem-solving and monolithic masculinity actually prevent them from gaining entry to the painting. "It's activated by paradox modulation," Rebis explains. "Meditate on *me*. Meditate on what I am. I am the avatar of contradiction: black and white, male and female, in one body."[44] As the Doom Patrol disappears into the canvas (to have yet another weird and inconclusive adventure), Booster Gold echoes the thoughts of the young Morrison: "Those guys give me the *creeps*."[45] The team's heterogenous gender and physicality may be a key component in their effectiveness, but it also sets them apart from their heroic peers and denies them access to the same kind of upwards plot trajectories: they are not men in tights; their stories will not be so simplistic, nor so satisfyingly resolved. Thus, anticlimactic bathos in the plot of *Doom Patrol* is not only mirrored by, but actually a function of the team's very make-up. This principle is further illustrated and strengthened by the fact that it holds true in reverse for Morrison: as the next section will show, classic heroes will invariably have classic adventures, and within this scheme, victory is inevitable.

The Justice League Always Wins: The Metaphysics of Bathos

One universally-acknowledged truth of the classic "oneiric" superhero narrative is that the good guys always win. As a result of his tenure on *Animal Man* and *Doom Patrol*, from 1996 to 2000 Morrison was given the responsibility of writing that most valuable DC Comics property, the Justice League of America. Anticlimax is manifestly not a feature of these stories: in fact, it is a recurring theme that no matter how grave the threat or slim the odds, by the end of the issue, the JLA will nonetheless have prevailed. This narrative determinism is even metatextually highlighted by Morrison in the series in issue #9, when the supervillain the Key attempts to harness the team's predisposition towards victory for his own ends:

> The Justice League *always* wins. So I had to make them win for *me*. I had to turn my problem into a *solution*. ... I'm waiting for them to *realize* they're

dreaming. I'm waiting for that inevitable Justice League *victory*. Because the accompanying psycho-electric *surge* will give me the means to take control of ... everything.[46]

This plan has an obvious, inherent flaw: Batman, Wonder Woman, Superman *et al.* are able to overcome the Key's artificial reality and defeat him because—as has already been established—*the Justice League always wins*. A darker turn on this theme is introduced in the one-shot story *JLA: Earth 2*. In this comic the team encounter Alexander Luthor, a refugee from an alternate Earth that is home to the moral opposites of the characters from the JLA's Earth ("Earth 1" in post–Crisis continuity). The good version of Luthor solicits the JLA's help to return to his own reality and fight their evil counterparts in the Crime Syndicate of Amerika. As the JLA set about imprisoning the Crime Syndicate members and cleaning up Earth 2, Owlman (the evil counterpart of Batman) points out the fruitlessness of the endeavor: "Luthor missed the flaw in his plan: he's brought his super *do-gooders* to a world where 'evil' always triumphs."[47]

When Wonder Woman laments the failure of their mission to rehabilitate the dark, mirror world, Batman tells her: "our methods *can't* succeed on this world. It's a law of nature. Everything we do is *ordained* to fail. Even *good* deeds go bad here, Diana."[48] When the Crime Syndicate cross over to Earth 1 to wreak havoc they discover the opposite is also true: "the glue that holds us together back home doesn't *work* here!" rages Owlman. "We're *ineffective!*"[49] The good JLA and evil CSA have no choice but to retreat to their own proper universes. The story ends with J'onn J'onnz's vague hope that their evil counterparts might have "learned something,"[50] yet the final panels show the Crime Syndicate members returning to their old corrupt, violent ways. Thus, in Morrison's vision of the post–Crisis DCU, the status quo is fixed and inelastic. Good will always prevail on Earth 1, and so the JLA's stories (in our universe) will always end in triumph. The very nature of the fictional world the JLA inhabit, and their status as its appointed heroes, preclude the narratives from anticlimax. Within this context, *Earth 2* shows Morrison at his most bleak, and most profoundly bathetic. While *Animal Man* and *Doom Patrol* demonstrate that atypical heroes never truly "win," the run on *JLA* establishes that victory itself is a hardwired feature of the conventional superhero narrative and thus as hollow as it is predictable.

If this story represents the bathos (in Pope's sense of nadir) of Morrison's treatment of the episodic narrative, then what alternatives exist for a writer of superhero comics? In *Doom Patrol* Morrison took his cue from the Dadaists in challenging the conventions and limitations of his chosen genre. This marks the beginning of Morrison's experiments with non-linear and fragmentary narratives. As we shall see in the following section, this kind of iconoclasm can generate its own problems, but also its own solutions.

Dada Is the Kingdom of NO: Iconoclastic Bathos

As stated in the introduction, bathos in Pope's sense of the term is always accidental. Yet, as Sara Crangle and Peter Nicholls write, post–1900 there is evidence for a turn to bathos which is deliberate, "where forms of artifice, vulgarity and hyperbole are welcomed and celebrated."[51] These critics go on to observe that "the 'nonsense' of dada offers perhaps the best example of this appropriation of the bathetic."[52]

As the conventional narrative of Dada's history has it, the movement was a reaction to the First World War, which the artists saw as "a direct product of the competitive urge of industrial capitalism, with its mechanized trench warfare as a grotesque and monstrous version of the productive process itself."[53] While Dada (like the term bathos) resists narrow definitions, it can be said to be concerned with such ideas as individualism, illogicality, multiplicity, fragmentation and, perhaps foremost, the urge towards iconoclasm. As one of the movement's self-appointed leaders, Tristan Tzara, wrote in his "Dada Manifesto 1918":

> I am against action; as for continuous contradiction, and affirmation too, I am neither for nor against them, and I won't explain myself because I hate common sense....
> Thus DADA was born, out of a need for independence.... People who join us keep their freedom. We don't accept any theories. We've had enough of the cubist and futurist academies: laboratories of formal ideas. Do we make art in order to earn money and keep the dear bourgeoisie happy?[54]

As Pope's *Peri Bathous* parodies Longinus' aspirational treatise on the Sublime, in contrast to the manifestos and "little magazines" of the Futurists and Vorticists, Tzara's text parodies the very idea of an artistic manifesto: "DADA DOES NOT MEAN ANYTHING."[55] In standing only for gleeful iconoclasm, Dada is often accused of being nihilistic or anti-art. The statements of those associated with the movement seem (perhaps provocatively) designed only to back this up. As Francis Picabia wrote in 1920:

> Dada itself feels nothing. It is nothing, nothing, nothing.
> It is like your hope, nothing.
> Like your heaven, nothing.

Like your idols, nothing.
Like your politicians, nothing.
Like your heroes, nothing.
Like your artists, nothing.
Like your religion, nothing.[56]

Morrison himself attests that his early work was strongly influenced by a Surrealist aesthetic.[57] *Animal Man* and *Doom Patrol* are littered with throwaway references and visual cues to Surrealism and Dada: the "stress psychecapes" of the Thanagarian art martyr Rokara Soh[58]; the grotesque bodily elision inflicted on the laboratory animals by B'wana Beast[59]; figures such as "Fear the Sky," a group of suit-wearing men with planets for heads, evoking the work of René Magritte[60]; and the Daliesque Huss.[61] Morrison's most sustained engagement with these movements is in the figures of the Brotherhood of Dada (itself an art-history joke, since, as we have seen, the Dadaists strongly resisted cohesion).

The Brotherhood of Dada is the Doom Patrol's recurring antagonist, a ragged collection of what its leader, Mr. Nobody, terms "super-powered outcasts ... with stupid names and even more stupid costumes."[62] In its original incarnation it includes the Fog, who is constantly interrupted by the voices of victims he has absorbed; the Quiz, who has every superpower you have never thought of; Sleepwalk, who only has powers when she is unconscious; and Frenzy, who can create a cyclone with two bicycle wheels attached to his back. As Tzara's manifesto lampooned the small-mindedness of manifestos in general, in positioning themselves as the Doom Patrol's antagonists, the Brotherhood of Dada point to the shallowness of comic-book villains, and the futility of such generic oppositions. From its initial appearances, the Brotherhood resists binary notions of morality. Addressing his newly collected cohorts in a lair composed of pop-culture detritus, Mr. Nobody tells them:

> "Good"! "Evil"! Outmoded concepts for an antique age. ... Look at us! Are we not final *proof* that there is no good, no evil, no truth, no reason? Are we not proof that the universe is a drooling idiot with no fashion sense? ... *From this day on, let unreason reign!*[63]

While the Brotherhood's initial plan of allowing Paris to be consumed by a sentient painting is sufficiently sinister to warrant superhero intervention, their second plan to reinvent themselves as avant-garde politicians is less easy to situate on the good-evil continuum. The Doom Patrol remain divided on the issue: Jane persists in seeing the Brotherhood's campaign as a necessary exposé of political corruption, while Cliff cannot shake the feeling that the whole ridiculous enterprise is something they should step in to oppose, "because if we *don't*... then the Brotherhood is *right* and there's no *point*. No point to *anything. I* can't live that way."⁶⁴

The Brotherhood's campaign speeches resound with iconoclastic bombast: they tout pointless policy initiatives like a plan to "add an extra inch and a half to rulers,"⁶⁵ cast aspersions on the very idea of an economy by describing money as "a scrap of colored paper with no intrinsic value."⁶⁶ In a probable homage to the UK's Monster Raving Loony Party they have as their campaign slogan: "Dada. Hey, you know it makes absolutely no sense."⁶⁷

This episode involves the complex interplay of several satirical elements. On the surface, it is just what the Brotherhood of Dada intends it to be: an iconoclastic statement, a parody that shows up the inherent ludicrousness and corruption involved in presidential electioneering and the entire political process. As Jane pointedly observes after watching Mr. Nobody's campaign broadcast, "the whole thing's a dumb circus, anyway. At least he's *admitting* it."⁶⁸ Yet in combining Dada with political satire, Morrison also exposes the ineffectual nature of both. Dada is accused of being anti-art in its lambasting of formalism and prevailing culture, replacing wholeness with fragmentation, reason with unreason, and significance with meaninglessness. It gleefully tears down icons, yet offers nothing to put in their place except tatty ephemera: signed urinals and nonsense verse. Likewise, political satire points out systemic failures and injustices without having to offer viable solutions. As Jonathan Coe observes on the limitations of this genre: "laughter is not just ineffectual as a form of protest ... it actually replaces protest.... [I]t's easier and much more pleasurable to laugh about a political issue than to think about it."⁶⁹ Thus, both approaches are "anti-establishment," but fail to provide constructive alternatives to the status quo and are therefore limited, perhaps even hollow.

As always with Morrison, there is a meta dimension to the implied criticism. While Mr. Nobody has promised that it is the Brotherhood's *raison d'être* to expose the shallowness of the traditional hero/villain opposition within comics, the radical overhaul of this genre convention is never actually delivered (in other words, the Dada manifesto is as full of empty promises as that of any would-be ruling party). In the "Magic Bus" episode, the Brotherhood is threatened by the U.S. government, which sends its own agent (the many-faced John Dandy) to put an end to Mr. Nobody's presidential campaign by assassinating him. Yet as he gives his affected rendition of dying, Mr. Nobody points to the true cause of his downfall as the general public, and their inability, or unwillingness, to embrace the unfamiliar: "God knows I *tried* as only a chimneypot can try, but they don't *want* strangeness and unpredictability in their lives. They tire of it so soon, though they never tire of *tedium*."[70]

We might read this as Morrison grumbling about the unadventurous palates of his comics' readership, but as yet another anticlimactic ending in a series riddled with bathos, it makes sense to interpret Mr. Nobody's complaint as symptom rather than cause. The Brotherhood of Dada typifies the trend in *Doom Patrol* towards what might be termed narrative profligacy. Morrison's creativity is in overdrive throughout the series: for example, in just one issue, *Doom Patrol* #31, we are introduced to such concepts as the Book of the Fifth Window, Baphomet the prophetic horse head, and a whole host of sinister villains: Fear the Skies, the Dry Bachelors, the Mystery Kites, Wynken, Blynken and Nod. The narrative opens too many avenues to be satisfactorily closed down within the episodic format, which then tends towards a satirical, anticlimactic ending (in this case, the aforementioned sinister forces are still de-creating the universe; the Doom Patrol have just managed to fix it so that they are now doing it "terribly, terribly slowly").[71] This profligate creativity produces a weariness in the reader, who begins to realize that nothing will come of the characters and concepts introduced in these narratives, and they will never be developed or even mentioned again. Fragmentation and multiplicity are simply too much for the episodic superhero narrative to usefully contain.

One very different solution to the problem of fragmentation is offered by what is arguably Morrison's most daring and complex work for DC: *Seven Soldiers of Victory* (2005–6). The concept for this series is a twist on the crossover "event," in which a number of comics titles tie in to tell a major storyline, and, of course, to boost sales by encouraging readers to buy beyond their usual pull-list. *Seven Soldiers* presents us with a motley collection of protagonists: Shining Knight, Guardian, Mister Miracle, Klarion the Witch Boy, Zatanna, Frankenstein, and the Bulleteer. These seven were deliberately chosen for being "characters with no baggage, who could be plunged into outrageous life or death situations with no guarantee that they would recover or even survive."[72] Generically self-aware, like all of Morrison's creations, the comic reinvents the superhero team-up by leaving the protagonists uninformed of their cooperation in the larger scheme of things: it is "the story of seven soldiers, destined to save the world from an evil queen yet never meet."[73] Their common enemy is the Sheeda, a time-traveling, culture-devouring race led by the unholy Gloriana Tenebrae. The Sheeda are variously seen as aliens or fairies (*sídhe* in Old Irish) by the human civilizations they attack, but it emerges that they are, in fact, "the *pinnacle* of *natural* selection ... the last living species clinging to life on a *dying* earth, consuming their own *history* to *survive*."[74] They are us from the future: a race grown so indolently capitalist and culturally barren that it turns to devouring its own ancestors.

While each of the protagonists fights against a different iteration of the Sheeda invasion, the disparate threads of their miniseries are brought together in the final bookending issue, *Seven Soldiers of Victory* #1. In some ways, this comic is exactly what a reader might expect from the climax of a superhero team-up story: the seven protagonists (albeit separately and unaware of their common purpose) fighting off the deadly foe amid the carnage of a besieged New York. Yet this ending is complicated by means of a number of unusual narrative devices. As signaled by the figure "The Time Tailor" presenting himself as the issue's narrator, the comic is a metatextual patchwork. On an artistic level, there is penciler J. H. Williams III's bravura demonstration of his mastery of other artists' styles (for example, the homage to Jack Kirby in the pages depicting Aurakles, the first and archetypal hero), as well as his employment of a variety of panel shapes, including those which appear to be layered or interlocking. On a narrative level, the comic switches between conventional linear storytelling and the use of other devices and styles, such as a page of Klarion's story told using lengthy captions rather than speech balloons, in a style perhaps meant to evoke a children's annual. Most intriguing is the use of *The Manhattan Guardian*, an intratext newspaper, to relate key events of the finale. Some of the paper's copy describes the battle itself, but levels of fictionality and authority compete to render its message ambiguous: "Hurricane Gloria Pummels Manhattan," reads a weather subheading (a reference to Gloriana Tenebrae, mistaken for a meteorological event?), while a Doonesbury-style comic strip called "Carla" seems to depict events happening to the Guardian's estranged wife as she attempts to flee the city. The paper includes the "Guardian Cryptic X-Word," as Morrison promises in his script, "containing answers to several *Seven Soldiers* mysteries."[75] It is left blank for the conscientious reader to fill in, indicating a need for active participation in the narrative, rather than mere passive consumption.

Marc Singer argues that the series as a whole resists linear reading strategies, requiring what one character in the text refers to as a "satellite" view, the ability to "read *Seven Soldiers* holistically as a single narrative connected by its repeating patterns, not as seven separate stories nor as one more conventionally linear narrative structured around unities of setting, character, or action."[76] As an emblem of this we might consider the set of images of Zatanna reaching up out of her own universe into a "dimensional lock."[77] In a splash page showing the action from Zatanna's

Fig. 2.1 "Whatever you are. Help me before it's too late." Morrison and Sook. From "Seven Soldiers: Zatanna" #4 © DC Comics. Used with permission.

perspective, we see the Seven Unknown Men gazing upon her dispassionately, the page borders that delineate their world lined with pens, cogs, and typewriter keys poised to stamp down on her. In an image shown from the opposite perspective (both that of the Seven Unknown Men and of the reader), the palm of Zatanna's hand breaches the borders of the panel is if she is reaching out of the comic (Fig. 2.1). "Whatever you are," she appeals, "help me before it's too late."[78]

The bald and besuited Seven Unknown Men may easily be read as another Morrisonian avatar—like him they are the unseen weavers of the protagonists' stories. Yet the image is metatextual in another way—it hearkens back to a key moment from *Animal Man*, a splash-page image of Buddy (who has gained awareness of the world beyond thanks to a mystical peyote trip) staring from the page in horror, shouting, "I CAN SEE YOU!"[79] In *Animal Man*, the reader is revealed as a sadistic voyeur who enjoys watching Buddy suffer. Zatanna, by contrast, trustingly holds out her hand and asks the people beyond her world to assist her. This they can do only by helping to complete the missing parts of the narrative. The ultimate ending of *Seven Soldiers*, its overall significance and the interrelation of its disparate episodes—all of these are resolutely left open for the reader to ponder, and to debate with others.[80] By structuring the text in this way, Morrison effectively devolves authority from writer to reader—an act which embraces Dada's iconoclastic practices of fragmentation and antiauthoritarianism without simply collapsing the narrative into meaninglessness.

Conclusion: Beyond Bathos

To take the "satellite view" of Morrison's work across his career in superhero comics, it becomes clear that there are both marked continuities and developments in his use of bathos.

Previous scholarship has already noted the prevalence of what I have termed anticlimactic bathos in early works such as *Doom Patrol* and *Animal Man,* especially in relation to plot. Indeed, much of Morrison's early work is concerned with the problem of how a superhero narrative should end. In pointing to the inflexible and repetitive nature of the conventional man-in-tights story with such formulas as "the JLA always wins," Morrison's narratives resist full-blown comics nostalgia. Yet "grim 'n' gritty" iconoclastic endings such as the death of Animal Man's family are also seen to be hollow and overly-simplistic in their valorization of violence as "realistic" or "adult" ("God help us if that's what it means"). While these early works expose the problems of writing within the superhero genre, they do not always provide satisfactory solutions. Morrison's initial attempt to craft a radically different kind of superhero narrative in *Doom Patrol*, as we have seen, leads to narrative fragmentation, where stories can only gesture towards closure by means of Cliff's acerbic quips. In later works, however, bathos is harnessed and made to work for, and with, the narrative: *Seven Soldiers* turns fragmentation into a strength by refusing to burden the series with an absolute or reductive ending.

As observed in the introduction, Pope's concept of bathos derives from a system in which the author stands as the ultimate crafter and arbiter of meaning, and where a work's success as art is entirely dependent on the abilities of its maker. From the beginning of his career at DC, Morrison satirizes the idea of the omnipotent artist, introducing creator figures who (like Crafty's god) are all authoritarian, shortsighted, and flawed. The answer, he suggests, is not to set up greater artist-gods, but to democratize the text. Whether a work like *Seven Soldiers* has meaning is dependent on the effort the reader puts in; its significance on how they choose to arrange and connect the narrative threads. The reader no longer sits back in derisive Popean judgment, but is implicated: and thus bathos, if it is anywhere, is in us.

Notes

1. Grant Morrison and Richard Case, *Doom Patrol* (New York: DC/Vertigo, 2004–8), 3.190.
2. Timothy Callahan, *Grant Morrison: The Early Years* (Edwardsville, IL: Sequart, 2007), 7.
3. Keston Sutherland, "What Is Bathos?," in *On Bathos: Literature, Art and Music*, ed. Sara Crangle and Peter Nicholls (London: Continuum, 2010), 9.
4. "Bathos, n. (2)," in OED Online. http://www.oed.com/view/Entry/16163?redirectedFrom=bathos (January 2, 2015).
5. "Bathos, n. (1a)," in Merriam-Webster Online (n.p.). http://www.merriam-webster.com/dictionary/bathos (accessed January 2, 2015).
6. "Bathos, n. (2)," in Collins Dictionary Online (n.p.). http://www.collinsdictionary.com/dictionary/english/bathos (accessed January 2, 2015).
7. Sutherland, "What Is Bathos?," 9.
8. Alexander Pope, *Martin Scriblerus' Peri Bathous, or, The Art of Sinking in Poetry* (Richmond: Oneworld Classics, 2009), 3.
9. Ibid., 2–3.
10. Ibid., 9.
11. Longinus, *On the Sublime*, trans. H. L. Havell (London: Macmillan, 1890), 2.
12. Grant Morrison and Chaz Truog, *The Animal Man Omnibus* (New York: DC Comics, 2013), 164, 650.
13. Ibid., 132.

14. Ibid., 135.
15. Ibid., 691.
16. Ibid., 695.
17. Ibid.
18. Ibid., 699.
19. Ibid., 703.
20. Ibid., 706.
21. Marc Singer, *Grant Morrison: Combining the Worlds of Contemporary Comics* (Jackson: University Press of Mississippi, 2012), 29.
22. Ibid., 21.
23. Morrison and Truog, *Animal Man Omnibus*, 703.
24. "Chapter 8: DC Comics Calling and Animal Man," *Grant Morrison: Talking with Gods*, dir. Patrick Meaney (Respect! Films and Sequart, 2010), DVD.
25. Umberto Eco, "The Myth of Superman," *Diacritics* 2, no. 1 (1972): 14–22 (17).
26. Morrison and Truog, *Animal Man Omnibus*, 692.
27. Ibid., 106.
28. Ibid., 443.
29. Grant Morrison, *Supergods: Our World in the Age of the Superhero* (London: Jonathan Cape, 2011), 26.
30. Morrison and Truog, *Animal Man Omnibus*, 696.
31. "A Word from the Author," in Morrison and Case, *Doom Patrol*, 1.186.
32. Ibid., 1.106.
33. Morrison and Case, *Doom Patrol*, 2.228.
34. Ibid., 3.63.
35. Ibid., 3.189.
36. Morrison and Truog, *Animal Man Omnibus*, 48.
37. Ibid.
38. Ibid.
39. Morrison and Case, *Doom Patrol*, 2.18.
40. Ibid., 2.121–2.
41. Ibid., 3.12.
42. Ibid., 2.55.
43. Susan Jeffords, *Hard Bodies: Hollywood Masculinity in the Reagan Era* (New Brunswick: Rutgers University Press, 1994), 25.
44. Ibid., 2.56–7.
45. Ibid., 2.57.
46. Grant Morrison and Howard Porter, *JLA: The Deluxe Edition* (New York: DC Comics, 2008–10) 1.206.
47. Grant Morrison and Frank Quitely, *JLA Earth 2* (New York: DC Comics, 2000), 63.
48. Ibid., 82.
49. Ibid., 80.
50. Ibid., 103.
51. Crangle and Nicholls, *On Bathos*, 5.
52. Ibid.
53. Richard Sheppard, *Aspects of European Dada* (unpublished thesis, 1979); quoted in Robert Short, *Dada and Surrealism* (London: Octopus Books, 1980), 17.
54. Tristan Tzara, "Dada Manifesto 1918," in *Seven Dada Manifestos and Lampisteries*, trans. Barbara Wright (London: Calder, 1977; repr. New York: Riverrun Press, 1981), 4–5.
55. Ibid., 4.
56. Francis Picabia, "Manifeste Cannibale Dada," *Dadaphone* 7 (1920); quoted in Short, *Dada and Surrealism*, 53.
57. "A Word from the Author," in Morrison and Case, *Doom Patrol*, 1.187.
58. Morrison and Truog, *Animal Man Omnibus*, 161.
59. Ibid., 34.

60. Morrison and Case, *Doom Patrol*, 2.131.
61. Huss appears in *Doom Patrol* #38. He sports a mustache similar to Salvador Dalí's and may be styled after the figures from *The Birth of Liquid Desires* (1932).
62. Morrison and Case, *Doom Patrol*, 2.26.
63. Ibid., 2.27.
64. Ibid., 5.28.
65. Ibid., 5.11.
66. Ibid., 5.23.
67. The Monster Raving Loony Party was established in the early 1980s by the ex-rock star "Screaming Lord" Sutch. Key policies include changing the name of the Isle of Man to "the Isle of Men, Women, Children, and Some Animals" and adding the Loch Ness Monster to the endangered species list. The party's slogan is "vote insanity: you know it makes sense." See Paul Sonne and Alistair Macdonald, "In the Longest-Running Joke in Politics, Life Imitates Farce," *The Wall Street Journal*, May 6, 2010; http://www.loonyparty.com.
68. Morrison and Case, *Doom Patrol*, 5.22.
69. Jonathan Coe, "Sinking Giggling into the Sea," *London Review of Books* 35, no. 14 (2013): 30–31.
70. Morrison and Case, *Doom Patrol*, 5.57
71. Ibid., 2.202.
72. Grant Morrison, "Introduction," in Grant Morrison *et al.*, *Seven Soldiers of Victory* (New York: DC Comics, 2006–7), 1.1.
73. Morrison *et al.*, *Seven Soldiers*, 4.177.
74. Ibid., 4.198.
75. "Seven Soldiers of Victory Part One: The Miser's Coat, extract and annotations," in Morrison *et al.*, *Seven Soldiers*, 4.221.
76. Singer, *Grant Morrison*, 226.
77. Grant Morrison and Ryan Sook, *Seven Soldiers: Zatanna* #4 (New York: DC Comics, 2003), 18.
78. Ibid., 16–17.
79. Morrison and Truog, *Animal Man Omnibus*, 511.
80. See, in particular, the extensive annotations to the text on fan forum Barbelith at www.barbelith.com.

The Writer and "the Writer"

The Death of the Author in Suicide Squad #58

ROY T. COOK

Grant Morrison's first major work in mainstream American comics is his run on DC's *Animal Man*, which stretches from issue #1 to issue #26. The series takes a dramatic metafictional turn in issue #5, titled "The Coyote Gospel."[1] In this issue Animal Man (a.k.a. Buddy Baker) encounters the dying Crafty Coyote, who has ascended from the comic book fiction of Animal Man's reality to live (and die) in Baker's own.

This issue of *Animal Man* is justly regarded as a brilliantly complex, multi-layered metafictional narrative[2]—but it is more than that. While the narrative introduces certain mysteries that ultimately lead to Animal Man's encounter with his own creator—the Writer (a.k.a. Morrison himself)—the particulars of the Crafty tale are often taken to have little to do with the climax of Morrison's *Animal Man* narrative. Such a reading, however, underestimates the role that the Crafty tale plays both in *Animal Man*, and in Morrison's comics oeuvre more generally. *Animal Man* #5, when read carefully against Morrison's larger corpus of work, represents the first chapter in his ongoing development of a subtle account of the relation between creators and their characters.

This account of the nature of fictional creation is important to understanding both the ongoing narrative of *Animal Man*, and Morrison's later work, which continues to expand on the scheme first developed in "The Coyote Gospel." The particular part of this account that will be of interest to us is Morrison's idea that entities (both fictional and real) can travel from one "level" to another, and in particular, that we should understand Morrison to have travelled into Animal Man's world, and to thus be literally identical[3] to one of the fictional characters he created—the Writer.

The account of the relationship between creator and created that Morrison develops throughout this work, and upon which rests his identification of himself and the Writer, is flawed, however. In demonstrating this, I will rely on two rather disparate theoretical traditions. First, fleshing out an initially plausible version of Morrison's claim to be identical to the Writer requires understanding exactly what fictions ask us to do, and what makes something true in a fiction—for this task I draw on the front-running account of the nature of fiction within the analytic tradition: Kendall Walton's analysis of fictions as games of make-believe.[4] In the Waltonian view, fictions are sets of instructions regarding what we are meant to imagine (or make-believe) to be true. Properly understanding and assessing Morrison's claim to be literally identical to his fictional avatar—the Writer—requires attending carefully to exactly what these comics ask us to imagine.

Morrison's claim to be identical to his fictional avatar, however, brings with it an implicit corollary: that this identity affords the character (and hence Morrison himself) with exactly the sort of authorial authority denied to authors (and to their authorial avatars) by Roland Barthes. In "The Death of the Author"[5] Barthes denies that the intentions and personal history of a text's author play any special, privileged role in the interpretation of that text. Within such a view authors have no special authority with regard to determining the "proper" interpretation of their works. I will not concern myself here with whether or not Barthesian accounts of the nature of authorship (or alternative views that build upon or reject Barthesian orthodoxy)[6] are correct. Instead, I will examine whether the view of fiction developed by Morrison, and illustrated via his insertion of the Writer into *Animal Man*, provides a genuine challenge to Barthes' understanding of the role of authorship (regardless of whether Barthes' views on authorship are plausible otherwise).

What is particularly interesting with regard to Morrison's account, and its ultimate failure, is that the *reductio ad absurdum* does not require mobilizing sophisticated accounts of the metaphysics of personal identity or the philosophical nature of fictional truth (although as we shall see, careful reflection on the nature of fictional truth and the role of authorial avatars is critical to properly formulating and understanding Morrison's views in the first place). Rather, the view of fiction and authorship that Morrison develops, and the challenge to Barthesian rejections of authorial authority implicit in this view, are both refuted in *Suicide Squad* #58, which provides a narrative counterexample in comic book form.

Authors, Avatars and Anthropologists

Morrison was not the first author to explore the connections between various levels of DC continuity and the real world: a similar blurring of the boundaries between distinct fictional worlds occurs much earlier, in Silver Age issues of *The Flash*. In his first Silver Age appearance in *Showcase Comics* #4 ("Mystery of the Human Thunderbolt"), the new Flash, Barry Allen, reads about the exploits of the Golden Age Flash in a comic book, suggesting that the Golden Age Flash is merely a fictional character within Silver Age DC continuity.[7] In *The Flash* #123 ("Flash of Two Worlds"), however, Jay Garrick, the Golden Age Flash, visits Barry Allen's reality and the two Flashes team up.[8] Thus, the Golden Age Flash is both fictional character and real person relative to the (fictional) perspective of the Silver Age Flash. Morrison describes the impact these comics had on readers (and on himself):

> There were inevitably philosophical ramifications for the reader. If Barry lived on a world where Jay was fictional, and we lived in a world where Barry was fictional, did that mean that we, as readers, were also part of Schwartz's elegant multiversal structure? It did indeed, and it was soon revealed that we all lived on Earth-Prime.[9]

Morrison's account of the connection between creators and the fictional characters they create can be seen as a continuation, of sorts, of this earlier, multi-level understanding of DC continuity and its relation to our own world.

Although, as already noted, Morrison's take on this theme is first developed in "The Coyote Gospel," it is perhaps easiest to begin with the more overt interrogation of these issues in *Animal Man* #25 and #26. I will not attempt to fully summarize these complex comics, but instead will remain content merely highlighting those aspects of the story that are relevant to the issues being explored here. In issue #25 ("Monkey Puzzle") Animal Man's spirit journey through the tropes and conventions of comic book storytelling concludes with his knocking on the door of a small cottage, and an authorial avatar of Morrison—the Writer—answering the door.[10] The next issue ("Deus Ex Machina") consists of the Writer explaining to Animal Man that the latter's life is nothing more than a result of the narrative choices made by Morrison while writing the comic.[11] In short, in these issues Morrison has, in some sense, "descended" from our (real) world to the (fictional) world inhabited by Animal Man (i.e., DC continuity) in order to engage in an exercise in authorial metafiction. The reader should take note of the careful way I have distinguished between the fictional character called the Writer and the real-life, human author named Morrison. The issues to be examined below hinge critically on the connections between these two entities.

"The Coyote Gospel" also depends upon, and is clearly meant to focus on, similar jumps between different "levels" of reality. In this case we do not have a "descent" of creator into his created world, but instead have a character that is fictional relative to Animal Man's world (i.e., one that might appear in funny animal comics read by Buddy Baker or, perhaps, his kids) "ascending" from the level of creation (Crafty's world) to the level of creator (DC continuity). Although Animal Man is not a comics creator, it is nevertheless clear from the narrative (in particular, from the shift in artistic style between that portion of the narrative that occurs in Crafty's world and that portion of the narrative that occurs in Animal Man's world) that Crafty is intended to be understood, at least initially, as fictional relative to Animal Man's perspective. Thus, issue #5 and issues #25 and #26 involve interactions between different "levels" of fiction—in both cases we have interactions between creation-level entities and created-level entities. Of particular interest is the fact that Animal Man himself plays both roles within the tripartite levels of reality constructed by Morrison in this narrative—in his interactions with Crafty, he is on a par with Crafty's creators (interacting with an agent from a narratively "lower" level), while in his interactions with the Writer he is not creator-level but created (interacting with an agent from a narratively "higher" level).

This complex narrative structure raises difficult questions regarding the nature of, and interactions between, fictional characters from different narrative "levels" of a particular fiction. In particular, different claims are true relative to these different worlds: "Animal Man exists" is false in the real world (he is merely a fictional character, after all), but is true in DC continuity (in other words, "within DC continuity, Animal Man exists" is true). Of course, we have to be careful here: there is some sense in which superheroes *do* exist in the real world—as ideas, as cultural constructs, perhaps even as abstract objects—as Morrison himself notes of Superman:

> Actually, it's as if he is more real than we are. We writers come and go, generations of artists leave their interpretations, and yet something persists, something that is always Superman.[12]

Here, however, we are interested in a literal reading of the claim "Animal Man exists"—that is, the reading that entails the existence of a superpowered being who dresses in orange and blue and has the powers of animals. Clearly *that* object doesn't exist in the real world, even if ideas of such do.

Along similar lines, "Crafty Coyote exists" is false in the real world (which, quite strikingly, does not seem to contain many talking animals), but is true in Crafty's world (in other words, "Within the fiction of Crafty's world, Crafty Coyote exists" is true). By issue #5, however, "Crafty coyote exists" is not only true from the perspective of Crafty's world, but also true from the perspective of DC continuity. In short, within DC continuity, Crafty is both a fictional character whose exploits Animal Man might read about, and a real person with whom he can interact.

Although Crafty's appearance changes from one context to another, there is no question that it is a *single* character that both lives in Crafty's world and interacts with Animal Man in the world of DC continuity. Morrison, by virtue of his role as author, has sufficient control over the interactions of these different levels of fictionality, and over the facts regarding the identity of a character (such as Crafty) when "ascending" from one fictional world (Crafty's world) to another (DC continuity) to ensure that this is so. What is less clear, however, is the relationship between the Writer—Morrison's authorial avatar, a fictional character that appears within DC continuity—and Morrison himself—the flesh-and-blood human writing both the story of Animal Man and that of Crafty.

There are a number of different forms that authorial avatars can take, and different roles that such avatars can play. Two distinctions are immediately apparent. First, authorial avatars can be distinguished based on whether they are *first-* or *third-person*—that is, on whether the author inserts a version of himself, or inserts a version of some other author or artist into the narrative. The Writer (in *Animal Man*, at least) is a first-person authorial avatar, while Morrison's appearance as one of the Architects in Brian Azzarello's *Doctor 13* backup stories from the 2006 *Tales of the Unexpected* miniseries is a third-person authorial avatar.[13]

Second, we can distinguish between those authorial avatars that are meant to be genuine representations of the author (what I shall call *replicative authorial avatars*) and those that are intended to "indicate" the author in a less direct sense (*resemblance authorial avatars*).[14] Both the Writer (again, in *Animal Man* but not necessarily elsewhere) and *Doctor 13*'s Morrison-as-Architect are replicative authorial avatars, since they are clearly meant to be depictions of Morrison himself. Morrison has also inserted resemblance authorial avatars—both first- and third-person— into his comics. For example, Morrison has claimed, at various times, that creation of King Mob from *The Invisibles* involved either an alien abduction (more on this below), or a magical spell, or both.[15] As a result, according to Morrison the direction of control between creator and created became inverted: Whenever King Mob became injured or ill in the comic, Morrison would contract similar symptoms (almost dying of an infection at one point).¹⁶ Nevertheless, Morrison never claims that he is in fact the same person as King Mob. On the contrary it is clear that we are not meant to understand King Mob as being identical to Morrison. Rather, King Mob is a fictional *surrogate* of sorts for the real-life Morrison: he is meant to reference, or to remind us of, Morrison, but he is not meant to be Morrison himself.¹⁷

Third-person resemblance authorial avatars are also not hard to locate in Morrison's work. For example, Simon Bisley's cover for *Doom Patrol* #36 features a bearded Flex Mentallo who looks very much like a very angry Alan Moore.¹⁸ Again, we are not meant to understand this as implying that Flex Mentallo really is Moore, but are instead to recognize that this authorial avatar, in virtue of its resemblance to Moore, is a playful reference to well-publicized disputes between Morrison and Moore.¹⁹

These distinctions fall far short of a full taxonomy and analysis of the different ways that authorial avatars can be inserted into fictional texts, but it suffices for our purposes. The instance of primary concern here—the replicative, first-person authorial avatar we have been calling the Writer—is particularly complex because Morrison claims that the Writer is to be understood, in some sense, as literally the same person as Morrison himself, just as the Crafty who inhabits Crafty's world is the very same character as the Crafty that later visits DC continuity. The question, then, is this: can Morrison make it the case that the Writer literally *is* Morrison (as he claims), rather than merely being a fictional version of Morrison?

Morrison describes his role as author, and in particular his authorial function with respect to *Animal Man*, in terms of a distinction between opposing conceptions of author-as-missionary and author-as-anthropologist:

> As I began to think of the DC universe as a place, it occurred to me that there were two ways to approach it: as a missionary or as an anthropologist ... missionaries ... attempted to impose their own values and preconceptions on cultures they considered inferior—in this case, that of the superheroes. Missionaries liked to humiliate the natives by pointing out their gauche customs and colorfully frank traditional dress [...]
>
> Anthropologists ... surrendered themselves to foreign cultures. They weren't afraid to go native or to look foolish. They came and they departed with respect and in the interests of mutual understanding. Naturally, I wanted to be an anthropologist.
>
> In *Animal Man* I created, with the help of my artistic collaborator, Chaz Truog, a paper version of myself that could be integrated with the 2-D DC universe. I sent my avatar onto the page surface to meet the Animal Man character and confirm suspicions he'd been having that his life story was being written by some demiurgic Gnostic overlord.... The implication was that our own lives

might also be "written" to entertain or instruct an audience in a perpendicular direction we could never point to, interacting with us in ways we could scarcely understand but that could be divined in the relationship of the comic world to the world of the creator and audience.[20]

This passage is ambiguous: on the one hand, Morrison describes projecting, not necessarily himself, but rather an authorial avatar (first-person, replicative), onto the page. On the other hand, he describes the situation as one involving mutual understanding between author and fictional character: Morrison does not merely write Animal Man coming to understand his fictional, created status, but instead enters the fictional world (in some literal sense) in order to explain things to Animal Man.

If we take Morrison at his word, then the DC universe is not just a creation that can be described and manipulated by the author. In addition, it is a real place that can be entered and explored—one where fictional characters can interact with persons from the real world, and not just vice versa. This does not sound unreasonable if taken metaphorically: first-person authorial avatars (whether replicative or resemblance) provide a straightforward means for authors to insert their opinions and personality (or, at the very least, what they wish us to take to be their opinions and personality) directly into narratives. But Morrison clearly means something more than mere metaphor. In a 2001 interview with *Newsarama*, he explains that

> *Animal Man* was an early attempt to descend into the real DC universe. I figured that if I put myself into a comic, it could be considered an actual voyage into the 2D comic book reality, wearing a suit to make myself look like one of them—a drawing. Exploring the place a little, I found that I could talk to characters; influence lives (even lives of famous characters who'd existed in this little paper universe long before I was born, like Superman for instance) and affect the structure of the "continuity." After *Animal Man*, I realized that I didn't have to enter that world looking like myself but that I could go in wearing different "fiction suits" as I came to call them. A fiction suit being simply any character we create as a disguise to allow us to wander around in the 2D four-color continuity cosmos without freaking out the natives the way I did Buddy Baker.[21]

Thus, according to Morrison, he (Morrison, not some fictional authorial avatar) entered DC continuity and interacted with the fictional characters living there. In short, Morrison is claiming to be *the very same thing* as his replicative first-person authorial avatar.

Although we have to wait until *Animal Man* #25 to meet the Writer, the "artist" of Animal Man (presumably penciler Chaz Truog) appears twice within "Crafty's Tale." Furthermore, these two appearances occur in two different "levels" of fictionality: the first in Crafty's world (as the "god" of Crafty's world, who exiles Crafty to DC continuity), and the second in (or perhaps "above") DC continuity (as the brush that fills in the blood in the final panels of the issue). Thus, *Animal Man* #5 already involves the *artist* "entering" these fictional realities, and the theme of creator-as-anthropologist is already fully at work in this earlier story even though Morrison (as the Writer) would not venture into DC continuity until many issues later. Although Morrison is not explicit about this, there seems to be no reason to doubt that we should also view these artist-avatars as instances of genuine identity, in which case, on Morrison's account, he cannot only insert himself into his comics, but can insert his collaborators into them as well.[22]

In order to see why we should take Morrison's claim to have entered the world of DC continuity seriously, it is helpful to look briefly at one of the more controversial episodes in Morrison's autobiography: his supposed interaction with otherworldly beings while taking drugs during a trip to Kathmandu.[23] Morrison reports that these entities grew our own universe in some sort of cosmic nursery, and goes on to describe their relation to our own reality as follows:

> Television talks about the "fourth wall" of the set as being the screen itself. If so, this [Morrison's "cosmic" experience] was a glimpse beyond the fifth wall of our shared reality. Five-dimensional intelligences could, as a condition of their geometrically elevated positions, get inside our skulls quite easily, and we might expect their voices to come from inside. They, in turn, could hear our thoughts as easily as we can read Batman's private inner monologues on a 2D page.[24]

Now, for our purposes we need not make any judgments regarding whether this episode was what Morrison claims it was, or was merely a drug-induced hallucination. What is important is that Morrison believes that the relationship between the "visitors" and ourselves is analogous to the relationship between ourselves and fictional characters—in particular, the fictional characters of *Animal Man* and the world of DC continuity. Just as our own world is a fiction (that is, a created narrative) relative to the world of Morrison's visitors, but is presumably no less real as a result, the fictional worlds inhabited by Animal Man or Crafty are, in Morrison's view, no less real—that is, no less sensible, tangible, and, importantly, visitable— than our own.

Given Morrison's otherworldly experience in Kathmandu, and the resulting revelation that the real world (as well as the world of the visitors) is no more or less real than the world of Animal Man or of Crafty, Morrison seems to conclude that he has the same, or a similar, sort of control over identity claims between the real world and DC continuity as he does with regard to identity claims holding between inhabitants of Crafty's world and DC continuity. Just as it is non-problematically the case that the Crafty that inhabits Crafty's world is the very same character that later enters DC continuity (regardless of the fact that the former is fictional relative to the latter), Morrison seems to believe that he can make it the case that he is literally identical to the Writer in an exactly parallel manner. This is possible in virtue of the fact that, according to his revelation, the metaphysical relations between Crafty's world and DC continuity are (roughly)[25] the same as the relations between DC continuity and the real world (which are, in turn, roughly the same as the relations between the real world and the world of the visitors): in each case, the former is "fictional" relative to the latter.

We now have the basic building blocks of Morrison's understanding of the nature of fiction: first, fictional worlds are no less "real" than the world that we readers of fiction inhabit. Second, our own world has exactly the same status relative to the world of Morrison's visitors as the fictional world of DC continuity has to our own. Third, one can travel from one such reality to another, playing the role of authorial anthropologist, and engaging directly with the inhabitants of that other world. Thus, the pages of *Animal Man* #25 and #26 are not, in Morrison's view, a description of what it might be like if Morrison were able to enter DC continuity and interact with Animal Man. Rather, they are meant to be understood as a sort of documentary report of what actually did happen when he in fact entered that world.

Morrison, Metaphysics and Make-Believe

While the proceeding section provides a careful, quite literal, reconstruction of Morrison's pronouncements regarding of the nature of fiction and the connections between creator and created, two objections almost immediately spring to mind. The first is that the suggested relationship—literal identity—between Morrison (the real person) and his authorial avatar (the Writer) is incredibly implausible. It is hard to see how any reasonable account of either the nature of personal identity (i.e., what makes a person the same from one time or situation to another) or of the nature of fictional truth could sustain a view where a single three-dimensional, flesh-and-blood human was somehow literally identical to a multiply-instanced, two-dimensional, printed character in a fiction.[26] Closely related to the first objection is a second: surely, regardless of whatever suggestive and sensational comments he might have made, Morrison almost certainly does not believe that he is, in fact, identical to the Writer. Morrison presumably has not had the sorts of experiences that would be required were the literal identity thesis true: for example, he surely does not have memories of meeting Animal Man in person, or of being constituted of paper and ink, or of being two-dimensional. Thus, a more plausible reading of Morrison's claims would be useful.

Fortunately, we can construct such an interpretation by understanding Morrison's identity thesis, not as a claim about reality (i.e., as the claim that the Writer really is identical to Morrison), but instead as claim about *what we are meant to imagine* when experiencing and evaluating the fiction. One influential framework for understanding the nature of fiction is that developed by Kendall Walton in *Mimesis as Make-Believe*.[27] Walton argues that a work of fiction should be understood as providing the rules for a certain kind of game of make-believe: assertions in the fiction (whether prose or pictorial) are understood as prescriptions regarding what we are meant to imagine to be true when playing the relevant game of make-believe, and experiencing the fiction (e.g., reading a comic) amounts to competently playing the make-believe game described by the fiction.

Real people, including real authors, often appear within fictions. According to the make-believe account of fiction, our default convention when experiencing such fictions is that we are meant to imagine that most or all of the actions and events that happened to the real person are also actions and events that we should imagine having happened to that person's fictional *doppelgänger* (unless such prescriptions are subverted by other aspects of the work). For example, if Abraham Lincoln appears in a historical novel, then (unless the novel indicates otherwise) we are meant to imagine that this character was president of the United States, that he lived in a log cabin, that he was assassinated, etc., regardless of whether the novel mentions any of this explicitly. Note, however, that the converse inference is not licensed: we are not meant to believe that everything that happens to Lincoln in the novel also happened to the actual, real-world Lincoln.

We can now understand Morrison's claim to be identical to the Writer as an instruction to imagine even more of the Writer: not only are we meant to imagine that actions and events that actually happened to Morrison also happened to the Writer (i.e., that the Writer is a fictional *version of*—that is, a replicative first-person avatar of—Morrison); we are also meant to imagine that the Writer really is literally identical to Morrison—

that is, we are meant to imagine that the Writer (a fictional character) is the same person as the real-world, flesh-and-blood Morrison—and hence we are meant to imagine that everything that happened to the Writer also happened to Morrison. This requires that we imagine the Writer to have once inhabited the (i.e., our) real world, to have made his "anthropological" trip from the real world to the fictional world, and to have later returned (furthermore, we are meant to imagine that the Writer is aware of all of this). Note that, although the claim that Morrison really *is* identical to the Writer might be metaphysically absurd, and his genuinely believing this claim unlikely, there seems to be nothing immediately problematic about our *imagining* it to be true.

This suggests that the Writer might have a special authority with regard to the thoughts, attitudes, and opinions of Morrison himself—an authority perhaps not shared by other sorts of first-person authorial avatars lacking this additional identity element. After all, competently experiencing the fiction in question—that is, competently interpreting *Animal Man*—requires that we imagine that Morrison's actual beliefs and biography are also the Writer's beliefs and biography (and vice versa). In short, if we are meant to imagine that the Writer is identical to (rather than merely similar to, or an analogue of or surrogate for) the real-world Morrison, then Morrison's actual beliefs and biography become a part of the fiction.

Discussion of the life and intentions of the author naturally brings us to Roland Barthes, and the pun embedded in the subtitle of this essay. In "The Death of the Author"[28] Barthes challenged the idea that authorial intention and authorial biography are essential ingredients for interpreting fictions, arguing that such works, once completed and made public, can be understood and assessed completely independently of the details of their creation and of their creator's intentions and influences.[29] Barthes does not claim that authorial intention and authorial biography must be ignored. Instead, he jettisons the privileged role traditionally accorded to intention and biography while retaining the idea that they are part of a plurality of legitimate interpretative resources.[30] Barthes was mindful of the complicating fact that authorial avatars sometimes appeared in a text, but resisted the idea that that they brought any sort of special authorial authority with them, arguing in "From Work to Text" that

> it is not that the Author may not "come back" in the Text, in his text, but he then does so as a "guest." If he is a novelist, he is inscribed in the novel like one of his characters, figured in the carpet; no longer privileged, paternal, aletheological, his inscription is ludic. He becomes, as it were, a paper-author: his

life is no longer the origin of his fictions but a fiction contributing to his work; there is a reversion of the work on to the life (and no longer the contrary).[31]

Morrison's insertion of the Writer into *Animal Man* can be read as a response to Barthes' widely influential rejection of the author's centrality to interpretation and meaning: Morrison is suggesting that the Writer is not *merely* a Barthesian "paper-author," since the paper-author (the Writer) and the actual author (Morrison) are (or are to be imagined to be) identical. By making his own actual beliefs and biography, rather than a defeasible report of such via a similar but non-identical authorial avatar of the more common sort, a part of the story, Morrison seems to have guaranteed that the meaning of *Animal Man* cannot be separated from the details of its creation, or from the intentions of its creator, since both creation and creator (rather than mere representations of such) are, in some sense, parts of the text itself.

Of course, formulating a plausible take on Morrison's claim to be literally identical to the Writer is one thing—defending it as correct is another. In fact, a refutation of Morrison's "anthropologist" account of the nature of fiction, of his claim to be identical to the Writer (even on the non-literal understanding just outlined), and of his implicit challenge to Barthes' denial of authorial authority already exists. What is most notable about this refutation is that it does not take the form of a philosophical essay. Instead, Morrison's account of the nature of fiction, and his understanding of the connection between the Writer (created authorial avatar) and himself (creator of that avatar), is refuted by another comic featuring the Writer.

Suicide Squad and the Death of the Author

The comic in question is *Suicide Squad* #58 ("Suicide Attack"), written by John Ostrander.[32] The comic tells the story of the eponymous group—a special squad of incarcerated supervillains who take on suicide missions in exchange for commuted prison sentences (explaining, in the process, how it is that supervillains who are captured in one issue are back on the streets only a few issues later). In this issue a special Suicide Squad is recruited by Black Adam to attack Circe's island fortress. The Writer—now equipped with a small word-processor—is one of the characters that make up this rather odd assault team.

As the team prepares for its mission, the Writer explains to his teammates that he (i.e., Morrison) is no longer in full control of the actions of the Writer:

> But you see, my problem is this—once I actually wrote *myself* into the story, *technically* I became part of the *continuity* and now someone else in controlling *me*—as I used to control my characters! It's *horrible!*[33]

On the next page he continues to explain his predicament:

> And so I script what's going to happen here on the computer, you see, and then it happens, unless reality goes too fast. But *sometimes* the writer who's now writing me *intervenes* and then I see what's about to happen.[34]

At this point, we see Black Adam's dialogue on the Writer's screen, whereupon we are given a panel with Black Adam delivering that same dialogue. The Writer concludes his explanation with "See? I *knew* he was going to say that!"[35]

At this point, Ostrander is already showing us some cracks in Morrison's understanding of the role of the Writer. Although the Writer speaks of inserting himself into the story, thus reflecting Morrison's imperative that, when reading the comic, we imagine that the Writer really is Morrison himself, the Writer's comments regarding his (i.e., Morrison's) loss of control over the words and deeds of the character suggest that the Writer is not literally Morrison at all—that is, imagining him to *be* (rather than merely *represent*) Morrison is not compatible with imagining the events as they are presented on the page. The Writer, in this issue, speaks as if he were a first-person authorial avatar (as he indeed was during his appearances in *Animal Man*), but his loss of control demonstrates that, since scripted by Ostrander, he has now been transformed into a third-person avatar.

Furthermore, the fact that it is Ostrander that is putting words in the Writer's mouth, and on the Writer's screen (and furthermore, that the Writer realizes this), throws some doubt onto the kind of anti–Barthesian authorial authority that the Writer might be thought to provide. Clearly, we are not meant to take the Writer's assertions and writings in *Suicide Squad* #58 as having any special claim to being accurate reports of the thoughts and motivations of Morrison. On the contrary, the Writer's complaint that "now someone else in controlling *me*—as I used to control my characters!" shows that he is aware that his own intentions and actions can no longer be taken to be—and hence can no longer be coherently imagined to be—either the intentions and actions of Morrison himself nor the result of Morrison's authorial efforts. In short, his words are no longer his own.

Things get even more interesting, however, a few pages later. The team assembled by Black Adam is, at this point, now engaged in a battle with various beasts protecting the island. The Writer is diligently typing the action and sound effects on his word processor:

> Amazon nearest writer gets hit by stray bullet. Pawingggg! Werebeast attacking Writer bursts into flame due to spontaneous combustion. Fwoomp! Yarrrgh![36]

At this point, the Writer gets stuck, quietly saying "Bugger! Writer's Block!" and, in the next panel, "I think I'm about to...?" He is promptly torn to pieces by another werebeast.[37]

Such is the rather inglorious death scene provided for the Writer by Ostrander. But is there is any sense in which we are to imagine that Ostrander also killed Morrison, or even some part of Morrison? The answer to this question is complex. On the one hand, there seems to be no reason that we cannot imagine that it is not only the Writer but also Morrison that dies during this issue of *Suicide Squad*—after all, we can imagine all sorts of false things about a person. But it is less clear that we can simultaneously imagine that the Writer dies *and* imagine that the Writer is identical to, and hence has all the same properties as, the real-world Morrison. After all, the Writer (the fictional character) dies at the hands (and maws) of werebeasts—as does perhaps a fictional avatar of Morrison—but the real, flesh-and-blood Morrison remains with us, writing comics to this day. To imagine that they are literally the same, yet have such distinct properties, would be a gross violation of Leibniz's Law, which states that identical objects are indiscernible. Thus, Ostrander's story provides a snappy, definitive refutation of Morrison's claim that we should (or even can coherently) imagine when reading stories involving the Writer that the latter is literally identical to the real-world Morrison and travelled from our world into DC continuity. Ostrander also refutes the corollary—that we must (or should, or even can) imagine that the Writer has the same beliefs and biography as Morrison—thereby defusing any anti–Barthesian authority that might be associated with the character.

The argument I have presented proceeds as follows: when reading the stories within which the Writer appears, we cannot coherently imagine that the Writer is identical to the real-world Morrison, since Ostrander kills the Writer, but does not kill (or in any detrimental way affect) Morrison himself. One might object that the character called the Writer in Morrison's comic is not, in fact, the same character as the character who goes by that name in Ostrander's comic.[38] In short, the suggestion is that we only need to imagine the Writer being identical to Morrison when it is Morrison who is writing him—the character called "the Writer" in Ostrander's comic might be a separate character altogether.

This sort of objection involves a rather substantial violation of the standards governing identity conditions for fictional characters in comics, however. What is fictionally true or false in a narrative is governed by, among other things, the norms and conventions at work in the production and consumption of the type of narrative in question, and comics are no exception.[39] According to standard practice within comics, an apparent depiction of a particular previously established character in fact depicts that character—that is, it is true in the fiction that the character is who she appears to be—so long as the author intends her to be that character (and so long as this presumption is not undone by later revelations that the character in question was being impersonated by some other fictional character, or other sorts of ret-conning). Ostrander clearly intends the character depicted in *Suicide Squad* #58 to be the very same character as is depicted in *Animal Man* #25 and #26, and in my experience readers usually take him to be such. As a result, there seems to be little motivation for denying that the Writer in *Animal Man* and the Writer in *Suicide Squad* are the very same character.

But perhaps this is too quick. The Writer is, it must be admitted, no ordinary character, but is a replicative authorial avatar. In addition, a critical part of the story just outlined regarding how *Suicide Squad* #58 undermines Morrison's account of the nature of fiction is that the Writer changes in a fundamental way from one story to the other. This change is not constituted merely by the fact that the character is scripted by different creators in the two stories. In addition, the Writer is a first-person authorial avatar in *Animal Man* #25 and #26, while in *Suicide Squad* #58 the Writer is a third-person authorial avatar. One might object to the account just given by suggesting that such different meta-narrative properties imply that there really are two distinct characters here—the Writer$_{AM}$ appearing in *Animal Man* and the Writer$_{SS}$ appearing in *Suicide Squad*—thereby trumping the conventions that govern identity conditions for more commonplace fictional characters just discussed.

While such a suggestion is not incoherent, it seems to introduce more problems than it solves. Writer$_{SS}$ is clearly connected *in some significant sense* to the Writer$_{AM}$—after all, Ostrander is using the Writer$_{SS}$ to metafictionally comment on Morrison's work on *Animal Man* and, in particular, on the role of the Writer$_{AM}$ in that work. If they are not the same character, then we need to explain what sort of connection does hold between these two characters. The only plausible answer is that the Writer$_{SS}$ is a third-person replicative avatar of the Writer$_{AM}$. In other words, just as Morrison introduced the Writer$_{AM}$ to represent himself in *Animal Man*, Ostrander introduced a new character—the Writer$_{SS}$—to represent the Writer$_{AM}$ in *Suicide Squad*. Such a proliferation of avatars begins to look rather epicyclic, however—at this point both common sense and theoretical parsimony suggest (but, admittedly, do not entail) that they are the same character after all.

Furthermore, this objection fails to block the arguments given above. Even if the two instances of the Writer are not really the same character, it is extremely plausible that we are meant to imagine that the Writer$_{SS}$ is identical to the Writer$_{AM}$ when reading *Suicide Squad* #58 (just as we are meant to imagine that Morrison is identical to the Writer$_{AM}$ when reading the relevant issues of *Animal Man*). But then, when assessing the larger story containing both occurrences of the Writer (that is, some surveyable sub-fiction of DC continuity containing *Animal Man* #25 and #26 and *Suicide Squad* #58), we are meant to imagine that Morrison is identical to the Writer$_{AM}$, and we are also meant to imagine that the Writer$_{AM}$ is identical to the Writer$_{SS}$. But then, by the transitivity of identity, we must imagine that Morrison is identical to the Writer$_{SS}$, and we are right back to the problem already addressed: this is something that we cannot, in fact, coherently imagine.[40]

Morrison and the Writer's Resurrection

So what has gone wrong with Morrison's attempt to "identify" the Writer and himself? The most obvious and straightforward explanation is that, contrary to the testimony of Morrison's Kathmandu visitors, the analogy upon which Morrison's account depends—that is, the claim that the relationship between DC continuity and the real world is (roughly) analogous to the relationship between Crafty's world and DC continuity, and is also (roughly) analogous to the relationship between the real world and the world of the visitors—fails. Morrison, as an inhabitant of the real world, and as creator both of (parts of) DC continuity and of Crafty's world, has a substantial amount of control over what is true in these worlds, and in particular, over the connections between them. Like the rest of us, however, he has a great deal less control over what is true in the real world, and over what is true regarding the connections between the real world and DC continuity.

It would be remiss to conclude this essay without touching on Morrison's own reaction to *Suicide Squad* #58. When, in the *Newsarama* interview quoted earlier, the interviewer asks Morrison what he thought of his "death" at Ostrander's hand, he responded that:

I think it probably served me right after everything I'd put Buddy Baker through. I just come back from the dead, stronger and stranger, like everyone else in comics.[41]

Thus, Morrison refuses to abandon the claim that he really is (i.e., we should imagine him to be identical to) the Writer, and (perhaps tongue-in-cheek, perhaps not) suggests that, in some sense, he died and has come back from the dead. Of course, superheroes are notorious for dying and then being almost instantly resurrected, "stronger and stranger." I leave it to the reader to evaluate Morrison's claim to have similarly risen.[42]

Notes

1. Grant Morrison and Chaz Truog, *Animal Man* #5 (New York: DC Comics, 1988).

2. See Marc Singer, *Grant Morrison: Combining the Worlds of Contemporary Comics* (Jackson: University Press of Mississippi, 2011) and Timothy Callahan, *Grant Morrison: The Early Years* (Createspace Publishing, 2012) for in-depth discussions of Animal Man.

3. The phrase "x is literally (or genuinely) identical to y" should be read in the straightforward mathematical sense—i.e., as "x and y are the very same object."

4. Kendall Walton, *Mimesis as Make-believe: On the Foundations of the Representational Arts* (Cambridge: Harvard University Press, 1993).

5. Roland Barthes, *Image, Music, Text*, trans. and ed. Richard Howard (London: Fontana, 1977).

6. For a good overview of Barthes' views on authorship, and of accounts of authorship based on or reacting to Barthesian orthodoxy, see Sean Burke, *The Death and Return of the Author: Criticism and Subjectivity in Barthes, Foucault, and Derrida* (Edinburgh: Edinburgh University Press, 2010).

7. Robert Kanigher, Carmine Infantino, and Joe Kubert, *Showcase* #4 (New York: DC Comics, 1956).

8. Gardner Fox and Carmine Infantino, *The Flash* #123 (New York: DC Comics, 1961).

9. Grant Morrison, *Supergods: What Masked Vigilantes, Miraculous Mutants, and a Sun God from Smallville Can Teach Us About Being Human* (New York: Spiegel & Grau, 2011), 112.

10. Grant Morrison and Chaz Truog, *Animal Man* #25 (New York: DC Comics, 1990).

11. Grant Morrison and Chaz Truog, *Animal Man* #26 (New York: DC Comics, 1990).

12. Morrison, *Supergods*, 14.

13. Brian Azzarello and Cliff Chiang, *Doctor 13: Architecture and Mortality* (New York: DC Comics, 2007).

14. This terminology is, so far as I know, novel, although the ideas obviously are not. Resemblance first-person authorial avatars are also sometimes called surrogates, a term I will use in its more everyday sense.

15. See Morrison, *Supergods*, 253–63 for the alien abduction version, and Grant Morrison, interview by Daniel Epstein, Suicide Girls, February 27, 2005, archived at https://suicidegirls.com/girls/anderswolleck/blog/2679166/grant-morrison/ for the magical version.

16. Morrison, *Supergods*, 283–5.

17. In fact, King Mob is arguably not a character based on Morrison but a character that Morrison attempts to become post-creation. See Morrison, *Supergods*, 287.

18. Grant Morrison and Kelley Jones, *Doom Patrol* #36 (New York: DC Comics, 1990).

19. Timothy Callahan, *Grant Morrison*, 178. Moore also appears, in a similar role, in one of the portraits hanging in the Bearded Gentleman's Club of Metropolis in Grant Morrison and Vince Giarrano, *Doom Patrol* #45 (New York: DC Comics, 1991).

20. Morrison, *Supergods*, 218–9.

21. Grant Morrison, interview by Matt Brady, "Magic, Fiction Suits, and Putting Buddy Through Hell...: Grant Morrison on Animal Man," *Newsarama*, June 7, 2001, archived at https://sites.google.com/site/deepspacetransmissions/interviews-1/2000–2005/news arama-grant-morrison-on-animal-man. Morrison is drawing something like the replicative-versus-resemblance distinction, where replicative first-person avatars are the result of entering the fiction as oneself, while resemblance first-person avatars are the result of entering the fiction disguised in a "fiction suit." Note that the Writer is not a fiction suit.

22. This example points to an ambiguity in the taxonomy presented earlier: is the god of Crafty's world a first-person authorial avatar, since drawn by Truog, or a third-person authorial avatar, since first scripted by Morrison?

23. Morrison, *Supergods*, 272–8.

24. Ibid., 276.

25. This qualification is necessary, since these distinct "worlds" are disanalogous in some respects: Crafty's world and DC continuity are two-dimensional, the real world is three-dimensional, and the world of Morrison's visitors is five-dimensional (see Morrison, *Supergods*, 277).

26. For good surveys of various front-running accounts of personal identity and of fictional truth, see *Stanford Encyclopedia of Philosophy Online*, s.v. "Personal Identity," by Eric T. Olsen, accessed July 19, 2013, http://plato.stanford.edu/entries/identity-personal/ and s.v. "Fiction," by Fred Kroon and Alberto Voltolini, accessed July 19, 2013, http://plato.stanford.edu/entries/fiction/ respectively. None of the accounts surveyed in these articles is compatible with the literal identity of the Writer and Morrison.

27. Kendall Walton's *Mimesis as Make-Believe* is the standard account of fiction along these lines. For a useful extension of these ideas to pictorial fiction, see Patrick Maynard, *Drawing Distinctions: The Varieties of Graphic Expression* (Ithaca: Cornell University Press, 2005).

28. Barthes, *Image, Music, Text*, 142–8.

29. Recall that I am not interested in the correctness of Barthes' views, but only in whether Morrison's account of the nature of fiction, and his implementation of this account via the Writer, provides a genuine challenge to Barthes' views.

30. For a useful overview of the subtleties of Barthes' (evolving) views on authorship, see Burke, *The Death and Return of the Author*, 39–50.

31. Barthes, *Image, Music, Text*, 161.

32. John Ostrander and Geof Isherwood, *Suicide Squad* #58 (New York: DC Comics, 1991).

33. Ibid., 10.

34. Ibid., 11.

35. Ibid.

36. Ibid., 16.

37. Ibid.

38. Will Brooker, amongst others, did so object. Thanks are due to him for emphasizing the importance of addressing this point.

39. For a further discussion of how the norms and conventions of comics (and other serialized art forms) determine identity conditions for characters (and other issues of "canonicity"), see Roy T. Cook, "Canonicity and Normativity in Massive Serialized Collaborative Fiction," *The Journal of Aesthetics and Art Criticism* 71, no. 3 (2013): 271–6.

40. Note that a structurally similar argument will work if the Writer$_{SS}$ is a replicative avatar meant to represent Morrison himself, rather than representing the Writer$_{AM}$.

41. Morrison, "Magic, Fiction Suits, and Putting Buddy Through Hell...."

42. An early version of this paper was presented at the "Grant Morrison and the Superhero Renaissance" conference at Trinity College, Dublin, September 2012. The final version benefitted greatly from the collegial feedback received there, and especially from comments by Will Brooker, Darragh Greene, Tim Pilcher, and Kate Roddy.

"Let me slip into someone more comfortable"

The Imaginary Adolescence of the Superhero

Keith Scott

> Do I contradict myself?
> Very well then I contradict myself,
> (I am large, I contain multitudes.)
> —Walt Whitman, "Song of Myself"[1]

> Whatever I am, that's what I am not.—Grant Morrison, *Talking with Gods*[2]

Poseur, Prophet, Perpetual Adolescent: Navigating Grant Morrison

Who, or what, is Grant Morrison? The savior of the modern comics or a moderately talented *pasticheur* of Philip K. Dick and Alan Moore? A visionary, or a chemically-addled neo-hippy, fuelled by "a rocket-driven roller-coaster of LSD, cannabis, mushrooms, DMT, 2CB, ecstasy and champagne?"[3] One of the most talented authors in his field or "a shit writer that [sic] so far up his own hole that his nose is his Adam's apple?"[4]

Discussion of Morrison the man rather than the writer may seem to invite the worst sort of *ad hominem* criticism, but the two cannot be separated. Perhaps more than any other writer in comics, he has sought to collapse the boundary between his life and his work, and asserted the centrality of a dynamic, complex interrelationship between "fiction" and "reality" as simply different facets of a single state. As Daniel Dennett observes, "our fundamental tactic of self-protection, self-control, and self-definition is not spinning webs or building dams, but telling stories, and more particularly concocting the story we tell others—and ourselves—about who we are."[5] Morrison puts it more succinctly: "We live in the stories we tell ourselves."[6] Our sense of self is inherently formed as a text, woven from the various stories, myths, and ideologies we are exposed to from birth; the tales we tell and are told become essential elements in the formation of our identity. Our "reality" is always already partially fictional:

> Self-narration is—and this needs stressing—an interpretative activity and not a simple mirroring of the past. In this respect, even fictions can provide us with characters and plots that we may identify with and which disclose ourselves; our experience of literature and film should readily prove this point.[7]

What, then, is the nature of Morrison's formative fictions? Throughout his career to date, he has produced what appears at first sight to be a wildly heterogeneous range of work; consider only his early work, which moves from farce to space opera to psychodrama and back again, or (more often) melds the genres together in a truly breathtaking manner. Add to this his seemingly encyclopaedic knowledge of British and American comics, and a frighteningly broad range of background reading, and it is easy to see why many readers find his work rebarbative, no more than a series of in-jokes, fanboy obsession and obscurantism. While it is undeniably true that a work such as *Final Crisis* (2008) can be initially off-putting, the reading of Morrison's work as a whole as unapproachable is, I think, utterly mistaken.

Like many British readers who were born in the 1960s and 1970s, I first encountered Morrison's work in the pages of *2000 AD*, with *Zenith* (1987), the story of a teenage superhero juggling the conflicting demands of battling multidimensional horrors and managing a career as a pop star and media icon. Writing in 2007, Douglas Wolk identified

> the hallmarks of Morrison's work ... reality-bending metafictional freak-outs dressed up in action-adventure drag; metaphors that make visible the process by which language creates an image that in turn becomes narrative; a touch of feel-good self-improvement rhetoric; faith in the power of pop and popularity to do magic; and skinny bald men who are stand-ins for Morrison himself, heroically conquering sadness and making the world evolve.[8]

Even twenty years before this, Morrison had done all this and more. What Wolk misses is the depth and complexity of Morrison's fictional universe (or rather universes; *Zenith* already features parallel Earths, pocket universes, and all the cosmic tropes that will mark the later work), and the way in which the text is filled with and formed by a myriad of other texts, from H. P. Lovecraft and William Blake to *The Beano* and *The Dandy*. Everything we might expect to see in Morrison's later work is already present in *Zenith*, and his writing as a whole can in many ways be seen as variations on the thematic and formal features he develops here. Morrison's writing can be seen as fractal (patterns which repeat on a greater or larger scale) or hologram-like (the totality is present within even a fragment of the whole). His stories are one story, his heroes are one hero, and in what follows I hope to make some pertinent comments about the nature of both the "what" and the "why" of his work; however, we must also consider briefly the "how" of his narrative process, as this is vital to a true understanding of his work.

One of Morrison's finest qualities as a writer is his honesty regarding his influences; consider the letters pages of the original monthly run of *The Invisibles* (1994–2000), where he frequently cites the texts (literary, musical, cinematic) that influenced each issue. In an interview with Graeme McMillan at the time he was beginning his run on *Batman and Robin*, when the vogue was for an unremittingly grim, post–Miller, post–Burton "Dark Knight," he states:

> Of course, one of my all-time favourite Batman panels was written by Haney and drawn by Jim Aparo and shows Batman strolling down the sunlit streets of Gotham, checking out the mini-skirted girls and accompanied by the line to end all lines: "Yes, Batman digs this day!"[9]

Morrison's recall of the panel is all but perfect; Batman is strolling "along one of Gotham's poshest avenues one April day,"[10] emitting the thought balloon, "Sheer magic! Winter's over and pretty girls are blossoming like flowers! Delicious."[11]

That Morrison chooses this image seems to me emblematic of his vision of the superhero. At first sight purely comic, a moment of Silver Age lightness and pure silliness (entirely fitting with the tone of *The Brave and The Bold* in contrast to *Batman* or *Detective Comics*), it is in fact remarkably incongruous. The Batman we see here is not the softer, more rounded Batman of the Silver Age; this is the demon-horned Dark Knight of Denny O'Neill (or even Bob Kane's original), profoundly out of place on a summer street. Significantly, this issue of *Brave and Bold* was published after DC began a deliberate attempt to rework Batman, moving him away from the Day-Glo, pop art-inflected heroics of the Silver Age. Two years before this,[12] Robin had been dispatched to college, the Batcave closed, and Bruce Wayne moved his center of operations to the heart of Gotham City, "to strike fear into the new wave of gangsterism sweeping the world."[13] Morrison shows us a Batman caught between Caped Crusader and Dark Knight Detective, both comic and entirely serious, and this is central to what he does with his heroes. Flex Mentallo is a noble, courageous figure and a ludicrous, high camp bodybuilder; Zenith is the defender of the multiverse and a teenage pop star wannabe; and Superman is both the quasi-divine guardian of Earth and (in *Action Comics* 2011–13) a defiantly blue-collar "champion of the oppressed, and the hero of the downtrodden."[14] As Wolk writes: "What Morrison tells us, every chance he gets, is that a higher-dimensional construct (like the complete version of the world in which we readers live) can be correctly perceived only from a multiple perspective."[15] And it is this sense of multiplicity which marks his best work, and above all what he does with heroes. Morrison's worlds are not constructed along binary oppositions, but are highly complex, multilayered and polysemous; his heroes walk between worlds, fluid, protean, and liminal. In this chapter I argue that this magical liminality evident in Morrison's work is bound up with adolescence; a concept which exists for the writer both as a developmental stage in human language and behavior, and as a unique perspective, a lens through which characters may view the world in a manner that is simultaneously optimistic and savagely critical.

Teenage Dreams So Hard to Beat: Transition, Transformation, Transcendence

> When I was a child, I spake as a child, I understood as a child, I thought as a child: but when I became a man, I put away childish things.[16]

> "And what is the use of a book," thought Alice, "without pictures or conversation?"[17]

Despite the proliferation of academic works in recent decades devoted to multimodal texts or (in Eisner's terminology) "sequential art,"[18] the status of the "comic book" as cultural debate is still contested; the reasons for this are complex and varied, but seem to me to lie largely in the way in which (in the Western, Anglophone world at least) children are led into literacy through a gradual progression away from images and towards the written word. From card books of simple pictures to pictures with a single word as label, through the readers with increasingly more complicated vocabulary the child moves to the world of pure text and (the term is highly significant) "real books."[19] If we accept this cultural paradigm, which has been the dominant model for at least two hundred years, then a work which deploys both text and images will inevitably be seen as more "childish" or "immature" than one which features text alone. Whether this is still the predominant view is doubtful; comics have become viewed as a "respectable" form, as evidenced by the growth of comics studies as an academic discipline, but traces of it still remain, as a visit to any school or bookshop will make clear. "Picture books" and "graphic novels" are consigned to discrete sections, and in the children's section of a bookstore, texts will be classed by intended reading age, and books will contain progressively fewer images as the age of the intended reader increases.

Throughout the twentieth century, comics were overwhelmingly seen as no more than "kids' stuff," and anyone seeking to use the medium to convey more adult issues was viewed as at best misguided, and at worst perverse. This is of course a nonsensical argument, as no medium is any more "mature" than any other, but it lies at the heart of much of the criticism in previous decades of those who attempted to create comics not aimed at children; message was confused with medium, and comics written for adult readers were read as if they had been conceived to warp the tender minds of children. This can be seen above all in the work of Fredric Wertham whose *Seduction of the Innocent* (1954) uses the horror comics of the 1950s as a starting point for a diatribe against the comic book in general. The first thing to note is that the horror comics were of course never designed for a readership of children. In his seminal study of boys' stories, E. S. Turner quotes publicity material from one of the publishers of the horror comics, which plays on the idea that these are very definitely *not* wholesome children's entertainment:

> Imagine—you are selling a nice line in Komfy Kiddies' Komics and Dainty Dailies when a parcel of putrid platter dithers slimily in at the back door. You hold your nose and cut the string and your reeking ration of horror has arrived.[20]

Wertham is guilty of a fundamental category error. However, this is merely one aspect of his reading of comics, and he goes on to develop a sustained argument in which he views those comics which were aimed at children as inherently corrupting fantasies of rebellion against the social certainties of Eisenhower's America:

> How can they [children] respect the hard-working mother, father or teacher who is so pedestrian, trying to teach the common rules of conduct, wanting you to keep your feet on the ground and unable even figuratively speaking to fly through the air? Psychologically Superman undermines the authority and dignity of the ordinary man and woman in the minds of children.[21]

In short, Wertham attacks "irresponsible images," as indeed the term *manga* is often translated.

This is a fundamental misunderstanding of the nature of the comic book; it is not a childish medium, but it occupies to this day a complex and deeply liminal position in culture. This is entirely fitting, when we consider how the comic strip itself relies on liminality in order to render the reader complicit in the events it depicts, by filling in the actions that occur between the frozen images in the panels[22]; combining text and image, reality and fantasy, youthful escapism and gritty reality, it belongs to the realms of both childhood and adulthood, and to neither; it (and Morrison's work in particular) should, I believe, be read as an *adolescent* form, and this should be seen as a strength, not a weakness. The use of the term "adolescent" is not meant to be in any way a dismissal of Morrison's work as immature; rather, I would argue that his writing, like adolescence, exists in an indeterminate region, mixing modes, genres and attitudes, where horror and graphic violence can coexist with tenderness, raucous humor and pure play. Adolescence, moreover, is a time of physical, emotional and social change, as the individual moves from one zone of identity to another, "a period when individuals are neither institutionalised as children nor accepted into adult roles and society."[23] It embodies a state of perpetual uncertainty, "a liminal phase, an ambiguous stage where he or she is in a certain sense placed outside society, 'betwixt and between' two stable conditions."[24] The adolescent is, to use Lovecraft's term, "the lurker at the threshold,"[25]

> Engaged in a struggle to emancipate himself from his parents. He, therefore, resists any dependence upon them for their guidance, approval or company, and rebels against any restrictions and controls that they impose upon his behavior. To facilitate the process of emancipation, he transfers his dependency to the peer group whose values are typically in conflict with those of his parents ... he is ambivalent, frightened, unpredictable, and often irresponsible.[26]

This liminal position should not however be seen as a purely negative and transitory phase; rather, as Penelope Eckert points out in her study of the language of multicultural adolescent peer groups: "adolescents are society's transition teams, reinterpreting the world, resolving the old with the new, substrate with superstrate, culture with culture, local with transnational."[27]

Moreover, "by virtue of their transitional place in the life course, adolescents are in a particularly strong position to respond to change in the conditions of life, and in so doing bring about lasting social change."[28] The marginal status of adolescence on a social level offers a freedom from constraint, and in this "temporary autonomous zone" (in Hakim Bey's phrase) its members have an opportunity to innovate both culturally and linguistically. Far from being merely a hiatus between childhood and adulthood, adolescence and its corresponding iconoclastic, questing mindset offers a position for challenging and original critiques of the world on an artistic level.

In his study of horror fiction, Stephen King argues that

> most great writers have a curious childish look to their faces ... part of them has never accomplished the imaginative going-away that is so much a part of growing up, of establishing the tunnel vision so necessary for a successful career as an adult.[29]

There is an undeniable truth here (an imaginative writer must seek to look beyond the conventional pieties of established, adult society), but Kingsley Amis makes a sharper point when he states:

> To the pre-pubertal eye all grown-up behaviour is so fantastic as to defeat discrimination; the youth in his last year at school is already taking out naturalization papers for the adult world. It is the boy in his early teens who sees that world with the delighted, faintly hostile astonishment of the tourist, who is entertained to the limits of endurance by its quaint, tribal customs, its grotesque ritual dances, its capering, scowling, gesticulating witch doctors. And if he later becomes a novelist, he must strive to recapture, not indeed the undifferentiating vision of childhood, but the adolescent's coldly wondering stare.[30]

The Morrisonian superhero plays a similar role; from Superman and Batman to the Invisibles, he or she embodies rebellion against conventional society, a vision of the world which is brighter (and darker—adolescence is a time of extremes) and more imaginatively rich than the mundane realities of the world of parental values. A character such as Captain Marvel is clearly a wish-fulfillment figure for a child, the alter-ego of the handicapped, orphaned pre-adolescent Billy Batson; Spider-Man and Superman are based in the desire of the adolescent to transcend his or her status as wimpish nobody (Peter Parker/Clark Kent) and, as with the hero of the Charles Atlas advert who inspires Morrison's creation of Flex Mentallo, go on to become alpha male. Above all, there is Batman, who is the perfect example of the psychodrama played out so often in comics. Bruce Wayne is born to a life of riches and comfort, and a childhood which dramatizes to perfection Jung's reading of pre-adult life: "In the childish state of consciousness, there are as yet no problems; nothing depends upon the subject, for the child itself is still wholly dependent upon its parents."[31]

However, this prelapsarian state of grace cannot last for ever; Oedipus kills Laius, Zeus slays Cronos, and Thomas and Martha Wayne must also die to usher the young Bruce into adulthood—or rather, adolescent liminality, as he constructs an identity which is plural, both and neither Bruce Wayne or Batman. He is both the boy forced to grow up before his time and "the boy who never grew up," eternally trapped in the limbo of becoming. Life as a "Betwixt-and-Between,"[32] in J.M. Barrie's terms, is an existence of perpetual uncertainty. For the Invisibles, identity is eternally fluid, something to be put on or changed as easily as clothing. Thus, Morrison's Batman shows the perils of life on the margins, as the character is subjected to a series of assaults on his identity, just as family, education and society seek to mold the adolescent.

Morrison's work is, in the terms outlined above, profoundly adolescent in its world-view: anarchistic, idealistic, cynical, and heartfelt in equal measure; his heroes, slipping perpetually between uncertain identities, are perfect examples of the "betwixt and between" nature of the teenage years. For Morrison, adolescence is not a physical state, but a state of mind, and his work as a whole is a sustained attempt to return an adult reader to the constant questioning of the *status quo* that is an essential part of youth. The most obvious example is Dane McGowan/Jack Frost in *The Invisibles*, the embodiment of *non serviam* teenage rebellion, but all Morrison's heroes, from Sebastian O to Animal Man and onwards, stand against any attempt to toe the party line. Whether utopians, anarchists, mutants or magicians, these characters defiantly reject consensus reality and seek to write their identity upon the world. Just as the Romantics praised the innocent, unclouded perception of the child, so Morrison wishes the reader to look beyond the way things are (or appear to be), to consider how they might be, a vision of the world which is imaginative, dreamlike and magical. Even his occult explorations show him resisting the conventional, rejecting the traditions of Western magic (or "Magick") and turning to the willfully heterodox theories of "Chaos Magicians" such as Phil Hine. As Morrison states:

> I discovered Chaos Magic in the early '80s and, as far as I was concerned, it was Punk Magic.... I didn't have to know all the correspondences of the Tree of Life or read a hundred dusty exegeses on the Quabalah to practice sorcery. I didn't have to rely on the ridiculous ceremonial pomp of Victorian magic, as typified by the rituals of the Golden Dawn and its offshoots. ... I've never been particularly interested in controlling people; magic, for me, is a working technology for exploring alternate realities, breaking down behavioral programs, coming to an understanding with Death and having a laugh.[33]

The adolescent rejects the comforting certainties of childhood and the banalities of adulthood, seeking to create a new social contract, a brief moment of autonomy before full insertion into the mundane. Fantasy, imagination and daydreaming are essential aspects of the adolescent mindset, part and parcel of the process of constructing potential identities, and a "magical" world-view (by which I mean a rejection of a model of the world rooted in purely concrete, empirical data) is inseparable from this period of life. As Heinz Streib puts it, magic is not a feature of "childish[ness]," but "remains one of the forms of logic in adolescence and adulthood."[34] The villains of Morrison's fictional universe, conversely, seek to constrain, confine, and control the individual; language is for them a tool of domination, rather than liberation. As Sir Miles Delacourt puts it in *The Invisibles*:

> There is a spell word implanted in the brain of every English-speaking child, the root mantra of restriction, the secret name of a mighty hidden demon: "eybeesee-dee-ee-eff-geeaitcheye-jai-kayell-emenn-ohpeequeue-are-ess-tee-youveedouble-you-ex-wyezed." That name and all the names it generates were designed to set limits upon humanity's ability to express abstract thought. What you see depends entirely upon the words you have to describe what you see. Nothing exists unless we say it.[35]

Morrison's villains are trapped by a simple-minded version of the Sapir-Whorf Hypothesis, the belief that we can only comprehend what our language allows us to express. Confronted by the glossolalic head of John the Baptist, the Myrmidons hear only what their repressive, dictatorial culture lets them hear. Morrison wants us to use our uniquely human gift of language to move beyond the conventional, in a truly heroic, magical act of transcendence. To accept any party line, any monolithic interpretation of reality, is to collapse into stasis and sterility. The magicians of *The Invisibles* "spell" new possibilities into being; in *Final Crisis*, Superman sings defiance to the crushing conformity of the Anti-Life Equation.[36] Communication and creation go hand in hand. Reliance on any single tool or belief system inevitably leads to disaster in Morrison's worlds; the secret is to be able to move easily from one system to another as the need arises. In the world of *The Invisibles*, magic works, but so does science, or martial arts, or a well-placed bullet. Magic can offer a useful short cut, a means of breaking the established boundaries of consensus reality; as the Drummer puts it in Warren Ellis' *Planetary*: "Magic is the cheat codes for the world. Sending a signal to reality's operating system, see?"[37]—but its true value is as a way of showing that other ways of conceiving reality exist.

The Morrisonian world-view is therefore, to use Louis MacNeice's term, "incorrigibly plural."[38] It seeks to embrace plurality, to engage left brain and right brain simultaneously; logic and paradox, magic and science, reality and fantasy must all be adopted in order to truly apprehend the nature of existence. The language we and Sir Miles Delacourt use is clumsily conveyed in only 26 letters; the Invisibles have an alphabet with 64 characters, expressing a metalanguage which can take its users so much further, "the keys to a wider world which you have not been educated to comprehend."[39] The *Invisibles* issue "Counting to Ten" is the essential text to consult if we wish to understand Morrison's ideas of the transformational power of language: bombarded by the weaponized alphabet of Cell 23, the heroes are subjected to a quasi–Situationist act of mental *détournement*, as every aspect of their identities as "rebels" or even "heroes" is called into question. To read this as simply an act of brainwashing is to miss the point; the Invisibles are both heroes and clichéd images of heroism and rebellion, acts of discourse, which must continually be challenged to avoid the descent into stereotype. We are what we say we are, or, in Morrison's words, "the stories we tell ourselves"; he wants us to see that these stories (which are embodied in language) are fictions, and can be rewritten, to allow us to rebuild "your little house called 'me.'"[40] In their dramatization of a move away from a fixed model of identity, couched in a series of stable narratives and ideologies, Morrison's superheroes offer just such a model of transition, transgression and transcendence; in short, a move "up, up and away." What lies beyond is liberation.

"Every man and every woman is a star"[41]: *From Mortals to Supergods*

> ANIMAL MAN. Your world must be so terrible. It seems so grey and bleak... How can you possibly live in a world without superheroes?
>
> GRANT MORRISON. We get by.[42]

In March 1940, George Orwell published "Boys' Weeklies," a study of the then-popular magazines *The Gem* and *The Magnet*. The essay castigates these stories as archaic, riddled with appalling assumptions about class and race, and entirely out of place in a world riven by war. In a justly famous passage, he sums up their world-view:

> The year is 1910—or 1940, but it is all the same. ... The King is on his throne and the pound is worth a pound. Over in Europe the comic foreigners are jabbering and gesticulating, but the grim grey battleships of the British Fleet are steaming up the Channel and at the outposts of Empire the monocled Englishmen are holding the niggers at bay. ... Everything is safe, solid and unquestionable. Everything will be the same for ever and ever.[43]

Just as Fredric Wertham attacked the corrupting influence of horror comics in *Seduction of the Innocent,* or contemporary critics inveigh against Harry Potter, so Orwell condemns popular literature as mindless, outdated, and appallingly simplistic in its reading of the world. Why this essay matters to us is that the author of these stories replied to Orwell's attack. In his response, Charles Hamilton (a.k.a. "Frank Richards," "Hilda Richards," "Martin Clifford," and many more) argued:

> Every day of happiness, illusory or otherwise—and most happiness is illusory—is so much to the good. It will help to give the boy confidence and hope. Frank Richards tells him that there are some splendid fellows in a world that is, after all, a decent sort of place. He likes to think himself like one of these fellows, and is happy in his day-dreams.[44]

Hamilton's defense of escapist literature as a source of aspirational, positive, anti-nihilist paradigms is all-but identical to Morrison's; his comics are far more than mere entertainment. In *The Invisibles*, he has Shelley argue that "as poets, it is our duty to turn our faces from the mire, to look up and tell our fellow men that we have seen a better world than this."[45] As Meaney writes in *Our Sentence Is Up*, "This is why he [Morrison] writes superhero comics: through writing some of the last purely heroic characters left in our society, he hopes to channel their hopes and inspiration into our reality."[46]

In an interview with Dylan Ratigan at the time of *Supergods*' publication, Morrison outlines his aims succinctly:

> We're kind of growing up in a world where the mass media narrative, the story that children are told and that we're all being told, is a story of ecological catastrophe and planetary doom and extinction of the human race, and I felt that was quite a dark story to learn ... my feeling is that these heroes, like they always do, have risen in response to an emergency, and the emergency is almost a kind of psychological emergency for our culture, and right now we're returning to some of the very basic ideas of optimism and hope and positivity that we have, and these superheroes offer images of a human future where we might actually survive and pull through.[47]

In short, Morrison is engaged in an act of mimetic engineering, transmitting moral messages through the form of the superhero, which (in his view) occupies a position in his cultural and psychological landscape analogous to that of saints and gods in other eras. God is dead, the Supergods walk among us. As he says:

> In Superman, some of the loftiest aspirations of our species came hurtling down from imagination's bright heaven to collide with the lowest form of entertainment and from this union something powerful and resonant was born, albeit in its underwear.... He was Apollo, the Sun god, the unbeatable supreme stuff, the personal greatness of which we all know we're capable.[48]

The question Animal Man asks his creator with which I began this section is in fact profoundly mistaken; we do live in a world with heroes, godforms which intersect with our world through the two-dimensional plane of the printed page, springing from the basic human need to reify what Abraham Lincoln termed the "better angels of our nature."[49] As *All-Star Superman* shows, a world without Superman will always create one, to fill the aspirational void.

Morrison's work is driven by three "M's": multiplicity, magic, and the more-than-mortal. His heroes are less super- than trans-, inter- and meta-humans, conduits for slippage from one realm of experience, epistemological or ontological model, to another. As I have sought to show, the multiple identities of his heroes and their journeys from one plane of existence to the next (and the recurring trope of movement from the picture plane to our "real" universe), reify the philosophical concerns of Morrison, the author. Characters slip between worlds, or insert themselves into new identities, each as provisional as the last. These concerns can be observed in any and all of his comics, both mainstream and experimental, but the work which perhaps best sums up his conception of the hero is *Flex Mentallo* (1996). A love-letter to superheroes, and filled with references to his earlier works, this is where Morrison most clearly expresses the liberating, transformative power of the superhero as a tool for the liberation of the human consciousness: "We made the comics because we knew. Somehow we knew something was missing and we tried to fill the gap with stories about gods and superheroes...."[50] Again, we see a turn to the adolescent imaginary as a way of carrying childhood fantasy into the realm of adulthood. The central character, another one of Morrison's fictionalized self-images, finds himself caught, unable either to return to a world of pure fantasy or to surrender to brute realism, and the work as a whole is an attempt to bridge the gap between two apparently irreconcilable worldviews. Critics such as Marc Singer have argued that *Flex Mentallo* fails in its attempt to demonstrate the true potential of the superhero form, and ultimately becomes lost in a navel-gazing act of artistic recycling: "an ultra-post-futurist Flex will only be a combination of past interpretations, not a new direction."[51] Others have derided the work as merely another example of Morrison's love of stylistic and formal complexity over the pleasures of plain narrative.[52] This seems to me to be a fundamentally flawed reading of the text; while the lack of immediately familiar characters can be dislocating for a reader, it is clear that at the heart of the work is a unifying idea which shines through.

At one point, Flex meets an aged janitor (quite clearly meant to be Billy Batson, the alter ego of DC's Captain Marvel), who gives him a crossword puzzle, which was originally given to *him* as the source of his superpowers:

> He said I should speak aloud the last word I wrote down.
> He claimed it was the word God said: the word that brought the universe and consciousness into being.⁵³

The final clue is half-completed, reading: "SHA_A_." Eventually, the crossword finds itself in the "real" world, completed by Wally Sage, the young man who created Flex in a childhood drawing. He fills in the missing letters, and the worlds elide.

Throughout the series, Wally reflects the *odi et amo* relationship between readers/critics and the comic form, and the work as a whole is a sustained debate between the dismissal of the superhero genre as: "Pathetic fucking power fantasies for lonely wankers who've had so much sand kicked in their faces they look like the opening credits of *Lawrence of Arabia*"⁵⁴ and the belief that it offers us a source of hope, dreams, and potential, with "no more barriers between the real and the imaginary."⁵⁵ The crossword clue is a hint to what Morrison is up to, as he sells a dummy to comic fans:

> SHA_A_. Ah, Captain Marvel, you're thinking. Wrongo. It's SHAMAN, the title of a magician who can bring miracles to our world.⁵⁶

Gregory Dickens above reads *Flex Mentallo* as a magical text, a spell which (like Billy Batson's magic word) liberates the reader into a vision of the world where dreams are as powerful and essential as reality, and argues that the reference to "SHAZAM" is merely an in-joke for the comics aficionado. This strikes me as an error; rather, this is both fannish reference and a call to magic, and a demonstration of Morrison's alchemical vision of art, where the apparently insignificant and worthless becomes a portal to the transcendent.

In Frank Miller's *The Dark Knight Returns*, his version of Superman as Reaganite stooge warns Batman that superheroes should stay hidden: "We must not remind them that giants walk the earth."⁵⁷ Morrison's work is a defiant riposte to this. His remodeling of the superhero to allow the return of humor, warmth, and above all sheer joy in the genre has been a huge benefit to comics, and the polymathic, catholic range of intellectual material he draws into his writing has set a challenge for other writers to follow. Silver Age lunacy combines with profoundly serious themes, always designed to promote a message of transformation and freedom through the imagination. Human and superhuman overlap and combine; at his best, Morrison offers us not just a superhero renaissance, but a return to the ideal of the Renaissance Man, outward-looking, forward-thinking, and eternally optimistic. While it is easy to sneer at Morrison's interest in self-help philosophies such as Neuro-Linguistic Programming, and his willingness to share a platform with a New Age guru such as Deepak Chopra (whose *The Seven Spiritual Laws of Superheroes* is directly inspired by Morrison's work),[58] this is part and parcel of his belief that as individuals and as a species, we are ripe for development. He has dubbed *The Invisibles* a "spell," and his use of the superhero can (and I believe should) be read as an alchemical act, the transformation of the base matter of ink and paper, words and pictures into a transcendent artform, which itself seeks to transform the reader. Magic is essentially an act of applied linguistics, the use of language to change our (perception of) reality; as Terence McKenna (an avowed influence on Morrison) puts it: "The real secret of magic is that the world is made of words, and that if you know the words that the world is made of you can make of it whatever you wish."[59]

The world is made of words; as Morrison puts it in *The Invisibles*: "Reality is all about Language. We can demonstrate."[60] His writing seeks not just to present the possibility of change, but to provoke it, deliberately shattering the barrier between reader and text, "fact" and "fiction," and offering the possibility of a more fluid, plural mode of existence. This is what the superhero has always done; it relies on the confusion of Self and Other, on hidden or dual identities, on characters who are themselves multiple and indefinable. Morrison wants his readers to construct their own "fiction suits" (a term which he has used repeatedly in interviews to describe his creative process, and which appears to be used for the first time in volume 3 of *The Invisibles*) and play with identity, in effect to transform themselves; this sense of transformation and transcendence is the key to understanding the attraction of the superhero for readers dissatisfied with or unsure of their own selves.

If forced to choose a single moment from Morrison's entire canon to sum up what the superhero represents for him, it would surely have to be a page from *All-Star Superman* #10. A long shot of a nondescript office building is followed by a close-up of a hand, penciling in the unmistakable form of Siegel and Shuster's Superman, and the words are spoken: "This is going to change everything."[61] As, of course, it does. Siegel and Shuster create the modern superhero, and change the publishing industry. Superman, in Morrison's eyes, changes his world, and ours, forever. As Superman and the reader learn, a world without superheroes is impossible, as they are an essential part of the human psyche, eternally present to remind us, as Superman, earlier in the same issue, reminds Regan, a despairing teenager, that "it's never as bad as it seems. You're much stronger than you think you are. Trust me."[62]

Defiantly and ludicrously idealistic, ridiculously optimistic, Morrison's superheroes are antidotes to cynicism and despair. Signifiers of a cluster of signifieds, they reject absolutism and monolinear thinking. In the multimodal communicative system of the comic, they embody Morrison's own ideas about the power of language (and art created in language) to restore some of the joy of youthful fantasy and imagination, while also retaining the adolescent's acuity and desire for radical change. They are idealistic, and idealized, but above all they are ideas, weapons systems for the battleground of the mind; in a world where belief systems (whether political, religious or economic) have led to untold misery, perhaps it is time for us all to stand with Morrison's Batman and declare that "Starting today, we fight ideas with better ideas."[63] Morrison's works are communicative acts, which employ text and image in a way which seeks to develop the potential of the comics form to convey these ideas. One of the challenges for those who study comics will be to develop a set of tools and heuristics for understanding the way in which the form functions; if we continue to examine these works through the critical lens of literary, textual studies, we will be heading up a blind alley. If we are to succeed in the task, we must engage with multimodality, with meaning which emerges from the interplay of words and pictures, and with a concept of a "work" which is the creation of multiple creators, rather than a single author. In short, we must consider how comics stretch and shatter the boundaries of traditional, criticism. Morrison shows us the way; as his heroes move from one identity to another, from common clay to supergod, so his comics break through the perceived limits of the form, even while apparently working within them. Comics are, I would argue, a language, and like any other language, they carry cultural and linguistic value; Morrison's comic dialect, like the metalanguage of *The Invisibles*, marks a deliberate attempt to go beyond the stereotypical, clichéd, and conventional, and communicate the vision of an existence transcending our world of binary oppositions and stale language use. "Up, up, and away," or, as Dr. Seuss puts it:

> In the places I go, there are things that I see
> That I never could spell if I stopped with the Z.
> I'm telling you this 'cause you're one of my friends.
> My alphabet starts where your alphabet ends![64]

Notes

1. Walt Whitman, "Song of Myself," in Walt Whitman, *Leaves of Grass: Reader's Edition*, ed. Harold W. Blodgett and Sculley Bradley (London: University of London Press, 1965), 88.

2. Grant Morrison, quoted by Steve Yeowell, in *Grant Morrison: Talking with Gods*, dir. Patrick Meaney (New York: Sequart, Respect! Films, 2010), DVD.
 3. Grant Morrison, interview with Daniel Robert Epstein, "Grant Morrison," *Suicide Girls*, March 4, 2005, http://suicidegirls.com/interviews/Grant%20Morrison/.
 4. Adam<#><#> [sic], May 5, 2012 (8:12 a.m.), comment on Wonder Warrior, "GRANT MORRISON SUCKS..[sic] and other stuff at DC," in *Comic Icons*, July 5, 2009, http://comiciconsonline.blogspot.co.uk/2009/07/grant-morrison-sucksand-other-stuff-at.html.
 5. Daniel C. Dennett, *Consciousness Explained* (London: Penguin, 1993), 418.
 6. Grant Morrison, *Supergods: What Masked Vigilantes, Miraculous Mutants, and a Sun God from Smallville Can Teach Us About Being Human* (New York: Spiegel & Grau, 2011), xvii.
 7. Anthony Paul Kerby, *Narrative and the Self* (Bloomington: Indiana University Press, 1991), 7.
 8. Douglas Wolk, *Reading Comics: How Graphic Novels Work and What They Mean* (Cambridge, MA: Da Capo Press, 2007), 258.
 9. Grant Morrison, interview with Graeme McMillan, "Grant Morrison Tells All About Batman and Robin," io9.com, January 7, 2009, http://io9.com/5301435/grant-morrison-tells-all-about-batman-and-robin.
 10. Bob Haney and Neal Adams, *The Brave and The Bold* #102 (New York: DC Comics, 1972), 1.
 11. Ibid.
 12. Frank Robbins and Irv Novick, *Batman* #217 (New York: DC Comics, 1969), in E. Nelson Bridwell, ed., *Batman from the 30s to the 70s* (New York: Crown, 1972), 299–320.
 13. Ibid., 303.
 14. Grant Morrison, interview with Dylan Ratigan, *The Dylan Ratigan Show*, MSNBC, July 28, 2011. Available at "SuperGods Author Grant Morrison; How Superman is a Role Model for Good Values," Youtube.com, accessed July 17, 2013, http://www.youtube.com/watch?v=jARfxM58m3c.
 15. Wolk, *Reading Comics*, 266.
 16. 1 Cor. 13:11 (King James Version).
 17. Lewis Carroll, *Alice's Adventures in Wonderland* (London: The Folio Press, 1961), 3.
 18. Will Eisner, *Comics and Sequential Art* (Tamarac, FL: Poorhouse Press, 1985).
 19. For discussions of the so-called "reading wars" and the debate concerning the relative merits of graded readers as opposed to "real books," see Michael O. Tunnell and James S. Jacobs, "Using 'Real' Books: Research Findings on Literature Based Reading Instruction," *The Reading Teacher* 42, no. 7 (1989): 470–7, and J. S. Kim, "Research and the Reading Wars," in *When Research Matters: How Scholarship Influences Education Policy*, ed. F. M. Hess (Cambridge: Harvard Education Press, 2008), 89–111.
 20. E.S. Turner, *Boys Will Be Boys* (London: Penguin, 1975), 289.
 21. Fredric Wertham, *Seduction of the Innocent* (London: Museum Press, 1955), 97–8.
 22. Cf. Scott McCloud, *Understanding Comics: The Invisible Art* (New York: HarperPerennial, 1994), 65–9.
 23. Alison Waller, *Constructing Adolescence in Fantastic Realism* (London: Routledge, 2011), 32.
 24. Thomas Hylland Eriksen, *Small Places, Large Issues: An Introduction to Social and Cultural Anthropology*, 3d ed. (Milton Keynes: Cram101, 2012), 125.
 25. H. P. Lovecraft and August Derleth, *The Lurker At The Threshold* (Sauk City, WI: Arkham House, 1945).
 26. Albert Bandura, "The Stormy Decade: Fact or Fiction?," *Psychology in the Schools* 1, no. 3 (1964): 224.
 27. Eckert, Penelope Eckert, "Language and Adolescent Peer Groups," *Journal of Language and Social Psychology* 22, no. 1 (March 2003): 115.

28. Ibid.

29. Stephen King, *Stephen King's Danse Macabre* (London: Fontana, 1985), 143–4.

30. Kingsley Amis, "City Ways," in *What Became of Jane Austen? and Other Questions* (London: Penguin, 1980), 134–40.

31. C. G. Jung, *Modern Man in Search of a Soul*, trans. W. F. Dell and C. F. Baynes (London: Routledge and Kegan Paul, 1961), 113.

32. J. M. Barrie, *Peter Pan and Peter Pan in Kensington Gardens* (Ware: Wordsworth Editions Limited, 2007), 206.

33. Grant Morrison and Jill Thompson, *The Invisibles*, 1 #13 (New York: DC/Vertigo, 1995), 25.

34. Heinz Streib, "Magical Feeling and Thinking in Childhood and Adolescence: A Developmental Perspective," *British Journal of Religious Education* 16, no. 2 (1994): 70

35. Grant Morrison and Phil Jimenez, *The Invisibles*, 1 #19 (New York: DC/Vertigo, 1996), 7.

36. Grant Morrison and Doug Mahnke, *Final Crisis* #7 (New York: DC Comics, 2009), 22.

37. Warren Ellis and John Cassady, *Planetary* #7 (La Jolla, CA: Wildstorm Productions, 2000), 14.

38. Louis MacNeice, "Snow," in *Collected Poems of Louis MacNeice*, ed. E. R. Dodds (London: Faber & Faber, 1966), 30.

39. Grant Morrison and Phil Jimenez, *The Invisibles*, 2 #13 (New York: DC/Vertigo, 1998), 7.

40. Grant Morrison and Frank Quitely, *The Invisibles*, 3 #12 (New York: DC/Vertigo, 2000), 18.

41. Aleister Crowley, "The Holograph Manuscript of Liber AL vel Legis" (1904), in U.S. Grand Lodge Ordo Templis Orientis, accessed July 17, 2013, http://lib.oto-usa.org/libri/liber0031.html?num=1.

42. Grant Morrison and Chaz Truog, *Animal Man* #26 (New York: DC Comics, 1990), 9.

43. George Orwell, "Boys' Weeklies," in *The Complete Works of George Orwell*, ed. Ian Angus and Peter Davison, vol. 12, *A Patriot After All, 1940–1941* (London: Secker & Warburg, 2000), 67.

44. Charles Hamilton ("Frank Richards"), in ibid., 84.

45. Grant Morrison and Jill Thompson, *The Invisibles*, 1 #5 (New York: DC/Vertigo, 1995), 3.

46. Patrick Meaney, *Our Sentence Is Up: Seeing Grant Morrison's The Invisibles* (Edwardsville, IL: Sequart, 2010), Kindle edition.

47. Morrison, *The Dylan Ratigan Show*.

48. Morrison, *Supergods*, 15.

49. Abraham Lincoln, "First Inaugural Address of Abraham Lincoln" (speech), March 4, 1861, in Yale Law School: The Avalon Project, accessed 27 October 2013, http://avalon.law.yale.edu/19th_century/lincoln1.asp.

50. Grant Morrison and Frank Quitely, *Flex Mentallo, Man of Muscle Mystery: The Deluxe Edition* (New York: DC Comics/Vertigo, 2012), 91.

51. Marc Singer, *Grant Morrison: Combining the Worlds of Contemporary Comics* (Jackson: University Press of Mississippi, 2012), 150.

52. See, for example, Sean Rogers, "Flex Mentallo and the Morrison Problem," *The Comics Journal*, January 8, 2012, http://www.tcj.com/flex-mentallo-and-the-morrison-problem/8/1/12.

53. Morrison and Quitely, *Flex Mentallo*, 23.

54. Ibid., 97.

55. Ibid., 95.

56. Gregory Dickens, "Review: Flex Mentallo," *Popimage*, accessed July 17, 2013, http://www.popimage.com/profile/morrison/012501flexrev.html.

57. Frank Miller, *The Dark Knight Returns: Tenth Anniversary Edition* (New York: DC Comics, 1996), 129.

58. Deepak Chopra, *The Seven Spiritual Laws of Superheroes* (New York: HarperOne, 2011). Morrison has appeared with Chopra at the San Diego ComiCon on two occasions, on July 19, 2006 and July 23, 2011.

59. Terence McKenna, "Alien Dreamtime with Terence McKenna" (speech), Transmission Theater, San Francisco, February 27, 1993, Deoxy/Video, accessed July 10, 2013, http://deoxy.org/t_adt.htm.

60. Grant Morrison and Phil Jimenez, *The Invisibles*, 2 #13 (New York: DC/Vertigo), 5.

61. Grant Morrison and Frank Quitely, *All-Star Superman* (New York: DC Comics, 2011), 245.

62. Ibid., 236.

63. Grant Morrison and David Finch, *Batman: The Return* (New York: DC Comics, 2011), 13.

64. Dr. Seuss (Theodor Geisel), *On Beyond Zebra* (New York: Random House, 1955), 4–5.

Parasitic Signifiers

The Invasiveness of Language in Grant Morrison's Comics

CLARE PITKETHLY

"How do we fight *words*?"—Grant Morrison and Phil Jimenez, *The Invisibles* 2 #13[1]

On the pages of a comic, words are positioned outside the speaking character, thus emphasizing an alien dimension to these words. It is this relation between the characters and language that will be the focus of this chapter, in a discussion of the unique potential of the comic to illustrate language's imposition from without. This potential is one that is demonstrated in the comics of Grant Morrison, as an invasive quality to language is continually emphasized in the writer's work. This is something that persists throughout his expansive body of work, with the writer's more recent superhero comics maintaining the same invasive quality to language as developed in earlier work. In order to emphasize this continuity, I will discuss Morrison's work in three chronological stages: firstly, his early American superhero comics, *Animal Man* (1988–90) and *Doom Patrol* (1989–93), works in which language is imposed upon his characters from without; secondly, *The Invisibles* (1994–2000), a work in which an inescapable dimension to language is illustrated by means of a coinciding of his characters with signifiers; and thirdly, his subsequent superhero comics, including *New X-Men* (2001–4), *The Filth* (2002–3), *Seven Soldiers* (2005–6), and *Batman* (2006), works in which this invasive dimension to language continues, but this time, by means of the materiality of words on the comic page. In each of these three stages, the specific quality associated with the invasiveness of language changes, from its exteriority to its inescapability to its materiality (all being visually emphasized on the pages of a comic), but despite this shift, the particular relation to language narrativized in the writer's work remains. Unable to escape such intrusive signifiers, this relation to language exemplifies that associated with psychosis in the work of psychoanalyst Jacques Lacan. Lacan's work offers a useful framework to discuss such a dimension to language, and in this essay, I will draw upon this aspect of his work to provide a context for the relation to language narrativized in Morrison's work, as I demonstrate the way in which this relation is achieved via an emphasis on the very status of language on the pages of a comic.

Signifiers Imposed by Another

To start at the beginning of Morrison's involvement with American superhero comics, toward the end of the writer's run on his first ongoing superhero comic book series, *Animal Man*, the titular character draws attention to a sense of estrangement from his words. As played out in the narrative of the comic, this character does not recognize himself in his words; it is just as if his words are the words of another, as if someone else is speaking through his mouth. To use the words of Animal Man (words that presumably would likewise appear alien to him): "I read my own words, my own thoughts, and I realize they're *not* mine after all. They were *never* mine."[2] The words of another are being imposed upon him, but he is not aware of just where these words are actually coming from. This dimension to language, of being spoken by something else, is one evocative of the function of the signifier in the work of Lacan, as he asks (as translated from the original French), "How can we not all sense that the words on which we depend, are in a way imposed on us?"[3] This alien dimension to language stems from the acquisition of signifiers from another, as when a subject enters language, he or she does so via someone else's words,[4] via signifiers imposed upon the subject from without. These signifiers, moreover, ultimately remain foreign to the speaking subject, as another's discourse inside the speaker, one speaking through his or her mouth.[5] Such an alien dimension to language is evoked by Animal Man's estrangement from his words, as another's signifiers are spoken through his mouth.

When Animal Man is faced with the question of just whose words they actually are, he goes in pursuit of an answer, hoping to elicit a satisfactory response to this question from someone else. This search for an answer leads him to a shadowy figure, a figure ultimately revealed to be the comic's writer. From within the narrative of the comic, Morrison's illustrated stand-in introduces himself to his character: "I'm Grant ... I'm the evil mastermind behind the scenes. I'm the wicked puppeteer who pulls the strings and makes you *dance*. I'm your *writer*."[6] As conveyed within the narrative of the comic, it is the writer who is the one imposing signifiers upon his character, or to use the words of Morrison's stand-in, words directed toward Animal Man: "you just say what you're written to say. *I* have to think this stuff up."[7] In this way, it is the writer who is positioned as the author of these signifiers, thus, ostensibly escaping subjection to someone else's words, ostensibly escaping being spoken by the discourse of another. As is evident in this narrative example, it is the characters on the pages of the comic that are subject to language as the discourse of another, a subjection that continues in Morrison's later work, and one that is emphasized by means of the very status of words in a comic.

The novel potential of the comic to illustrate an invasive dimension to language via the use of written words in speech balloons is evident in the dialogue of one particular character in Morrison's run on *Doom Patrol*.[8] In this comic, the speech of a villainous character named the Fog is relentlessly inundated by words imposed by others, via concatenating interruptions that appear in parenthesized text within the character's speech balloons, as apparent in the excerpt below:

> (Listen, are we ever going to get out of here?) Shut *up*! You can't (I only asked) *concentrate*, can you.... You just don't (I think he's) know what (asking a perfectly reasonable) to do next (question). Will you all be *quiet*, for God's sake! I'm trying to (creep!) I'm trying to be *menacing* here. There's nowhere to run ("nowhere to run!" what a cliché!) I'm going to swallow you (oh, not another one!) whole. Don't you feel (isn't it) like you're running in a *dream*? You get slower and (crowded enough) slower, no matter how hard you try (in here?).[9]

In the narrative of the comic, these interjecting words are quite literally the voices of others, others that were initially outside this character, but who had become incorporated within him after he ingested them. Unhappy to be inside him, these voices constantly interject and override his speech; they argue with him, refute his statements and protest against their imprisonment and sentencing within him. With so many voices inside him, all competing with each other, the Fog fights relentlessly to keep them all under control,[10] with the resulting conflict producing an effect of being split by these irreconcilable signifiers. It is the status of speech as written words on the pages of the comic that enables the production of such an effect, specifically, the use of parenthesis, punctuation unique to writing. As estranged words in parentheses invade this character's speech balloons, it is evident that it is something quite *other* that is speaking through his mouth. Thus, in *Doom Patrol*, the alien dimension to language narrativized in *Animal Man* is likewise emphasized, but this time, by means of the status of speech as writing in a comic.

The narrativization of such an invasive dimension to language continues in *The Invisibles*, as in one particular issue of the comic book series, this dimension to language is likened to that of a cancerous growth. In this issue of *The Invisibles*,[11] Ragged Robin tells Boy a story of a man who had been diagnosed with throat cancer; and to continue using the words of the character recounting the tale, "The cancer talks to him. It's stopped growing now and bonded to his vocal cords. There's some kind of new structure there. It takes control of his voice sometimes and describes other worlds or predicts the future."[12] Words spoken through this character's mouth are those of something else, some part of him that is beyond his control and that takes over his body, akin to a cancer. Such a cancerous dimension to language is identified in Lacan's *Seminar XXIII*: as translated, "the word is a form of cancer with which the human being is afflicted."[13] As a part of the subject, one that is beyond his control, and one that proceeds to takes over his body, there is an invasively cancerous dimension to language; and as Morrison's characters are afflicted by invasive signifiers, it is just such a dimension to language that is narrativized.

In *The Invisibles*, language is repeatedly attributed with the quality of being an affliction, after initially having been introduced early on in the series via a character inhabited by thoughts imposed from without (thoughts being dependent upon language, as articulated in Lacan's *Seminar XXIII*, "we do not think without words").[14] To draw upon the words of Morrison's character, as he attributes the imposition of thoughts upon him to the machinations of another:

> You can shout and call me crazy all you like but it won't change the *facts*. We're all *receivers*. Like cheap radios.... We think our thoughts are our own, but let me tell you, they're *not*. Our thoughts are *broadcasts* ... by our *masters* in the new world order.... When was the last time you had a thought that wasn't put there by them?[15]

In attributing his thoughts to another, and conceiving of them as being imposed from without, the dialogue of this character exemplifies a relation to language evocative of that associated with psychosis in the work of Lacan, as discussed in *Seminar III*: as translated, "the psychotic is inhabited, possessed, by language."[16] It is such a relation to language that persists throughout *The Invisibles*, as Morrison's characters are recurrently inhabited by words imposed from without.

Elsewhere in *The Invisibles*, such an invasive quality to language is tied to the very appearance of words on the pages of a comic, via an emphasis on the placement of speech in balloons positioned outside the speaking character. As illustrated on the cover of one issue of *The Invis-*

ibles,[17] the words of another are being imposed upon the pictured characters, an imposition that is emphasized via the externality of these words. This cover image (Fig. 5.1), drawn by Brian Bolland, pictures a narrative event from the comic's script,[18] and exemplifies the particular relation to language recurrent throughout Morrison's body of work. As illustrated on this cover, someone else's words have been cut out and pasted over the speech balloons of the pictured characters (these are words that appear to be typewritten, and thus are visually distinct from the kinds of lettering that usually adorn the pages of a comic), in an image that demonstrates the potential of the comic to illustrate an invasive dimension to language via an emphasis on the imposition of another's words from without. Now not only is language something that is imposed upon Morrison's characters within the narrative of the comic, but this very imposition is illustrated by means of the status of words on the comic page.

Inescapable Signifiers

There is an invasive quality to language on the pages of a comic, as illustrated on Bolland's cover,[19] a cover that not only emphasizes an alien dimension to language, but one that also emphasizes an inescapable quality to these words, as in their intrusion, these words cannot be avoided. The pictured characters are unable to escape the words imposed from without, these words being forced upon them in an unremitting way, and in contrast to the momentary quality of speech, the words on the comic page remain. In *The Invisibles*,[20] the imposition of obtrusive words upon the characters is attributed to another alphabet, the full 64-letter alphabet, which by means of its additional letters (letters that are missing from our inadequate 26-letter alphabet, or "slave language" as it is termed in the comic),[21] enables others to impose their words upon these characters, the imposed words being spoken through the mouths of these characters. In the narrative of the comic, these characters are not quite sure how to defend themselves against the invasive signifiers; or in the words of one character, "How do we fight *words*?"[22] The inescapable quality of the 64-letter alphabet words is also shared by the words on the pages of the comic, but it is not only by means of this other alphabet that the status of language in the comic is narrativized in Morrison's work, as such a quality to language also recurs in another form.

Elsewhere in *The Invisibles*, such an inescapable quality to language recurs by means of a word drug named Key 17,[23] a drug that affects the

Parasitic Signifiers (PITKETHLY)

Fig. 5.1 Cover. Morrison, Jimenez and Stokes. From "The Invisibles" vol. 2 #13 ™ and © Grant Morrison. Used with permission of DC Comics.

language-processing centers of the brain. Under the influence of this drug, when looking at a written word, the affected character does not see the signifier, but rather, he or she sees that to which the signifier refers. In one issue of *The Invisibles*,[24] an inescapable quality to language is emphasized by means of this word drug, as King Mob, under its influence, coincides with signifiers written by another, seeing fragments of his body instead of the written words. This character, while looking at scraps of paper falling down around his feet, each bearing the written word "finger," sees not the written words, but rather, he sees his own fingers, just as if they had been severed from his hands and discarded in the same manner as the written words had been.[25] An identical effect is also produced by a scrap of paper stuck to a mirror, one bearing the written words "diseased face." When King Mob gazes at the words adorning the mirror, the reflection he sees is that of a diseased face.[26] In both instances, the character coincides with another's signifiers[27]; he *is* those words, in a horrifyingly literal way.[28] In addition, a coinciding of character with signifier recurs again in *The Invisibles*, as Ragged Robin, a writer, is unable to distance herself from the words she writes. She is afraid to include herself in a story she is writing lest she cannot be separated from what is written on the page; or to draw upon the words of the character, "I'm scared if I write myself in, I'll never get out. They'll find me trapped here in my own words."[29] As Morrison's characters coincide with the written words on the page, they are swallowed up by the signifier, which is something all-consuming, something from which they are unable to escape.

The aforementioned means of subjection to language are appropriated by these characters in the concluding issues of *The Invisibles*, and are used as a means to overcome those who had subjected them to language.[30] By means of the word drug, these characters impose signifiers upon the comic's villains (notably, as featured in the narrative of *The Invisibles*,[31] the administration of a large dose of the word drug to Sir Miles, one of the series' villains, results in a psychotic episode and the consequent labeling, "You have become schizophrenic").[32] It is via the use of this word drug that the comic's villains are ultimately overcome,[33] and in doing so, as it is depicted in the narrative of the comic, Morrison's characters obtain a freedom from their subjection to another's signifiers.[34] This freedom is articulated in the concluding words of the final issue of the series, as one character quotes the following words (words accompanying an image that further provokes an association with language via its focus on the full stop at the end of the written sentence)[35]: "We allowed ourselves to be... sentenced. See! Now! Our sentence is up."[36] Within the context of the characters' battle to defend themselves against another's signifiers, it is worth noting that these final words are actually the words of someone else (it is another character's words that are being quoted); and as the series concludes with another's words being spoken, the alien dimension to language that had recurred throughout the series continues to be emphasized. Following *The Invisibles*, the sentencing of Morrison's characters to language is maintained throughout the writer's subsequent work, albeit by means of an additional quality attributed to the signifier, as will be demonstrated in the next, and final, section of this chapter.

Accosted by Material Signifiers

On the pages of a comic, words have a tangible quality to them; they can be garishly colored and can be given prominent or accentuated forms.[37] Such words demonstrate the potential of the comic to emphasize a material dimension to language,[38] and it is this very materiality that is narrativized in Morrison's more recent work. In emphasizing a material dimension to language, the writer's characters continue to be subject to invasive signifiers, but now, it is the signifier's physicality that is associated with its imposition. In his more recent work, his characters are affected by the material dimension to words in a comic, while the same relation to language evident in earlier work is maintained, albeit with a change in the particular quality associated with this relation. Such an imposition of material signifiers can be seen in *New X-Men*,[39] as derogatory words physically impact on one particular character, by means of their object-like status on the page. These words are hurled towards a character named Beast, and upon contact with them, he reels backward, a result of their overwhelming physical force. There is a particularly literal violence to these derogatory words, a violence resulting from their tangible quality on the comic page. Words are, in this instance, potentially lethal weapons[40]; they have a bodily impact, in the same way that a material object can have; and it is via such an emphasis on the materiality of words in a comic that Morrison's characters continue to be subject to an invasive dimension to language, as they are accosted by the signifiers on the page.

A material quality to language in the comic is emphasized again in *New X-Men*,[41] as the onomatopoeic sound-effect words of a comic book fight scene literally overwhelm the page. Such onomatopoeic words are conventionally used in a transient manner, as they signify momentary sound effects,[42] but in this particular instance, these words have an object-like quality to them. In the narrative of the comic, during the course of a fight scene, involving genetically engineered clones of the X-Man Nightcrawler, the accompanying "BAMF!" onomatopoeias—the sound effect associated with Nightcrawler's teleportations—are given a material status, as they outlast the momentary sound effects by persisting in subsequent images of the scene. Moreover, each new "BAMF!" piles over the previous ones, to the point that these words completely obscure everything else in the panel. Rather than simply signifying transient sound effects, in this instance, there is an emphasis on the word as a material object with a substance of its own. This particular quality to language is also narrativized in *Batman* #656,[43] via a fight scene that occurs in a modern art gallery. During the course of this fight, onomatopoeia stands in for accompanying sound effects ("BLAM!"); however, in the narrative of the comic, these words are literally material objects. The fight is occurring in the midst of an exhibition of comic book-style art, and the onomatopoeia that accompanies the fight scene is art that adorns the gallery's walls. As evident in both examples, such words are not so much substitutes for something else, but are more material things themselves.

While the ostentatious appearance of comic book onomatopoeia emphasizes the material quality to such words, all words on the pages of a comic have a materiality to them. This material quality to words in a comic is emphasized again in *The Filth*, as Max Thunderstone, a character termed "the world's first ever real-life *superhero*,"[44] displays his particular superpower, which consists of manifesting his thoughts as written words in fluffy white balloons floating above his head, in just the same way thoughts appear on the pages of a comic. Such a material quality to written thoughts in the comic is also narrativized in *Seven Soldiers*,[45] via a character that sees the thoughts of others as written words in fluffy white balloons floating above other characters' heads. While the thoughts of others intrude upon this character in the same way that they appear on the pages of the comic, the other characters in the narrative remain oblivious to these written words. While these examples from *The Filth*[46] and *Seven Soldiers*[47] emphasize a similarly material quality to thoughts, it is the latter example that maintains the particular relation to language discussed throughout this chapter, as it is manifestly the signifiers of another that are imposed upon this character from without.[48]

In *Seven Soldiers*,[49] as invasive signifiers plague the aforementioned character, by means of the intrusion of others' thoughts upon him, in the narrative of the comic, such an imposition of signifiers is likened to that in psychosis; to cite the words of this character, as he contemplates the appearance of words in this very way: "Maybe I'm schizophrenic or something. Maybe these are delusions."[50] With the material quality to thoughts on the pages of a comic compared to hallucinated signifiers, the potential of the comic to illustrate an invasiveness to language via its imposition from without, a dimension to language associated with psychosis,[51] is demonstrated in the narrative. In the comic, it is one signifier in particular that relentlessly plagues this character, and it is a signifier so inescapable that it even names him: the signifier is "ugly," while the character's name is "Uglyhead."[52] This coinciding of character with signifier repeats a dimension to language formerly emphasized in *The Invisibles*,[53] but now, in *Seven Soldiers*, such an inescapable dimension to language is emphasized by means of its very materiality in a comic, as Uglyhead is unable to escape the signifiers that appear on the page, in their imposition by another.

In conclusion, the comic demonstrates a unique potential to illustrate an invasive dimension to language, given the particular status of words on the page: the exteriority of a character's words can be drawn upon in emphasizing the intrusion of signifiers from without; their inescapable quality can be drawn upon in emphasizing a coinciding of characters with signifiers; and their materiality can be drawn upon in emphasizing an object-like quality to these words. An invasiveness to language, as illustrated by these means, is manifest throughout Morrison's work, with the writer drawing upon the unique potential of the comic to do this, via the recurrent subjection of his characters to signifiers imposed upon them by another.

Notes

1. Grant Morrison and Phil Jimenez, *The Invisibles* 2 #13 (New York: DC/Vertigo, 1998), 7.
2. Grant Morrison and Chaz Truog, *Animal Man* #25 (New York: DC Comics, 1990), 21.
3. Jacques Lacan, *Joyce and the Sinthome: The Seminar of Jacques Lacan, Book XXIII*, trans. Luke Thurston (unpublished manuscript, 1975–1976), seminar 7, Wednesday, 17 February 1976.
4. Bruce Fink, *The Lacaninan Subject: Between Language and Jouissance* (Princeton: Princeton University Press, 1995), 53.
5. As discussed by Fink in *The Lacaninan Subject*, this dimension of being subject to signifiers imposed from somewhere else is particularly evident in slips of the tongue (3–4).
6. Grant Morrison and Chaz Truog, *Animal Man* #25, 24; *Animal Man* #26 (New York: DC Comics, 1990), 2.
7. Morrison and Truog, *Animal Man* #26 (New York: DC Comics, 1990), 9.
8. Grant Morrison and Richard Case, *Doom Patrol* #27-#29 (New York: DC Comics, 1989–1990).

9. Grant Morrison and Richard Case, *Doom Patrol* #28 (New York: DC Comics, 1989), 17.
10. Ibid., 16–17, 21.
11. Grant Morrison and Phil Jimenez, *The Invisibles* 1 #17 (New York: DC/Vertigo, 1996).
12. Ibid., 14.
13. The use of the word cancer in this translation is consistent with the original French; see Lacan, *Joyce and the Sinthome*, seminar 7; see also, Jacques-Alain Miller, "Teachings of the Case Presentation," *Returning to Freud: Clinical Psychoanalysis in the School of Lacan*, trans. and ed. Stuart Schneiderman (New Haven: Yale University Press, 1980), 49.
14. Lacan, *Joyce and the Sinthome*, seminar 7.
15. Grant Morrison and Steve Yeowell, *The Invisibles* 1 #2 (New York: DC/Vertigo, 1994), 1.
16. This relation to language is held in contrast to that of the neurotic subject, who, by comparison, "inhabits language"; Jacques Lacan, *The Psychoses: The Seminar of Jacques Lacan, Book III*, trans. Russell Grigg (London: Routledge, 1993), 250.
17. Grant Morrison and Phil Jimenez, *The Invisibles* 2 #13 (New York: DC/Vertigo, 1998), cover.
18. The collaborative aspect of the comic should be noted, and the contribution of the many artists (pencilers, inkers, and letterers) to the production of these texts acknowledged. As I make reference to comic art in this chapter, it is to exemplify the relation of Morrison's characters to language, as it recurs throughout the writer's comic book scripts. All artworks discussed in this esssay are chosen for their illustration of this particular relation.
19. Grant Morrison and Phil Jimenez, *The Invisibles* 2 #13 (New York: DC/Vertigo, 1998), cover.
20. Ibid., 6–7.
21. Ibid., 7.
22. Ibid.
23. Elsewhere in *The Invisibles*, revisions of this word drug are called Key 23 and Key 64, but the function of these word drugs remains the same.
24. Grant Morrison and Phil Jimenez, *The Invisibles* 1 #18 (New York: DC/Vertigo, 1996).
25. Ibid., 4–5.
26. Ibid., 5; Grant Morrison and Phil Jimenez, *The Invisibles* 1 #19 (New York: DC/Vertigo, 1996), 22; Grant Morrison and Phil Jimenez, *The Invisibles* 2 #1 (New York: DC/Vertigo, 1997), 7.
27. An inability to gain a distance from the signifiers of another is indicative of a nonfunctioning of the reflective dimension of language, something that is associated with the psychotic structure in Paul Verhaeghe's *On Being Normal: A Manual for Clinical Psychodiagnostics*, trans. Sigi Jottkandt (London: Karnak, 2008), 223.
28. Briefly jumping ahead to Morrison's later work, a similar coinciding of character and signifier can be seen in *Vimanarama!* #3, as one character's facial features are literally replaced by the written word for each feature. For example, the word "eye" appears in place of an eye, and the word "finger" appears in place of each finger (this latter example directly reminiscent of the horrifyingly literal fingers in *The Invisibles*). See Grant Morrison and Philip Bond, *Vimanarama!* #3 (New York: DC/Vertigo, 2005), 5.
29. Grant Morrison and Chris Weston, *The Invisibles* 2 #20 (New York: DC/Vertigo, 1998), 21.
30. The use of language as a weapon in the battle between the comic's heroes and villains is discussed in Stephen Rauch, "We Have All Been Sentenced: Language as a Means of Control in Grant Morrison's *The Invisibles*," *International Journal of Comic Art* 6, no. 2 (2004): 350–63.
31. Grant Morrison and Sean Phillips, *The Invisibles* 3 #6 (New York: DC/Vertigo, 1999), 15; Grant Morrison and Sean Phillips, *The Invisibles* 3 #5 (New York: DC/Vertigo, 2000), 10, 18; Grant Morrison and Steve Yeowell, *The Invisibles* 3 #4 (New York: DC/Vertigo, 2000), 21.

32. Morrison and Yeowell, *The Invisibles* vol. 3 #4, 21.
33. Grant Morrison and Steve Yeowell, *The Invisibles* 3 #2 (New York: DC/Vertigo, 2000), 5–7; Grant Morrison and Frank Quitely, *The Invisibles* 3 #1 (New York: DC Comics, 2000), 16–17.
34. Furthermore, in addition to their use of the word drug to do so, a freedom from the signifier is also obtained as Morrison's characters shed their names, along with everything that accompanies such a label, as articulated in *The Invisibles* 3 #2 (20) and *The Invisibles* 3 #1 (2).
35. The rendering of these words as images is discussed in Christopher Murray's "Subverting the Sublime: Romantic Ideology in the Comics of Grant Morrison," in *Sub/versions: Cultural Status, Genre and Critique*, ed. Pauline MacPherson *et al.*, (Newcastle: Cambridge Scholars, 2008), 34–51 (45, 48); while in Marc Singer's *Grant Morrison: Combining the Worlds of Contemporary Comics* (Jackson: University Press of Mississippi, 2012), 126, the same panel is interpreted in terms of Lacan's Symbolic, Imaginary and Real, an interpretation reminiscent of Donald Ault's association of the former orders with the comic's words, images, and gap respectively in "'Cutting Up' Again Part II: Lacan on Barks on Lacan," in *Comics & Culture: Analytical and Theoretical Approaches to Comics*, ed. Anne Magnussen and Hans-Christian Christiansen (Copenhagen: Museum Tusculanum Press, 2000), 123–140.
36. Morrison and Quitely, *The Invisibles* 3 #1, 22.
37. In a comic, words can be treated as parts of images, as discussed by Scott McCloud in *Understanding Comics: The Invisible Art* (New York: HarperPerennial, 1994), 154.
38. An example of this potential to illustrate a material dimension to language is evident in *New X-Men* #121, as obtrusive green letters take form from splatters of slimy liquid, letters that proceed to spell out a message to the character pictured, in an image by Frank Quitely; Grant Morrison and Frank Quitely, *New X-Men* #121 (New York: Marvel Comics, 2002), 20.
39. Grant Morrison and Ethan Van Sciver, *New X-Men* #117 (New York: Marvel Comics, 2001), 13.
40. Such a potential for words to be lethal weapons is echoed in *Seven Soldiers: Shining Knight* #2, as articulated by a villainous character, "I kill with *words.*" Grant Morrison and Simone Bianchi, *Seven Soldiers: Shining Knight* #2 (New York: DC Comics, 2005), 8.
41. Grant Morrison and Marc Silvestri, *New X-Men* #152 (New York: DC Comics, 2004), 6.
42. In *Understanding Comics*, Scott McCloud identifies such words to be a desperate attempt to capture sound in a comic (134).
43. Grant Morrison and Andy Kubert, *Batman* #656 (New York: DC Comics, 2006), 10.
44. Grant Morrison and Chris Weston, *The Filth* #10 (New York: DC/Vertigo, 2003), 6.
45. Grant Morrison and Doug Mahnke, *Seven Soldiers: Frankenstein* #1 (New York: DC Comics, 2006).
46. Morrison and Weston, *The Filth* #10, 6.
47. Morrison and Mahnke, *Seven Soldiers: Frankenstein* #1.
48. In contrast, in *The Filth* #10, the world's first ever real-life superhero is ostensibly able to manifest his own words at will, evoking a similar command over language as that attributed to Morrison's stand-in in *Animal Man* #26, discussed previously in this essay.
49. Morrison and Mahnke, *Seven Soldiers: Frankenstein* #1.
50. Ibid., 7.
51. Lacan proposes, in *Seminar III*, that hallucinated signifiers in psychosis are foreclosed signifiers appearing in the Real (13, 86–87).
52. Morrison and Mahnke, *Seven Soldiers: Frankenstein* #1, 5.
53. As discussed previously with reference to *The Invisibles* 1 #18.

Part II
Thematic Analysis

From Shame into Glory in *The Filth*

David Coughlan

Grant Morrison's *The Filth* (2002–03) is, in many ways, a comic about abjection and shame: the shame of picking your nose, the shame of enjoying pornography, of masturbating, the shame of male pattern baldness, of the comb-over, the shame of violence, the shame of loving a cat, or letting that cat die of neglect.[1] In *The Filth*, that cat is Tony, and Tony's owner is one Greg Feely, and the comic is about Greg's perceived shame, but it is also about the shame of superheroes, and male shame in general. And it is about alchemy, about transforming the shit of shame into the gold of glory.

The Abject Alter-Ego

The Filth does not take place in what is known as the DC Universe, the world of Superman, Batman, and Wonder Woman. The only superheroes in the world of *The Filth* are those to be found in comic books until, that is, the appearance of Max Thunderstone, "man-made god" and "the world's first ever real-life *superhero*."[2] Max is explicitly conceived by Morrison as a comic-book hero made flesh, to the extent that one of his powers, as he explains, is "a consciousness so focused and so disciplined, it can actually manifest words in a *cloud* above my head,"[3] meaning his thoughts appear to those around him as if in a comic book's speech balloon. He is introduced in a full-page image which shows him standing full-length in a room where issues of the comic *Status Quorum* are scattered everywhere and the shelves are laden with comics and action figures.[4] He is clearly an action figure on a larger scale, shown stripped to the waist, his veins snaking over his superbly defined muscles. His physique conforms to Richard Dyer's description of comic book heroes' "bodybuilt bodies," "hard and contoured, often resembling armour,"[5] and, indeed, his weight-lifting equipment is visible too in the background of that first image. He has become a "god, driving a car of raw muscle"[6] which is appropriately suggestive of, and as, an image of phallic compensation given that, as Scott Bukatman observes, "with their thick necks, bulging veins, and protruding tendons ... these heroes really become enormous *dicks* sheathed in ... condoms."[7] Fittingly, Max has his own skin-tight costume, the word "Max" emblazoned across the chest.

As a true comic book hero, Max has a double identity too, for his real name is not Max Thunderstone but Maxwell Shatt. It is as Thunderstone, however, that the once chronically agoraphobic Shatt will "finally go *public*"[8] because, as Bukatman observes, the "costume and logo constitute the superhero as *publicly* marked."[9] Max is then, as he says, "outside and everyone can *see* me."[10] In this way, the double identity relates to private and public identities, but it relates also to adolescent and adult identities, particularly male identities. In fact, as I have shown elsewhere, the costumed identity "allows a structuring of these identities in relation to each other, with the private linked to the adolescent and the public to the adult" so that the comic book hero's costume "constructs him as a man exactly because it marks him as a public figure."[11] In contrast, within the terms of the dominant comic book masculinity, a man who settles for a private life or, more accurately, a life at home represents something of a failure, without real power. Compare, for example, Greg Feely with the dynamic figure of Max Thunderstone. The first image of Greg is not of some action man, but of a balding figure in an ill-fitting suit, buying kitty litter and pornography, and being laughed at by a couple of schoolgirls as the shop-keeper affirms in a matey way that there is "nothing like a good wank."[12] Outside the shop, he picks his nose, takes a look at what is produced, and eats it. Then, as he does most nights, he goes home to his cat, Tony, eats in front of the television, and masturbates over pornography before going to bed. Is there not something pathetic about poor, lonely Greg, the wanker?

Greg is an abject figure, in fact, and in a very literal sense. As Judith Butler notes, "Abjection (in Latin, *ab-jicere*) literally means to cast off, away, or out and, hence, presupposes and produces a domain of agency from which it is differentiated."[13] Only pages after he is introduced, Greg is revealed to be a fiction, an artificial personality or "para-personality,"[14] that his true self wears, like a pair of old slippers, during his downtime. In reality, it would appear, Greg Feely is Ned Slade, an officer of The Hand, a global secret agency, and once Ned is recalled to duty Greg must be cast off, fucked out of him by a fellow agent.[15] Greg is not a part of Ned, or not a part of what Julia Kristeva terms the "clean and proper" self,[16] the "I" that is constituted exactly by this act of expulsion which establishes the border between inside and outside, between self and other. As Noëlle McAfee explains, abjection is "rejecting what is other to oneself—and thereby creating borders of an always tenuous 'I'" or, as Kristeva puts it, "I expel *myself*, I spit *myself* out, I abject *myself* within the same motion through which 'I' claim to establish *myself*."[17] For Ned to be, Greg must be flushed out of his system; he comes "running out of [his] nose," as something that "smells awful."[18] Indeed, as that which "can be metaphorically related to what leaks or is expelled from the individual body and its various orifices, the abject is ... always related to matters that traverse the body's boundaries...: blood, pus, mucus, saliva, milk, urine, semen, feces, tears."[19] Masturbating, nose-picking Greg seems almost perverse in his disregard for the proper limits of the body. Normally, there is abjection where we recognize that which was once inside, and when, therefore, our sense of the boundary of our self, our identity, is disturbed or threatened. "What is abjected is radically excluded but never banished altogether. It hovers at the periphery of one's existence, constantly challenging one's own tenuous borders of selfhood."[20] What is abjected can be uncannily familiar, therefore, to the extent that Kristeva says that abjection "places the one haunted by it literally beside himself."[21] No sooner, then, has Ned been purged of Greg than he comes face-to-face with him again, in the bathroom, in the form of the Hand-assigned doppelgänger who will "keep Greg's life *warm*"[22] for him while he is on active duty (this is, after all, a world of para-personas, and *para* is Greek for "beside").

The process of abjection that Kristeva identifies as key to subject formation is also evident at the societal level: "It is as if dividing lines were built up between society and a certain nature, as well as within the social aggregate, on the basis of the simple logic of *excluding filth*, which, promoted to the ritual level of *defilement*, founded the 'self and clean' of each social group."[23] For Judith Butler, as Calvin Thomas clarifies, abjection "is concerned with the way the dominant patriarchal-heteronormative social order maintains itself ... by constructing arenas of abject powerlessness, lifelessness, and meaninglessness to which it consigns its marginalized others" or, in other words, it "is the mode by which Others become shit."[24] Maintaining this order, excluding filth, is exactly what the secret agency The Hand is about. It is explained to the semi-amnesiac Ned Slade that he works as part of The Hand's "supercleansing operations," based in The Crack and with a mission to enforce Status: Q "by removing and safely destroying all that is *not* Status: Q," all "threats to *social hygiene*."[25] Theirs is "the hand that wipes the arse of the world."[26] In this way, Morrison's *The Filth* engages with abjection, with Kristeva's account of how "excrement and its equivalents (decay, infection, disease, corpse, etc.) stand for the danger to identity that comes from without: the ego threatened by the non-ego, society threatened by its outside, life by death."[27] In place of the non-ego, Morrison has the "not-self" and the "anti-person"[28] for The Hand to face, so that, in the course of Ned's missions with The Hand, they take down the rogue agent Officer Spartacus Hughes, the murderous Doctor Arno Von Vermun, and the insane hardcore porn director Tex Porneau. Yet, they also neutralize Max Thunderstone, the Man-Made God. In what way, therefore, it must be asked, is a superhero filthy?

The Hypermasculine Self

It is Max who describes The Hand as "an organized gang of authoritarian monsters"[29] and reveals that it was his friend, Greg Feely, who found out about them in the first place, only to be brainwashed and recruited by them in the shape of Ned Slade. It is Ned, it thus emerges, who is the para-persona, and Greg is instead "not self ... a natural born *anti-person*" and "officially the world's most dangerous man."[30] It can be argued, however, that Max and Greg's attacks on The Hand are not what make them a danger to Status: Q but are only a symptom of that which really makes them a threat to the social order. Max, to start with, in his efforts to become the world's first superhero, conforms to an extreme form of heroic masculine identity commonly described as "hypermasculine,"[31] a form that is effectively defined by the body that, all but naked in its skin-tight costume, seems at the same time to present a hard, impenetrable shell, a total unit. The rigidity of hypermasculinity reflects the constricted form of traditional heroic masculinity, an ideal masculinity that leaves men "constrained by the force of, and their *fantasy* relation to, a dominant or hegemonic ideal of masculinity as tough, heterosexual, authoritative, successful."[32] Max's hypermasculine identity, therefore, actually locates him inside society's heteronormative patriarchy, and especially because it seems to exemplify a "clean and proper" body whose rigidly determined boundaries will brook no pollution.

Such hypermasculine selves are often presented[33] in terms of Klaus Theweleit's analysis, when discussing the German *Freikorps*, of the soldier male's "steel body," "all armor, speeding bullet, steel enclosure," a self and own body.[34] Importantly, in examining Theweleit's work, Jessica Benjamin and Anson Rabinbach comment on the "soldier's wish to destroy the mother, ... a wish to rid himself and the earth of all those maternal qualities of warmth and sensuality that could be called mother."[35] The hypermasculinity of the comic book hero is based on a similar repudiation, with Jeffrey Brown observing that "idealized masculinity ... remains dependent upon the symbolic split between masculinity and femininity, between the *hard* male and the *soft* other," so that "masculinity is defined by what it is not, namely 'feminine,' and by all its associated traits—hard *not* soft, strong *not* weak, reserved *not* emotional, active *not* passive."[36] This rigid masculinity, therefore, is defined by what is not self, by what it has excluded as filth, which here is that which it has identified as feminine. This is all the more significant because abjection, too, is first and foremost an exclusion of the maternal, as the child, in order to be as a unit, rejects its union with its mother. As Kristeva explains, "Abjection preserves what existed in the archaism of pre-objectal relationship, in the immemorial violence with which a body becomes separated from another body in order to be"; it confronts us "with our earliest attempts to release the hold of *maternal* entity even before ex-isting outside of her," because "the first 'thing' to be abjected is the mother's body, the child's own origin."[37] As a result, the mother is "coded as 'abject.'"[38]

It is not a coincidence, therefore, that the event that enables Maxwell Shatt to become Max Thunderstone, his winning $69 million in the lottery, is also the event that kills his mother, whose heart is too weak to handle the excitement. As he dons the costume of the heroic male, he shifts "from the field of maternal power to the realm of the patriarchy,"[39] and his clean and proper body will be untouched by femininity from this point on. Except, and this is the true reason that he is an enemy of The Hand, Max never manages to fully define his superheroic identity. As he says, "My body never seemed to get big enough or impressive enough to make my message convincing. It was fun to pose in my outfits in front of the *mirror* but the idea of actually going *outside* became more and more terrifying."[40] Moreover, this failure to meet the ideal of the heroic male is signaled by a kind of phallic failure, by his strangely-shaped penis which is "like a weird *mushroom* or something.... That's not *normal.*"[41] If hypermasculine heroes really are "enormous *dicks* sheathed in ... condoms," then Max is a sadly misshapen one.[42] The cracks in the hard contours of his body reflect a weakness in his psyche also. The comic book hero's costume marks him publicly as a man, but Max retains a clear attachment to his private life or, in fact, to his life as a boy with his mother. He launches his superhero career on his mother Irene's birthday, admitting, "she would have been 83 years old today, so this is quite an important date for me."[43] As he thrillingly fights his way into The Hand, he exclaims, "Oh Mum. This is incredible.

Mum. Dad. You'd be so *proud* of me if you could see me" and "Look at me, Mum!"[44] His love for his mother represents Max's contamination, his failure to shape a clean and proper self in the patriarchal and, perhaps especially, heteronormative mold. His repeated assertion that, finally, he is "*outside*. I'm outside and everyone can *see* me,"[45] suggests that Max might be gay, and that his superheroic exploits represent him coming out. From The Hand's perspective, therefore, it must be Shatt out, because, as Brown details, "in the misogynistic, homophobic, and racist view of this ideology [of idealized masculinity], the despised other that masculinity defines itself against conventionally includes not only women but also feminized men."[46] This is at least part of the reason as well that Greg is on the same team as Max. As Antony Easthope observes, the double identity as structured through comic-book heroes forces "a boy to choose between a better self that is masculine and only masculine and another everyday self that seems feminine."[47] Greg occupies the role of the everyday self in the comic book, and is intentionally contrasted with the heroic ideal. He is Feely *not* (Nick) Fury, he is emotional *not* reserved, he is all that is so-called soft *not* hard, weak *not* strong, passive *not* active. He finally realizes that Ned must be the para-persona when his doppelgänger lets Tony die, because if one Greg loved Tony then all Gregs should love Tony: "if Greg really *was* a *parapersona*, made by The Hand, there would have to be *rules* governing his behaviour."[48] The Hand learns to its cost that "all he cared about was the fucking cat."[49] Greg is just a big pussy, really.

In the end, it takes a para-persona to make a soldier male of Max; the obscenely violent and destructive character Spartacus Hughes (his initials ironically mark him as the true Super Hero) infects Max's body and earmarks it "for *devastation* at the hands of alcohol, tobacco, hard drugs, and voraciously *incurable STDs*" as he looks for "a degrading fuck to get me in the mood for some fancy ultra-violence."[50] This hypermasculine posturing is unreal. As Lynne Segal argues, "No one can be 'that male' without constantly doing violence to many of the most basic human attributes: the capacity for sensitivity to oneself and others, for tenderness and empathy, the reality of fear and weakness, the pleasures of passivity—all, of course, quintessentially 'feminine.'"[51] To be "that male" would mean closing the self to any contact, to anything that would come from outside. But, as Judith Butler points out, "for inner and outer worlds to remain utterly distinct, the entire surface of the body would have to achieve an impossible impermeability. This sealing of its surfaces would constitute the seamless boundary of the subject; but this enclosure would invariably be exploded by precisely that excremental filth that it fears."[52] There would be absolute containment followed by an absolute voiding, of the bowels, or balls, or bladder, polluting the clean male self. Yet, this explosion of filth somehow recalls Theweleit's account of the soldier in battle, when "the man appears not only naked, but stripped of skin; he seems to lose his body armor, so that everything enters directly into the interior of his body, or flows directly from it. He is out of control and seems permitted to be so. But at the same time, he is all armor."[53] Here, everything flows from the man even as he remains impossibly impermeable, or, in other words, the soldier male is here given permission to transgress the boundaries of the self in order to shore up the boundaries of that same fragile self. Kristeva might be considering a similar scenario when she writes that "it is as if the skin, a fragile container, no longer guaranteed the integrity of one's 'own and clean self' but, scraped or transparent, invisible or taut, gave way before the dejection of its contents. Urine, blood, sperm, excrement then show up in order to reassure a subject that is lacking its 'own and clean self.' The abjection of those flows from within suddenly becomes the sole 'object' of sexual desire."[54]

As Thomas notes, the "main if not sole representational arena in which semen regularly makes a literal appearance is the ejaculation scenes, or 'money shots,' of heterosexually oriented hard-core film pornography."[55] Morrison seems to be referencing exactly such scenes when, on the opening page of *The Filth*, he shows Spartacus Hughes, three times in the one panel, standing over the prone body of a woman covered in fluid and then references a *"One-Man Gangbang"*[56] just pages later.[57] Spartacus's claim that "it makes me feel quite ... *dirty*"[58] is an ironic one because such a scene preserves masculinity's "supposedly immaculate self-construction" even as it assigns femininity "the role of the discarded, humiliated self."[59] "The function of the money shot," therefore, as Thomas puts it, "is to help keep the processes ... that produce masculinity from turning it into shit," while the costs "of accession to the *corps propre* of the phallicized ego are the abjection or fecalization of the other."[60]

A Sick Society

The shame of man is twofold, therefore, and can be mapped onto the double identity of the comic-book hero. The everyday self looks to the heroic self and is ashamed that he fails to meet those ideals, and the heroic self looks to the everyday self and is ashamed of the violence he must inflict on his Other in order to be. Referencing Theweleit, Thomas comments that in the "most restrictive representational economy, nothing is allowed to come out of the male body except in the name of violence and domination" or, as Steve Connor puts it, man is "ashamed most of all of the violence that is inseparable from being a man."[61] And yet, neither Greg nor Max is ashamed and, perhaps even, has anything to be ashamed about. Greg, at least, is not ashamed of picking his nose, or wanking; Max seems not ashamed either of his mushroom-shaped penis, as he shows it to others to get their opinion. But, though Greg and Max are not ashamed, clearly they should be, or at least the social system expects them to be. Society tells them that, if they could see themselves as the abject creatures they are, they would be ashamed. Shame requires doubleness, a self and other, because "shame is the vicarious experience of the other's negative evaluation."[62] As such, as Sandra Lee Bartky explains, "it requires if not an actual audience before whom my deficiencies are paraded, then an internalized audience with the capacity to judge me."[63] Morrison indicates this by initially showing us Greg as if seen through the shop's and streets' security cameras, first buying pornography, then picking his nose; some pages later he looks up at a surveillance camera and asks, "What are *you* looking at?"[64] The implication is that Greg has failed to internalize the self-surveying, and therefore shame-producing, faculty of the superego required to preserve a clean and proper social body. Max, meanwhile, believes that his heroics are being broadcast live to the world, but learns that they are being streamed on an "internet snuff site"[65]; his heroics, like his penis, are something he should be ashamed about.

Why should Greg and Max be ashamed? Greg is an everyday man who kicks ass, and Max is a hero-in-the-making who still loves his mother, fighting against an oppressive, authoritarian regime. Except, even as The Hand are "tasked with preventing ... utopias from achieving realization," they also "neutralize dangerously antisocial individuals."[66] Morrison himself, in explaining The Hand, says, "Think of the way a human immune system works to regulate processes within the body. Think of Status: Q as the body's natural temperature and threats to Status: Q as fevers or illnesses which have to be contained by our own natural defenses. The 'body' in this case being Society and the immune system being the Hand."[67] It turns out that it was Greg, Max, and their allies who created the contaminated, infectious para-persona of Spartacus Hughes in an effort to destabilize Status: Q, but, as Greg is rightly told, "attacking The Hand is like fighting your own *immune system*."[68] Morrison's notion of the society as body can be related to the long-established idea of the body politic, which "conceived of social structure and process through the prism of the human body."[69] Moreover, when Morrison refers to Spartacus as "a cancer" and casts a police force as the immune system, he reflects the way in which "the discourse of the body politic in political philosophy is always accompanied by a reflection on the illness and diseases of the body politic," as when Plato writes that "when a person's unhealthy, it takes very little to upset him and make him ill.... The same is true of an unhealthy society. It will fall into sickness and dissension at the slightest external provocation ... while sometimes faction fights will start without any external stimulus at all."[70] The ways in which we understand how the body is harmed and healed inform our thinking about the welfare of the state also, and how we represent it. As Margaret Healy argues:

> Discourses of disease, in fact, inscribe social tensions.... All "bounded structures" (nations, societies, cities) must imagine their conditions of disunity—problems relating to boundaries, internal structures and the relationship between parts—in much the same way as they imagine the physical body's conditions of disharmony. When disunity is perceived, a shared set of metaphors is drawn upon to imagine the conditions of well-being and wholeness for both the social field and the individual body.[71]

The examples in Jonathan Gil Harris's analysis place a similar emphasis on the way in which the figure of the body is used to address problems relating to border issues; he shows that, "Western political rhetoric has amassed this century a sizeable lexicon loosely derived from pathological medicine whose terms (e.g. the 'purge,' 'foreign bodies,' 'infection,' 'containment,' perhaps even 'ethnic cleansing') presume an organic notion of nation or civil society."[72] For Harris, therefore, "the body remains a powerful constitutive metaphor—albeit one that remains largely occulted—in many twentieth-century discourses of national and social formation."[73] Catherine A. Holland, too, suggests that the "body may be made invisible to or transparent within the modern public realm, but it is nonetheless held in reserve as a political force that becomes visible (or is made visible) in the very moments when order itself is at its most vulnerable"; the body is "deployed by the very order that gains its coherence through the claim of having vanquished, exiled, or displaced it."[74] Just as a rigidly masculine self reacts to the shame of taint with the ejection and abjection of what is feminine and filthy, so a society whose boundaries are disturbed induces the bod(il)y to show up to restore them.

Should Greg and company, therefore, be ashamed of what they have done to the body politic? Or is it The Hand that should be ashamed, for recruiting Spartacus and equipping him with Max's recycled body? As Marc Singer rightly points out, "*The Filth* does not simply suggest, as many genre fictions do, that the roles of hero and villain are ambiguous or interdependent—it argues that these labels are useless in a world where everyone has the capacity for evil."[75] Yet it might be more accurate to say that everyone has the capacity for filth or, as Spartacus puts it, "all of this is *shit* ... we're all *shit* ... *anyone* can be Spartacus Hughes."[76] What *The Filth* does is take the ambiguity of its title, which is a slang term for the police as well as referring to that which requires policing, to show that the line between the clean and the filthy is not set. It is not the drawing of the border which excludes something as filth, but the exclusion of something as filth which draws the border. Filth is not filth before it is ejected from the system or, as Butler puts it, abjection "appears as an expulsion of alien elements, but the alien is effectively established through this expulsion."[77] Kristeva explains, "Filth is not a quality in itself, but it applies only to what relates to a *boundary* and, more particularly, represents the object jettisoned out of that boundary, its other side, a margin."[78] In terms of the body politic, therefore, it is only through the abjection of others that the police actions of The Hand can be interpreted as an immune system protecting the social body from an outside contaminant rather than as an autoimmune reaction attacking the body itself. The claim that "*anyone* can be Spartacus" recalls now that famous cry of protest and solidarity against oppression from Stanley Kubrick's 1960 film: "I'm Spartacus!"

The Shame Inoculation

Morrison's *The Filth* places the reader in a world where they can no longer tell if they are on the side of the police or of the perverted. This is a world properly inhabited by para-personas because as J. Hillis Miller details

> "para" is a double antithetical prefix signifying at once proximity and distance, similarity and difference, interiority and exteriority, something inside a domestic economy and at the same time outside it, something simultaneously this side of a boundary line, threshold, or margin, and also beyond it, equivalent in status and also secondary or subsidiary, submissive, as of guest to host, slave to master. A thing in "para," moreover, is not only simultaneously on both sides of the boundary line between inside and out. It is also the boundary itself, the screen which is a permeable membrane connecting inside and outside. It confuses them with one another, allowing the outside in, making the inside out, dividing them and joining them.[79]

Turned around, readers do not know whether they should be cheering on or shouting down Greg Touchy-Feely, the cat lover, or Greg Pedo-Feely, the suspected child molester. And Greg does not know himself: "They say

I killed Tony with neglect and came up with The Hand as an excuse for being an alcoholic pervert deep inside. I couldn't stand it if that were true ... I'd be so ashamed of myself."[80] To know Greg is to know abjection; "his abjection is due to the permanent ambiguity of the parts he plays without his knowledge, even when he believes he knows."[81] And to read *The Filth* is to know abjection because it is "not lack of cleanliness or health that cause abjection but what disturbs identity, system, order. What does not respect borders, positions, rules. The in-between, the ambiguous, the composite."[82]

Exposing his readers to the abject is exactly Morrison's intention in *The Filth*. As he says, "I'm deliberately injecting the worst aspects of life into my readers' heads ... in an effort to help them survive the torrents of nastiness, horror and dirt we're all exposed to every day."[83] Ultimately, therefore, he sees the comic introducing the reader to the worst of contemporary Western culture in order to prompt a life-affirming response. *The Filth* is intended "as a filter or cleansing plant—a colourful pseudo-kidney," Morrison says, "as some kind of purifying—or putrefying—poetry."[84] In a strange way, Kristeva can also see contemporary literature engaged in such a process:

> For the subject firmly settled in its superego, a writing of this sort is necessarily implicated in the interspace that characterizes perversion; and for this reason, it gives rise in turn to abjection. And yet, such texts call for a softening of the superego. Writing them implies an ability to imagine the abject, that is, to see oneself in its place and to thrust it aside only by means of the displacements of verbal play. It is only after his death, eventually, that the writer of abjection will escape his condition of waste, reject, abject.[85]

Morrison himself describes how, "during the twelve months of actually writing *The Filth* scripts I was so overwhelmed ... that I almost committed suicide on several occasions and spent most of the year in a state of intense psychological and physical distress. I can happily say that the ordeal is now over; I was able to process all this negative energy into my writing and emerge ... changed forever."[86] In Morrison's experience, abjection, as Kristeva writes, "is a resurrection that has gone through death (of the ego). It is an alchemy that transforms death drive into a start of life, of new significance."[87] Writing, and reading, *The Filth* means "rebirth with and against abjection."[88] The reader of *The Filth* has to learn that the "Crack runs through *everything*. And everyone."[89] The Crack in the armor of the clean and proper self leaves the ego exposed to the non-ego, and this injection of filth might mean a remedy or a poison; perhaps for this reason, the creator of I-Life "wondered if, instead of trying to *kill* diseases, we could *befriend* them."[90] And this applies also to the body politic, the dominant social order, which must remain open to those members of society it is ashamed to admit. Morrison laments those readers who cannot sympathize with the abject figure of Greg, "an ordinary, lonely man tending a sick animal," and it is exactly to "help cure these emotional deficiencies, *The Filth* can be seen [as] a healing inoculation of grime."[91] *The Filth* functions, therefore, as a shame inoculation also, allowing readers to know not the shame but "the value of powerlessness"[92] as the self is softened through imaginative sympathy with what has been cast outside. The ending of *The Filth*, and of *The Invisibles* and *Flex Mentallo* also, is concerned with those who too often seem discarded by society—the disabled, the homeless, the depressed, the suicidal—and symbolizes their successful reincorporation into a more open social body through the image of flowers sprouting from garbage bags. And all of this is achieved in *The Filth* through contact with the first thing to be abjected, the self's secret origin, and the Commanding Officer of The Hand, Mother Dirt. "Have you forgotten me?" she asks.[93]

Thomas also sees an ethical possibility in a "wilful pursuit of abjection as self-divestiture *in writing*" which "could allow abjective writing to become something other than the mode by which *others* become shit."[94] The power of writing in *The Filth* is seen in the image of an overdosing Greg, lying prone on his kitchen floor, still holding in his hand a pen which looms, massive in scale, over the micro-world of The Crack. The hand is poised to write, and can compose a suicide note or can spin an entire universe into existence. Readers can side with one or the other. The end of *The Filth* reproduces, in many ways therefore, the end of *Flex Mentallo*, but the shamanic word of positive transformation in that book is unwritten here. Readers must imagine it (in) themselves through contact with *The Filth*'s "superabundance,"[95] which shares in the excessiveness of the mother's body, the mother's dirt. "The message of *The Filth* is very clear," says Morrison: "I'd like readers to realize that even the most mundane existence—even the shabbiest, shittiest life you can live—can be redeemed into glory by the power of imagination,"[96] redeemed by The Hand of God, The Hand of Greg, The Hand of Grant.

Notes

1. *The Filth*, written by Grant Morrison, with art by Chris Weston and Gary Erskine, was published under DC Comics's Vertigo imprint in 13 parts from 2002 to 2003.
2. Grant Morrison and Chris Weston, *The Filth* #10 (New York: DC/Vertigo, 2003), 6.
3. Ibid., 6.

4. *Status Quorum* is a comic within the comic of *The Filth*, recounting the adventures of the eponymous superhero team, but it is also a world within that world. It exists as the paperverse, "an ongoing 2-dimensional narrative universe based on traditional American comic book fiction" within which imaginary technologies can be developed before being "harvested into 3-D existence." Grant Morrison, "The Paperverse," *Crack!Comics*, 7 December 2003, http://www.crackcomicks.com/the_paperverse.htm.

5. Richard Dyer, "The White Man's Muscles," in *The Masculinity Studies Reader*, ed. Rachel Adams and David Savran (Oxford: Blackwell, 2002), 263, 265.

6. Morrison and Weston, *The Filth* #10, 5.

7. Scott Bukatman, *Matters of Gravity: Special Effects and Supermen in the 20th Century* (Durham: Duke University Press, 2003), 61.

8. Morrison and Weston, *The Filth* #10, 6.

9. Bukatman, *Matters of Gravity*, 54.

10. Morrison and Weston, *The Filth* #10, 17.

11. David Coughlan, "The Naked Hero and Model Man: Costumed Identity in Comic Book Narratives," in *Heroes of Film, Comics and American Culture: Essays on Real and Fictional Defenders of Home*, ed. Lisa M. DeTora (Jefferson, NC: McFarland, 2009), 237, 238.

12. Morrison and Weston, *The Filth* #1, 2.

13. Judith Butler, *Bodies That Matter: On the Discursive Limits of "Sex"* (New York: Routledge, 1993), 243 n. 2.

14. Morrison and Weston, *The Filth* #1, 13.

15. Mixing the two names, Ned Slade and Greg Feely, gives Ned Feely, an indication that *The Filth* "was based on an unsold proposal for Nick Fury, Agent of SHIELD, Marvel Comics' premier super-spy." Marc Singer, *Grant Morrison: Combining the Worlds of Contemporary Comics* (Jackson: University Press of Mississippi, 2012), 183. In this context, the name Maxwell Shatt could well be a reference to Maxwell Smart from the *Get Smart* television series.

16. Julia Kristeva, *Powers of Horror: An Essay on Abjection* (New York: Columbia University Press, 1982), 8.

17. Noëlle McAfee, *Julia Kristeva*, Routledge Critical Thinkers (New York: Routledge, 2004), 45; Kristeva, *Powers of Horror*, 3.

18. Morrison and Weston, *The Filth* #1, 13, 14.

19. Calvin Thomas, *Masculinity, Psychoanalysis, Straight Queer Theory: Essays on Abjection in Literature, Mass Culture, and Film* (New York: Palgrave Macmillan, 2008), xii.

20. McAfee, *Julia Kristeva*, 46.

21. Kristeva, *Powers of Horror*, 1.

22. Morrison and Weston, *The Filth* #1, 15.

23. Kristeva, *Powers of Horror*, 65.

24. Thomas, *Masculinity, Psychoanalysis, Straight Queer Theory*, xii; Judith Butler, *Gender Trouble: Feminism and the Subversion of Identity* (New York: Routledge, 1999), 170.

25. Morrison and Weston, *The Filth* #2, 1, 2, 3. Status: Q, like *Status Quorum*, of course refers to the *status quo*, "the way it is." Ibid., 2.

26. Ibid., 3.

27. Kristeva, *Powers of Horror*, 71.

28. Morrison and Weston, *The Filth* #13, 1.

29. Morrison and Weston, *The Filth* #10, 9.

30. Morrison and Weston, *The Filth* #11, 18, 6.

31. See, for example, Jeffrey A. Brown, *Black Superheroes, Milestone Comics, and Their Fans*, Studies in Popular Culture (Jackson: University Press of Mississippi, 2001); Bukatman, *Matters of Gravity*; Rob Lendrum, "The Super Black Macho, One Baaad Mutha: Black Superhero Masculinity in 1970s Mainstream Comic Books," *Extrapolation* 46, no. 3 (2005): 360–72; Kenneth MacKinnon, *Uneasy Pleasures: The Male as Erotic Object* (London: Cygnus Arts, 1997).

32. Lynne Segal, "Back to the Boys? Temptations of the Good Gender Theorist," *Textual Practice* 15, no. 2 (2001): 239.
33. Brown, *Black Superheroes*; Bukatman, *Matters of Gravity*; Dyer, "The White Man's Muscles."
34. Klaus Theweleit, *Male Fantasies*, vol. 2, *Male Bodies: Psychoanalyzing the White Terror*, trans. Erica Carter and Chris Turner with Stephen Conway (Cambridge: Polity Press, 1989), 159, 192.
35. Jessica Benjamin and Anson Rabinbach, foreword to *Male Fantasies*, by Klaus Theweleit, xxi-xxii.
36. Brown, *Black Superheroes*, 169, 168.
37. Kristeva, *Powers of Horror*, 10, 13; McAfee, *Julia Kristeva*, 48.
38. Kristeva, *Powers of Horror*, 64.
39. Bukatman, *Matters of Gravity*, 55.
40. Morrison and Weston, *The Filth* #10, 8.
41. Ibid., 8.
42. Bukatman, *Matters of Gravity*, 61.
43. Morrison and Weston, *The Filth* #10, 7.
44. Ibid., 13, 18.
45. Ibid., 17.
46. Brown, *Black Superheroes*, 169.
47. Antony Easthope, *What a Man's Gotta Do: The Masculine Myth in Popular Culture* (New York: Routledge, 1990), quoted in ibid., 174.
48. Morrison and Weston, *The Filth* #11, 6.
49. Ibid., 18.
50. Morrison and Weston, *The Filth* #12, 3; Morrison and Weston, *The Filth* #11, 19.
51. Lynne Segal, *Slow Motion: Changing Masculinities, Changing Men* (London: Virago, 1990), 114.
52. Butler, *Gender Trouble*, 170.
53. Theweleit, *Male Fantasies*, 192.
54. Kristeva, *Powers of Horror*, 53. The skin here "invisible or taut" recalls the skin stripped from the soldier in Theweleit's description.
55. Calvin Thomas, *Male Matters: Masculinity, Anxiety, and the Male Body on the Line* (Urbana: University of Illinois Press, 1996), 19.
56. Morrison and Weston, *The Filth* #1, 10.
57. A defeated Max Thunderstone takes the place of the woman in the similar image which closes issue ten.
58. Morrison and Weston, *The Filth* #1, 1.
59. Thomas, *Male Matters*, 13, 22.
60. Ibid., 23.
61. Ibid., 18; Steve Connor, "The Shame of Being a Man," *Textual Practice* 15, no. 2 (2001): 213. In *The Filth*, Morrison gives us the example of Adam (Secret Original from the Status Quorum), a hero properly denying himself "the love of one good woman," Eve. Morrison and Weston, *The Filth* #3, 17. However, when Secret Original breaks through from his paperverse into the world of *The Filth*, he finds his "inwritten basic *decency*" so tested that now, he says, the closest he gets to loving Eve is checking out "alternative continuities where you let the entire Status Quorum gangbang you for money [in] sleazy hardcore comix." Ibid., 8, 18. "The truth is that a man," I have argued elsewhere, "fears his secret self fights not on the side of good but of evil." Coughlan, *The Naked Hero and Model Man*, 246. This is what Secret Original concludes: "I'm not a handsome hero anymore. I'm an ugly villain.... I'm a monster." Morrison and Weston, *The Filth* #12, 10.
62. Helen Block Lewis, "Shame and the Narcissistic Personality," in *The Many Faces of Shame*, ed. Donald L. Nathanson (New York: Guilford Press, 1987), 108.
63. Sandra Lee Bartky, *Femininity and Domination: Studies in the Phenomenology of Oppression* (New York: Routledge, 1990), 86.
64. Morrison and Weston, *The Filth* #1, 7.
65. Morrison and Weston, *The Filth* #10, 20.

66. Singer, *Grant Morrison*, 185.

67. Matt Brady, "A Healing Inoculation of Grime: Grant Morrison on *The Filth*," *Crack!Comics*, 12 July 2003, http://www.crackcomicks.com/the_filth_questions.htm.

68. Morrison and Weston, *The Filth* #13, 4. Morrison pushes his analogy to the extreme in the way that *The Filth* plays with scales and dimensions of space and time, placing worlds within worlds, and bodies within bodies. The Hand's base of operations, The Crack, for example, turns out to exist on a miniature scale, occupying a garbage-strewn slice of Greg's kitchen floor. More pertinently, Morrison also introduces I-Life, an engineered nano-species living out its brief life-span on a bonsai planet suspended over an artificial sun, then evolving in the body of a young woman called Sharon Jones, their Bio-Ship. A further example of radical scaling can be seen in the form of Alpha Sapiens, another member of the Status Quorum:

> Alpha Sapiens is Bill Tomney, an educationally-subnormal cleaner whose simple brain allows him to play host to the time-travelling micro-city of the Morlockoi. This minute, utopian society of tomorrow travels back in time to take over Bill's head.... Alpha Sapiens' primary mission is to arrange current events so that the world of today will eventually shrink and become the perfect, loving world of the majestic, miniaturized Morlockoi! [Grant Morrison, "The Status Quorum," *Crack!Comics*, 7 December 2003, http://www.crackcomicks.com/the_status_quorum.htm].

This brief narrative is a deliberately miniaturised version of some of *The Filth*'s own recursiveness, where, for example, the last seen evolution of the I-Life seems to replicate the forms and functions of The Hand with, as Singer notes, "a similar mission to coordinate Greg's bodily functions and preserve his health," in *Grant Morrison*, 192. This suggests that the I-Life of the future will go back in time to become The Hand that will recruit Greg who will save the I-Life that will become The Hand, and so on.

69. Jonathan Gil Harris, *Foreign Bodies and the Body Politic: Discourses of Social Pathology in Early Modern England* (Cambridge: Cambridge University Press, 1998), 1. For a brief history of the concept of the body politic, see A. D. Harvey, "The Body Politic: Anatomy of a Metaphor," *Contemporary Review* 275, no. 1603 (1999): 85–93.

70. Brady, "A Healing Inoculation of Grime"; Eugene Thacker, "*Nomos, Nosos* and *Bios*," in "Biopolitics," ed. Melinda Cooper, Andrew Goffey, and Anna Munster, special issue, *Culture Machine* 7 (2005), http://www.culturemachine.net/index.php/cm/article/view/25/32; Plato, *The Republic*, trans. Desmond Lee, 2d ed. (London: Penguin, 1987), 375 (VIII, 556e).

71. Margaret Healy, *Fictions of Disease in Early Modern England: Bodies, Plagues and Politics* (Basingstoke: Palgrave, 2001), 16–17.

72. Harris, *Foreign Bodies and the Body Politic*, 3.

73. Ibid..

74. Catherine A. Holland, *The Body Politic: Foundings, Citizenship, and Difference in the American Political Imagination* (New York: Routledge, 2001), xix, xx. Holland is discussing the body politic within an American context which is not alien to *The Filth*, despite its British setting. The characters Adam and Eve from the explicitly American *Status Quorum* relate to the New World as symbol of a new Eden, "purified of the contaminants of the European past," in ibid., xxi; see also Singer, *Grant Morrison*, 184–85 on utopianism in *The Filth*. In terms of the body politic, therefore, Morrison may also be thinking, in an American context, of Henry David Thoreau's view that "a corporation has no conscience; but a corporation of conscientious men is a corporation *with* a conscience." "Resistance to Civil Government," in *The Norton Anthology of American Literature*, gen. ed. Nina Baym, 7th ed., vol. B, *1820–1865* (New York: Norton, 2007), 1858. Thoreau is certainly there in the final issue of Morrison's *The Invisibles*, where the drum machines in the kids' trainers recall Thoreau's declaration that, "If a man does not keep pace with his companions, perhaps it is because he hears a different drummer. Let him step to the music which he hears," in *Walden*, in *The Norton Anthology of American Literature*, gen. ed. Nina Baym, 7th ed., vol. B, *1820–1865* (New York: Norton, 2007), 2041. *Nature*, by Thoreau's fellow transcendentalist Ralph Waldo Emerson, is also evident in

the same issue, both in the references to "nature" and in the idea that "the material world is the part of heaven we can *touch*," in Grant Morrison and Frank Quitely, *The Invisibles* (New York: DC/Vertigo, 1996–2002), 7.276.

75. Singer, *Grant Morrison*, 187.

76. Morrison and Weston, *The Filth #2*, 19. Also relevant in this context is Jacques Derrida's discussion of the "*pharmakos* (wizard, magician, poisoner), a ... character ... compared to a scapegoat. The *evil* and the *outside*, the expulsion of the evil, its exclusion out of the body (and out) of the city—these are the two major senses of the character and of the ritual" through which the "city's body *proper* thus reconstitutes its unity," in *Dissemination*, trans. Barbara Johnson (London: Continuum, 2004), 133, 134.

77. Butler, *Gender Trouble*, 169.

78. Kristeva, *Powers of Horror*, 69.

79. J. Hillis Miller, "The Critic as Host," in *Deconstruction and Criticism*, by Harold Bloom *et al.* (New York: Continuum, 1995), 219.

80. Morrison and Weston, *The Filth #12*, 17.

81. Kristeva, *Powers of Horror*, 84.

82. Ibid., 4.

83. Brady, "A Healing Inoculation of Grime."

84. Ibid.

85. Kristeva, *Powers of Horror*, 16.

86. Brady, "A Healing Inoculation of Grime."

87. Kristeva, *Powers of Horror*, 15.

88. Ibid., 31.

89. Morrison and Weston, *The Filth #9*, 9.

90. Morrison and Weston, *The Filth #2*, 11.

91. Brady, "A Healing Inoculation of Grime."

92. Thomas, *Male Matters*, 22.

93. Morrison and Weston, *The Filth #13*, 10. In *The Invisibles*, Barbelith is also said to be "like being in your mother," in Morrison and Phil Jimenez, *The Invisibles*, 5.229. The final issue of that series tells a story similar to *The Filth*'s, where "consciousness experiences the introduction of necessary inoculating agents ... as a form of invasion by hostile, bacterial forces. The inoculation is conceptualized ... as an invasion of threatening 'not-self' material" but we should not be anxious; this material is "only all the things you left *outside* when you were building your little house called 'me,'" in Morrison and Quitely, *The Invisibles*, 7.277, 282.

94. Thomas, *Masculinity, Psychoanalysis, Straight Queer Theory*, xiv.

95. Singer, *Grant Morrison*, 196.

96. Brady, "A Healing Inoculation of Grime."

"The Jungian Stuff"

Symbols of Transformation in All-Star Superman

DARRAGH GREENE

> Man is the only creature who can see his own death coming; and, when he does, it concentrates his mind wonderfully. He prepares for death by freeing himself from mundane goals and attachments, and turns instead to the cultivation of his own interior garden.—Anthony Storr, *Solitude*[1]

What is the nature of humanity's relationship to eternity? In the early sixth century AD, the Roman philosopher and statesman Boethius coined this famous definition of eternity: *interminabilis vitae tota simul perfecta et possessio*, that is, "the whole, simultaneous and perfect possession of boundless life."[2] The formula was expressed in relation to the eternality of God, but could it have some bearing on human nature and destiny? While *All-Star Superman* (2006–8), like any sophisticated text, may be read in many ways, few would disagree that it is fundamentally a story about death, and this theme is heightened and deepened when the one dying is the archetypal invulnerable superhero, Superman. In this essay, I will explore from a Jungian perspective *All-Star Superman*'s indirect answer to my opening question. "But why from a Jungian perspective?" the reader may ask. Morrison himself in his memoir-cum-history of superhero comics, *Supergods* (2011), explicitly states his intention (dating from his tenure on DC Comics's super-team title *JLA* in the mid–1990s) to write "Jung comics," by treating the characters "as specific human personality defaults, [which] could function in a wider therapeutic context."[3] He carries over this vision to *All-Star*'s Superman who is constructed to be "a divine Everyman, Platonic man sweating out the drama of ordinary life on an extraordinary canvas."[4] As such, and according to a Jungian perspective, he presents a model of humanity's own dual nature: a limited ego on the edge and in the midst of, but rooted to, an unlimited Self. This Self is the equivalent of the God-Image in man or, perhaps, as Jung sometimes vacillated, God Himself.[5] In this way, in Morrison's hands, Superman's enforced yet voluntary death and subsequent solar-stellification figures forth the apotheosis of humanity's essential vital force, "the best that the human spirit has to offer."[6] His struggle and passion, the revealed paradoxical vulnerability of the invulnerable, is symbolic of each human being's own difficult transformation via a never-ending individuation from being an isolated and defensive ego to becoming a sublime and infinite Self that is, in effect, superhuman or like unto a god. What will be of most interest in this reading of the comic is the character of this unified Self, which is self-sufficient but not isolated. For the paradoxical end of individuation, it turns out, is life lived with and, moreover, for others.

The Mythos of Superman

Morrison believes that stories are ethically and politically potent: "Writers and artists build by hand little worlds that they hope might effect change in real minds, in the real world where stories are read. A story can make us cry and laugh, break our hearts, or make us angry enough to change the world."[7] Furthermore, he maintains, and as Nicholas Galante notes elsewhere in this volume, "that people respond emotionally to deep mythical patterns whether or not they recognize or 'understand' them as such."[8] Morrison, thus, fastens on the reader's feelings by means of the affective vehicle of myth, thereby bypassing more rational modes and disciplines of persuasion. Indeed, in the notes to *All-Star Superman*, he explains how it tells the story of:

> Superman as star, or solar "deity," hence our opening shot of Superman framed by solar flares and the structure of the story which traverses one epic "day"— dipping below the horizon in issue six so that Superman, like all good solar myth heroes, can journey through midwinter's longest night and the upside-down underworld before rising again in issue nine, revitalized.[9]

And in *Supergods*, he reveals more concerning the "deep mythical pattern" that informs *All-Star Superman*:

> The twelve-issue format allowed us to present Superman with a mythic twelve labors, following the sun's path across the day, as well as the changing seasons in a year. Each issue featured a complete story, and they all connected to make a twelve-part final adventure for Superman, facing his death, composing a last Will and Testament while settling his affairs and trying to ensure the world would prosper when he was gone.[10]

And later again in the same book, he writes of how the metaphors of angels and gods, "as our role models and intermediaries on the road to 'God' or 'cosmic consciousness,' we can just as easily call them superheroes."[11] It is abundantly clear, then, that Morrison himself considers the rich resources of myth as an especially potent means of engaging and changing readers; and moreover, that the superhero functions as a symbolic figure who points and maps the way towards larger and heightened consciousness that can transform both the reader and the world. A second focus, therefore, of this essay will be on the question of just how re-working myth can effect political change.

Morrison's "mythical method," to borrow a phrase from T. S. Eliot, bears a striking affinity to Jung's thinking concerning mystery, symbol, and myth.[12] "Great art till now has always derived its fruitfulness from myth, from the unconscious process of symbolization which continues through the ages and, as the primordial manifestation of the human spirit, will continue to be the root of all creation in the future," Jung writes in "The Undiscovered Self."[13] In fact, Jung's very conception of mythology was influenced early on by the Sanskrit scholar Friedrich Max Müller, who contended, as Jung's biographer Ronald Hayman writes, "that among the *Aryans* ... all mythological systems were based on the orbiting of the Earth around the sun, and on the sun worship that developed from primitive man's perception of his dependence on it."[14] Thus, for Jung solar myths were the key to all Western mythologies. Furthermore, he suggested that the longing for the sun has been turned towards God, but not the external God: "To honour God, the sun or the fire is to honour one's own vital force, the libido."[15] In this way, the monomyth is always heliocentric and, moreover, always about *you*—as Horace put it, *de te fabula narratur*.[16]

From the time of his break with Freud, it was Jung's conviction that there is a collective or universal foundation to the human psyche that is to be found expressed in mythologems and religious images discoverable in all cultures. Arguing for the existence of this collective unconscious, he writes:

> There is good reason for supposing that the archetypes are the unconscious images of the instincts themselves, in other words, that they are patterns of instinctual behaviours.... The hypothesis of the collective unconscious is, therefore, no more daring than to assume there are instincts.... The question is simply this: are there or are there not unconscious universal forms of this kind? If they exist, then there is a region of the psyche which one can call the collective unconscious.[17]

His discovery of such a foundation led him to emphasize the mythopoeic capacity of the dynamic unconscious process. For him, mythically resonant art and literature bespeak indirectly in compelling stories enigmatic and uncanny messages concerning the deep, recurring truths of how we both see and experience our lives in the world.[18] Mythos not logos, it follows, is the *via regia* both to and from the unconscious, for our lives are the stories we tell ourselves which themselves, both grown out of and expressing the myriad types of situation encountered in the world, originate beneath the threshold of consciousness. Indeed, Jung wrote that "the collective unconscious is an image of the world."[19] Mythos, mythologem, monomyth: it is story, the narrative drive of thought and imagination, which underpins life and the unconscious universe.

Jung holds that we are not engendered as *tabulae rasae*; rather, our psyche is already inscribed with an array of archetypes that incline us to experience the world according to certain inherited schemes or patterns. To be clear, these archetypes in the collective unconscious are themselves strictly without content and, in a sense, formless. They are structuring tendencies that supply us with an instinctual heritage:

> Archetypes are not determined as regards their content, but only as regards their form and then only to a very limited degree.... The archetype in itself is empty and purely formal, nothing but a *facultas praeformandi*, a possibility of representation which is given *a priori*. The representations themselves are not inherited, only the forms, and in that respect they correspond in every way to the instincts, which are also determined in form only.[20]

So, for instance, the archetypes "mother" and "father" structure the initial experience of *my* mother and *my* father, primarily, and then mothers and fathers, generally. In effect, Jung's conception of the psyche bridges the gap between the *a priori* universal and the *a posteriori* particular. The archetypes, the temporally evolved origin of our present categories, of how we divide up our world and see things, are key to this bridging theory.

The archetype is a kind of "cognitive invariant,"[21] a formless pattern or template. From the Greek, "archetype" means "prime imprinter." According to Jung, archetypes tend to structure our experiences according to patterns going back through all of human history and probably animal history too. Robin Robertson writes, "Jung liked to compare an archetype to a riverbed which has slowly been formed over thousands of years."[22] Indeed, on the subject of invariant knowledge or that which stands fast for us, Wittgenstein employs the same analogy:

> The mythology may change back into a state of flux, the river-bed of thoughts may shift. But I distinguish between the movement of the waters on the river-

bed and the shift of the bed itself; though there is not a sharp division of the one from the other.... And the bank of the river consists partly of hard rock, subject to no alteration or only to an imperceptible one, partly of sand, which now in one place now in another gets washed away, or deposited.[23]

Both psychologist and philosopher were concerned to explore and determine the fundamental principles or grounds of our knowledge and life and posited that there is, in some sense, an inherited or already-existing template or background for how we live now, namely, that set of diverse activities distinctive of the human being.

Rooted in the archetypes, myths are not deceptive or lying fictions. On the contrary, they can be means of indirectly showing us who and what we are in our world. Most importantly, employed and/or interpreted aright, they can be the powerful means of effecting personal change—what Jung calls individuation—and ultimately of changing the world:

Whenever the collective unconscious becomes a living experience and is brought to bear upon the conscious outlook of an age, this event is a creative act which is of importance for a whole epoch. A work of art is produced that may truthfully be called a message to generations of men.[24]

All-Star Superman strives to be just such a transformative work, being envisioned and constructed to change for the better the individual and so by extension society, and its "mythical method" is foundational for this therapeutic, ethico-political purpose.

"[M]any secular myths are degutted versions of sacred ones," contends Terry Eagleton.[25] *All-Star Superman*, however, does not fall into this category, for it distills, appropriates, reconfigures, and most crucially retains the dark viscera of the most potent of conscious-expanding myths, namely, that of the self-sacrificing solar god. Nor is the treatment of this deep mythical pattern reductive as Marc Singer makes clear: "Evoking diverse sources both secular and religious, ancient and modern, *All-Star Superman* operates according to several complementary narrative logics ... presenting a multivalent, multiply redundant, prismatic mythology rather than a single symbolic organizing scheme."[26] The guts of the myth of the solar god treat of the problem of death, and whether and how it has any meaning. Is death the absence and negation of life that drains existence of meaning, or might it hide a more redemptive aspect? In essence, Superman's perennial battle is with the evils of death, absence, and nothingness in all their myriad aspects.

Battle or conflict is essential to myth, romance, and fairy tale, and Jung sees conflict in dreams and the psyche as signs of the heroic struggle to individuate, to become full and particular selves. For him, as social beings we are all connected yet individual, and so individuation is not solipsistic, for it is of the essence of the world that its constituent related parts become themselves in their interrelated particularity. The personal is the political. Conflict, and above all, the transcendence of conflict, is the engine of individuation for enhanced and widened consciousness:

> Conscious and unconscious do not make a whole when one of them is suppressed and injured by the other. If they must contend, let it at least be a fair fight with equal rights on both sides. Both are aspects of life. Consciousness should defend its reason and protect itself, and the chaotic life of the unconscious should be given the chance of having its way too—as much of it as we can stand. This means open conflict and open collaboration at once. That, evidently, is the way human life should be. It is the old game of hammer and anvil: between them the patient iron is forged into an indestructible whole, and "individual."[27]

The myth of the dying solar god, and his extravagant, gratuitous and unselfish self-sacrifice for the good and well-being of others, reveals to us the secret solution to the riddle of death. Jung, as we have seen, insists that conflicts are not resolved through one side defeating the other; rather, the conflict itself is transcended. And so it is, ultimately, in the conflict between life and death. Life does not win over death, nor vice versa; rather, the conflict is to be transcended by virtue of a synthesis that connects the particular to the universal, the finite to the infinite, for the archetype of the Self is not subject to nor bound by time or the processes of generation and corruption. The aim of individuation is, thus, to transcend the transient and achieve the transcendent: "the self comprises infinitely more than the mere ego.... It is as much one's self, and all other selves, as the ego. Individuation does not shut one out from the world, but gathers the world to one's self."[28]

All-Star Superman's plot expresses the process of ego development or individuation, and the major characters, be they the hero or his helpers, senders, objects or villains, represent or psychologically personate what Jung called the complex functions or sub-personalities of the personal psyche. These complexes—which Morrison, the reader will recall, terms "specific human personality defaults"—are autonomous, seeming to possess a will, a life, and a personality of their own. According to Jung, each complex in the personal unconscious connects fundamentally to an archetype in the collective unconscious. The major complexes he identified are those of the mother, father, persona, ego, anima/animus, and the shadow. Of these, the most important complex is the ego, for it is the vehicle of conscious awareness and personal identity. All the complexes, in a sense, orbit and are circumscribed by the Self, about which Jung wrote: "It is not only the centre but the whole circumference which embraces both consciousness and unconsciousness; it is the centre of this totality, just as the ego is the centre of the conscious mind."[29] He also called the Self the archetype of archetypes, and that its goal is completeness or wholeness. The ego's development, the path of individuation, connects, more and more, the limited to the unlimited, by gathering what is unconscious into consciousness as the psyche strives for wholeness. This is Jung's answer to the question of what is humanity's relation to eternity, and we shall see that *All-Star Superman* tracks and expresses the same answer.

The Individuation of a Supergod

All the major complexes already mentioned are represented by the chief characters introduced in the opening issue of *All-Star*, while it is the sun that symbolizes the Self. Most obviously, Superman stands for the ego; Clark Kent the persona, which is the ego's adaptation to the social environment; Lex Luthor the shadow, which is the anti-persona and anti-ego; and Lois Lane the anima, which is the universal image of woman in a man's psyche. Finally, Leo Quintum, futurist and philanthropist, stands for the wise old man, a complex connected with superior insight and the Self that, together with the shadow and anima, is key to the process of individuation. Robertson calls these the "archetypes of development."[30] Each is encountered in deeper levels of the unconscious, and they must be worked through in series in the course of personal development and psychic growth. The shadow concerns those traits and actions that have been ignored or denied by the conscious ego, and it is usually made manifest in dreams as a frightening and often evil figure of the same sex as the dreamer. The anima personifies the image of the eternal feminine in man, and it proffers a link to the impersonal unconscious. Finally, the Self is concerned with wholeness, the goal of individuation, and it is made manifest as a figure of wisdom, male or female, and sometimes as animals or abstract figures.[31]

If we consider the cover to the first issue of *All-Star*, in which Superman sits, with his back to the reader, atop the cumulus clouds over Metropolis while looking directly at us over his right shoulder, we note that the single vanishing point for the whole image is the sun, rising over the world-city. Superman's body is orientated to the sun, and I suggest that he is inviting us to see the world from his perspective, and identify with him as he embarks on his confrontation with and transformative journey into the Self. The first-page origin story continues this invitation to the reader to identify with the hero where in the fourth panel, the baby Kal El's perspective is ours, looking up at Pa and Ma Kent. The double-page spread that follows shows Superman in the chromosphere of the sun, representing the stable and established ego, separate from but orbiting the vast Self, which is the source of its vitality, the burning energy of the soul. As Quintum's assistant, Agatha, says of Superman: "I know every cell in his body is a living solar battery, evolved to store raw energy from the sun."[32] In a similar way, the ego draws its energy from the Self, and a fully developed and differentiated ego is the necessary and real starting point of adult individuation.

Superman saves Quintum's mission to map the sun, or comprehend the Self, which shows how the ego and the wise old man, who occupies a nodal position in connection with the Self, work together in the process of individuation. That work is, from one perspective, thwarted by the shadow, and from another spurred by it, for the shadow is also a key complex in the work of individuation. The ego shuns time and death, believing in its immortality, whereas the shadow is touched with intimations of mortality, and so concerning Superman, Luthor says, "I'm getting older and … and he isn't."[33] The genetically modified human suicide bomb makes Luthor's link with death explicit from the beginning, by announcing to the crew of the Ray Bradbury: "Death. Courtesy of Lex Luthor."[34] Later, in issue #5, Luthor says to Clark Kent, who is interviewing him on death row, "There's no deep psychology behind the struggle between Superman and me. It's all very simple. How would you feel if someone deliberately stood in your way, over and over again? If it wasn't for Superman, I'd be in charge on this planet!"[35] Underpinning Luthor's explanation, however, is precisely the relationship between the ego and the shadow. Superman's never-ending struggle with Luthor is the perennial struggle of the ego, that is, who we choose to be, against the anti-ego or shadow, who we choose not to be, but which potential lies always within us. And the ultimate choice of the anti-ego is death, suicide, for that guarantees the annihilation of its opposite. The whole thrust of *All-Star Superman* seeks to transcend this opposition between being and non-being, the choice to live or die, by finding a third way, which is the re-birth into what Superman himself, in issue #12, calls neoconsciousness and what, coming to the same thing, Jung terms *unio mystica* with the *unus mundus*.

As Pistorius the organist says to Emil Sinclair in Hermann Hesse's *Demian*, "When we hate someone we are hating something that is within ourselves, in his image. We are never stirred up by something which does not already exist within us."³⁶ The shadow possesses some quality, ignored and denied by us, which we must integrate into our personality or conscious selves. Indeed, shadow issues are encountered at the first stage of individuation when unconscious potential is actualized through the ego's conflict with the shadow. Robertson explains:

> Shadow figures usually appear first as non-human: aliens from another planet, vampires, zombies, half-animal/half-human creatures, etc. They confront us with their unwanted, though unavoidable presence. Over time, these dream figures evolve and become fully human, of the same sex as ourselves, but villainous, evil, despicable.... Later, they evolve still further into pitiful people whom we view as not particularly significant figures—but whom we tolerate as part of our everyday lives. Still later, the Shadow figures evolve into friends, relatives, lovers. Finally, if we have learned to integrate their unwanted character traits into our personality, they no longer have to be personified in the unconscious. We have changed and they are part of us.³⁷

At this point, it should be noted that the archetype of evil is different from the shadow, and is explored by Morrison in the figure of Darkseid in *Seven Soldiers* (2005–6), *Final Crisis* (2008–9), and *The Return of Bruce of Wayne* (2010). Above all, Darkseid yearns for anti-life, which is pure nothingness and unmeaning. As Sebastian Barry writes in his novel *The Secret Scripture*, "The devil's own tragedy is he is the author of nothing and architect of empty spaces."³⁸ By contrast, the shadow contains positive possibilities rejected by the ego as well as negatives—in fact, Jung maintained that the shadow was ninety-per-cent gold.³⁹ Hence, Superman keeps insisting that there is good in Luthor—in issue #10, for instance, he visits Luthor on death row, and tells him: "Lex, I know there's good in you."⁴⁰

In the great conflicts of myth and romance, the psychological attitude of the protagonist is regularly found to be opposite to that of the antagonist. Hence, for instance, in the *Iliad*, Achilles is an introvert who shuns the other Greek heroes and is prone to confining himself to his tent whereas his chief rival Hector is an extraverted favorite of the Trojan public and loving family man. And in the *Odyssey*, the cyclops Polyphemus is an island-dwelling, unsocial introvert who devours rather than welcomes the strangers whom he discovers in his cave, while Odysseus is an extravert who tricks him and makes good his and his crew's escape so as to continue his homeward journey and many adventures in the wide world. Finally, in the medieval romance *Sir Gawain and the Green Knight*, Gawain is the reflective hero, who only takes on his quest after much rumination, whereas the Green Knight is bold and direct in his challenges and game playing. Similar to these cases, in *All-Star Superman*, Superman is an introvert who yearns for the quiet life, epitomized by the prized privacy of his Fortress of Solitude, as distinct from the extraverted Luthor who requires constant stimulation and is forever in danger of boredom. In effect, Luthor's reaching out to the world invariably calls Superman out of his retreat.

The shadow, furthermore, is the bearer of the inferior function, which "personifies everything that the subject refuses to acknowledge about himself and yet is always thrusting itself upon him directly or indirectly—for instance, inferior traits of character and other incompatible tendencies."[41] Morrison's Superman is a feeler, someone who recognizes the value of people and things whereas Luthor coldly identifies and classifies. Luthor's unfeeling thinking, thus, is Superman's inferior function. When Superman discriminates, he does so by weighing values. He does not think from first principles as Luthor does. Thinking, rather, is his route into the unconscious and its wealth of possibilities.[42] So, how does Superman integrate the shadow or inferior function; that is, how does he become a thinker? The answer is that when death touches him, Superman starts to think: he makes preparations for his demise, produces his last Will and Testament, and plans for a world without him.

Superman, as a feeler, evaluates. He feels the worth of human life, of all sentient life; and after his integration of his unconscious shadow potential, he feels exquisitely his connection to all lives. Indeed, his final sacrificial act affirms that connection. Furthermore, feelers deal in memories; by comparing past situations to the present, they see through to the emotional truth hidden in the confusion of data and information. On this point, Robertson writes: "Feelers are able to deal with the fuzziness of life."[43] An extraverted, egotistical thinker like Luthor wants to remodel, and so reduce, the world to his own image, which is his own conception of what is right and true, according to the facts as he sees them. Superman, on the other hand, has no grand plan to forcibly change the world; rather, he sees what is of value in it as it stands. Luthor, then, is the bearer of Superman's inferior function, namely, extraverted thinking. Through conflict with this personification of extraverted thinking, Superman forever makes his initial connection to the collective unconscious and the other major archetypes of development. Moreover, Luthor's strange gift to Superman, death, proves the spur to ultimate individuation. The attentive reader, thus, should infer how conflict with the implacable "other" marks the start of any pathway of self-development.

Returning to Luthor's suicide bomber, while aboard Quintum's ship, he berates Superman: "You have no right to limit my ambitions, fascist! No right at all to stand in the way of my self-realization!"[44] To this, Superman replies, "You misunderstand. I'm here to help with that."[45] There is a double meaning here, as he ejects the suicide bomber from the ship, allowing him to explode in space. But the statement also reveals his function in the book as a whole, which is to push at limits and achieve self-realization himself, and thereby light others to theirs. This is made plain when in issue #9, Lilo, one of the Kryptonian astronauts, accuses Superman of inaction: "You could have built a New Krypton in this squalor. You could have laid the foundation stones of tomorrow."[46] Superman's reply to her accusation is: "What right do I have to impose my values on anyone?"[47] The Kryptonian astronauts, powerful, proud, and narcissistic, are sociopathic Nietzschean supermen. They lack empathy, and do not understand the meaning of sacrifice for others. If Superman is to succeed on his journey of Self-realization, it has to be by avoiding the sterile narcissism of the Kryptonian astronauts.

To tie everything together, then, in the Jungian perspective on this key opening scene, Superman is the ego; and Quintum's ship, the Ray Bradbury, standing for the personal unconscious, contains the three most important complexes for individuation: the shadow, the anima, and the wise old man, while the sun represents the Self. Superman's journey to the sun or Self begins the process of individuation. In issue #2, he says to Lois: "My trip to the sun did more than triple my strength.... It tripled my curiosity, my imagination, my creativity."[48] The process is further and coincidentally spurred by the ego's recognition of death, which is the ambiguous gift of the shadow: the trip to the sun has overloaded Superman's cells with solar energy, and they are slowly breaking down.

Death and the Transformed Self

From the first issue of *All-Star Superman*, the overt thematic question of the whole work is, how is Superman to solve the problem of his own death? Jung, at the end of his life, concluded that the crucial problems cannot be solved; instead, they may be transcended. In this connection, while looking back over his career as an analyst, he wrote, "the greatest and most important problems of life are all fundamentally insoluble. They must be so, because they express the necessary polarity inherent in every self-regulating system. They can never be solved, but only outgrown."[49] This insight informs issue #2's episode of the Ultrasphinx's "unanswerable question": "What happens when the unstoppable force meets the immovable object?"[50] The question puzzles Superman, for no synthesis seems possible. Then, all at once, Superman's answer is inspired by a moment of syzygy[51] between ego and anima, when his eyes meet Lois's, and the *coniunctio oppositorum* occurs by dint of a raising of consciousness, outgrowth, and transcendence. Superman's answer to the Ultrasphinx's question is: "They surrender."[52] Moreover, it is in the surrender to his death that Superman's self-sacrifice and self-dispossession leads to radical remaking and transfiguration. As Eagleton writes:

> Only the good are capable of dying.... In this sense, how you die is determined by how you live. Death is a form of self-dispossession which must be rehearsed in life if it is to be successfully accomplished. Otherwise it will prove to be a cul-de-sac rather than a horizon. Being-for-others and being-toward-death are aspects of the same condition.[53]

Although he has been preparing for it and working towards it, Superman's metamorphosis can only occur in connection with death. In dying, he transforms from terrestrial to solar god. Death is necessary to the process. Indeed, in his death-dream, Superman's father, Jor-El, tells him, "Your body is undergoing a mutation, a conversion to solar radio-consciousness."[54] Jor-El explains, "Neither matter nor energy nor consciousness can be destroyed."[55] Why not? Luthor, representative of Superman's shadow, intuits the answer in a flash: "The fundamental forces are all yoked together by thought alone."[56]

Superman's apotheotic stellification at the end of the book reunites matter, energy, and consciousness or spirit in a *coniunctio oppositorum*. Completion of the *opus* of individuation comes with the achievement of the union of the whole man with the *unus mundus*, that is, the world without differentiation. Of the *unus mundus*, Jung wrote that it was the "eternal Ground of all empirical being, just as the Self is the ground and origin of the individual personality, past, present and future."[57] At the moment of full realization of the Self, in its complete possession all at once of illimitable life, a window opens on eternity. Superman's final, total self-realization in its nature transcends the limited conception of the bounded ego. The mysterious and invisible essence of likeness to God may only be figured forth or illuminated by allegory or symbolism. In our final view of Superman, in issue #12, we see a new symbol, a Version 2.0 of the Vitruvian Man, which combines the idealism, futurism, and imagination of Leonardo Da Vinci and William Blake's convictions concerning human possibility, progress, and happy destiny. Superman at the heart of our sun, charges and renews our star, and thus our world, with his spirit. In this way, he radiates the ineffable essence or idea of man transcendent, the *homo altus* of spiritual alchemy, enlightened and ever-living for the good of all.

What is important in Morrison's vision of Superman, then, is that he provides a model to imitate. His superpowers are alien, but his virtue issues from a form of life that is fundamentally human. In Aristotelian terms, he is the magnanimous or even magnificent man.[58] He possesses all the virtues; in essence, he is morally good. Aristotle comments how gods are autonomous and lone beings, needing no others.[59] Superman, not born but bred and raised among us, is ever morally cognizant of being in community with others. He is never going to become like *Watchmen*'s Dr. Manhattan, a man who, upon developing superhuman powers, steadily loses his humanity and connection to others. In this case, Alan Moore, the self-avowed anarchist, seems to subscribe to Lord Acton's infamous apothegm: "power tends to corrupt and absolute power corrupts absolutely. Great men are almost always bad men."[60] But as Eagleton reminds us, power as the means of transformation and change can be employed for noble ends.[61] In this sense, Morrison's counter-response to Moore's dark vision of the essential immorality of power proffers a sanguine corrective concerning the best ethical potential of the social, interdependent, and interrelated human being that aligns with the soaring humanistic oratory of Pico della Mirandola in the *Oration on the Dignity of Man* (1486).

Taking the foregoing into account, I return now to the original question with which I opened this chapter, namely, what is the nature of humanity's relationship to eternity? The transcendence of the ego in full Self-realization is the end of all Jungian individuation—except that its fulfillment is always denied, cut short by death. A translation and conservation of being, if possible, however, would circumvent death. Only nothing is impossible, as Leo Quintum says, in issue #1, and there is always a way, as Superman says again and again through the whole book. In the end, Jor-El confirms their beliefs with the science: "Matter, energy: these things cannot be created or destroyed ... nor can consciousness."[62] In this way, Morrison's *All-Star Superman* implies that whatever is conceivable is possible; and if it is possible, then in the synthesis or unification of the modes of possible and the actual, by and in our thought, which yokes together the fundamental forces, we may see the whole world within ourselves, and our whole selves within the world, there being no essential difference between these two aspects of being.[63]

Superman's death, therefore, is but the end of the limited ego, while it is the explosion and expansion of the Self, whereby he radiates the conditions by which others may follow him and make the same journey from ego to Self. On the world Superman created and gave life to, Earth Q, the

Neoplatonist humanist Pico della Mirandola exhorts all to realize a new form of life:

> Let us not yield sovereignty even to them, the highest of the angelic hierarchies! Become instead like them in all their glory and dignity. Imitation is man's nature and if he but wills it, so shall he surpass even imagination's greatest paragons.[64]

All-Star Superman shows its readers that their only limits are the ones they set on themselves. By extending their curiosity, imagination, and creativity, they can look out on eternity and see their true home there. As Jor-El says to Superman, in the final issue, while the latter's consciousness approaches the realm of the dead:

> You have shown them the face of the Man of Tomorrow. You have given them an *ideal* to aspire to, embodied their highest aspirations. They will race, and stumble, and fall and crawl ... and curse ... and finally ... they will join you in the sun, Kal-El.[65]

A cynical reader, of course, might demur and dismiss Morrison's notion of unlimited human potential as dewy-eyed and impossibly romantic. Does Morrison overestimate human altruism? I think not, for throughout the book, he has looked squarely at all the myriad challenges to virtuous living, and even for Superman, who acts as exemplary model, these challenges are not easily overcome. Evil, "the hole in things,"[66] is real enough in its consequences: suffering, repudiation of value, annihilation of meaning, and, of course, death. But Superman's passion, affirmation of value and meaning, and transcendence of death expresses the reality of an alternative path.

Superman and Our Better Selves

The critical question that remains is, how does myth, and specifically Morrison's myth of *All-Star Superman*, become a reforming tool for political ends, for transforming tomorrow? Few would disagree that men and women are deeply conditioned by their circumstances, by historical and contextual ideology. There is, thus, conditioning from without; but against the Foucauldian or the postmodernist or any other proponent of social constructionism, a Jungian would say, there is conditioning *within* too by dint of the archetypes. It is crucial that whereas external conditions—for instance, those imposed by an unjust social or legal system—can warp a person artificially, the in-built conditions of the archetypes align with just the kind of creatures we are. Human beings share certain distinctive needs across all times and cultures: the need for food and water; for clothing and shelter; for security, friendship, and love; for meaning.[67] The archetypes are born of, and evolved from, the embodied experiences across eons of just this type of being. Myth, generated by the archetypes, always bears within it a radical critique of any form of life fashioned of false consciousness. Myth, thus, explodes illusions of insalubrious ideologies and recalls us to our authentic selves because the archetypes, whether expressed in dreams or myths, function to recall men and women to their deepest needs, and of these, the need to flourish, to live well, is the most natural of all. In effect, as social, story-telling beings, our myths are where, to borrow Wittgenstein's phrase, explanations for us come to an end. They are the riverbed of our understanding of ourselves. When life and society go awry, it is myth that lights up our moral emotions and in which all powers of rebirth and regeneration are to be found. And renewal, *renaissance*, always takes the form of fresh stories, including the modern myth of Superman, constructed out of the old.

Morrison's artistic alchemy is two-fold: *All-Star Superman* transforms its reader by widening, deepening, and universalizing the idea of the superhero by means of the "mythical method" of structuring and archetypal symbolism. In addition and at another level, Morrison conjures this same transformative opus by turning to a neglected and repudiated corner of culture, namely, comic-book superheroes, and transmuting popular ephemera into literary and artistic gold. On the edge of mainstream aesthetic practice, he constructs a rich counter-culture of radical narratives studded with hieratic symbolism rooted in the shared archetypes of the species. This edge, which is the horizon of all rejected potential, is paradigmatic of the shadow that is, as Jung stressed, ninety-per-cent gold. In fact, there is an analogy here between the process of shadow integration and one of the use-features of literature that, according to Mark Edmundson, "open[s] us up to the manifold voices and vocabularies we may contain or may borrow...."[68]

On the same point, he refers to Shakespeare's work as paradigmatic in this regard since it "teaches us how to draw on different aspects of ourselves, different indwelling voices, to create a coherent variety and richness that represent an alternative to monolithic official versions."[69] In remaking the superhero, by broadening and enriching its principal representative, Morrison is engaged in the mutually reinforcing activities of fashioning radical art and panning for hidden riches relevant to the whole of society.

Morrison, moreover, re-imagines the superhero—reconfigures its idea—not in order to recoup its former Silver Age glories when he was a child, reading American superhero comics in the Glasgow of the 1960s. Unlike Kurt Busiek and Mark Waid, representative reconstructionists of the genre,[70] Morrison is not interested in retooling the idea of the superhero in order to appeal to older comics readers eager for a wised-up return to the adventure and fun of their childhood. Busiek and Waid take on board the challenge and criticisms of deconstruction, but they work to conserve and reposition their memory of the superhero in an adult space where such work is only ever nostalgia and escapism. By contrast, Morrison remakes the superhero with serious ethical, political, and artistic ambition. The point is never merely to entertain the reader, by pandering to her nostalgia or desire for easy consumption; rather, he constructs stories, fashions and deploys ideas, which are meant to shake her up and change her.

In the 1980s, Moore created comics in order to attack what he saw as the reactionary ideology of the superhero, and this involved a biting critique of the contemporary ethical and political culture that informed the hegemony of heroism, and so the superhero, target of the deconstruction, was diminished. His revisionist superhero work, especially *Watchmen*, devalues and reduces the superhero myth to that of an adolescent power fantasy; its model reader is disabused of his illusions concerning both the worth and nature of the superhero. By means of genealogical analysis and deconstructive critique, Moore systematically strips away value and meaning from the idea of the superhero as so much illusion, thereby shrinking it to the bare essence of a naked hunger for power. He, thus, debunks the idea of the superhero as a dangerous, infantilizing ideology to be grown out of.[71] But Morrison shows how that kind of reading of the superhero mythos is mistakenly reductive. *All-Star Superman* is, in a certain sense, a twelve-issue riposte to the twelve-issue *Watchmen*. Both start with a countdown to death, but treat death differently. While *Watchmen* tends to the repudiation and evacuation of meaning, *All-Star Superman* tends to its affirmation and multiplication. Indeed, Morrison strives to re-enchant the world with meaning, not by imposing one totalizing or grand narrative, but by opening up and multiplying meaning to the nth degree, implying that everyone has his or her own story, and imagination is the only limit to where those stories may take them.

In conclusion, Morrison sees the idea of the superhero as a vehicle for the critique of the prevailing selfish and self-loathing ideologies of the present-day world. For him, the imaginary is, in true Romantic tradition, an inexhaustible repertoire for resistance to the various stagnations of our current culture and society. In Morrison's hands, the superhero attains radical transfiguring purpose. He achieves this end—in *All-Star Superman* above all other works—by tapping into the archetypes of myths and dreams that serve as the bridge to our personal and collective ever newer, other, and better selves.

Notes

1. Anthony Storr, *Solitude* (London: HarperCollins, 1997), 169.
2. Anicius Manlius Severinus Boethius, *De Consolatione Philosophiae* V, pr. 6, in Boethius, *The Consolation of Philosophy*, trans. S. J. Tester (Cambridge: Harvard University Press, 1973), 422–23.
3. Grant Morrison, *Supergods: What Masked Vigilantes, Miraculous Mutants, and a Sun God from Smallville Can Teach Us About Being Human* (New York: Spiegal & Grau, 2011), 292–93.
4. Ibid., 411.
5. See C. G. Jung, *Answer to Job*, in *Collected Works* 11, ed. Herbert Read, Michael Fordham, and Gerald Adler, trans. R. F. C. Hull, Bollingen Series XX (Princeton: Princeton University Press, 1959–79), par. 757.
6. Morrison, *Supergods*, 293.
7. Ibid., 409.
8. Grant Morrison and Dave McKean, *Arkham Asylum: A Serious House on Serious Earth* (New York: DC Comics, 2004), 51.
9. Grant Morrison and Frank Quitely, *All-Star Superman* (New York: DC Comics, 2011), 296.
10. Morrison, *Supergods*, 410.
11. Ibid., 414.
12. See T. S. Eliot, "*Ulysses*, Order, and Myth," *The Dial* 75, no. 5 (Nov 1923): 480–83.
13. Jung, "The Undiscovered Self (Present and Future)," in *Collected Works* 10, par. 585.
14. Ronald Hayman, *A Life of Jung* (London: Bloomsbury, 1999), 133.
15. Ibid.
16. Horace, *Satires*, I.1.69–70, in Horace, *Satires, Epistles and Ars Poetica*, trans. H. R. Fairclough, rev. ed. (London: William Heinemann, 1929), 8–10.
17. Jung, *Collected Works* 9 i, pars. 91–92.
18. For more on Jungian perspectives on myth, see Steven F. Walker, *Jung and the Jungians on Myth* (New York: Garland, 1995) and Robert A. Segal, *Jung on Mythology* (Princeton: Princeton University Press, 1998).
19. Jung, *Collected Works* 7, par. 151.
20. Jung, *Collected Works* 9 i, par. 156.
21. Robin Robertson, *Introducing Jungian Psychology* (Dublin: New Leaf, 1992), 39.
22. Ibid., 110.
23. Ludwig Wittgenstein, *On Certainty*, ed. G. E. M. Anscombe and G. H. von Wright, trans. Denis Paul and G. E. M. Anscombe (New York: Harper & Row, 1972), 15e, §§ 97 and 99.
24. Jung, *Collected Works* 15, par. 153.
25. Terry Eagleton, *Reason, Faith, and Revolution* (New Haven: Yale University Press, 2009), 28.
26. Marc Singer, *Grant Morrison: Combining the Worlds of Contemporary Comics* (Jackson: University Press of Mississippi, 2012), 261.
27. Jung, *Collected Works* 9 i, par. 522.
28. Jung, *Collected Works* 8, par. 432.

29. Jung, *Collected Works* 12, par. 41.
30. See Robin Robertson, *C. G. Jung and the Archetypes of the Collective Unconscious* (New York: Peter Lang, 1987).
31. In Hermann Hesse's Jungian *Bildüngsroman*, *Demian*, Emil Sinclair's Self is symbolized serially by a blue and gold sparrowhawk, then the faintly androgynous and ageless Max Demian, and finally Max's mother, Frau Eva.
32. Morrison and Quitely, *All-Star Superman*, 12.
33. Ibid., 15, panel 4.
34. Ibid., 10, panel 5.
35. Ibid., 124, panels 3–4.
36. Herman Hesse, *Demian*, trans. W. J. Strachan (London: Peter Owen, 2006), 124.
37. Robertson, *Introducing Jungian Psychology*, 113–15.
38. Quoted in Terry Eagleton, *On Evil* (New Haven: Yale University Press, 2010), 62.
39. See Jung, *Collected Works* 9 ii, pars. 422–23.
40. Morrison and Quitely, *All-Star Superman*, 239, panel 3.
41. Jung, *Collected Works* 9 i, par. 513.
42. For more on Jung's classification of modes of judgment and perception, see Jung. *Psychological Types*, in *Collected Works* 6; and Daryl Sharp, *Personality Types: Jung's Model of Typology* (Toronto: Inner City Books, 1987). For a pair of classic studies on the inferior function and feeling function, respectively, see Marie-Louise von Franz and James Hillman, *Lectures on Jung's Typology* (Woodstock, CT: Spring Publications, 1998).
43. Robertson, *Introducing Jungian Psychology*, 95.
44. Morrison and Quitely, *All-Star Superman*, 17, panel 2.
45. Ibid., panel 3.
46. Ibid., 207, panel 5.
47. Ibid.
48. Morrison and Quitely, *All-Star Superman*, 42, panel 3.
49. Quoted in Anthony Stevens, *On Jung*, 2d ed. (London: Penguin, 1999), 51.
50. Morrison and Quitely, *All-Star Superman*, 69, panel 1.
51. See Jung, *Collected Works* 9 ii, pars. 24–40.
52. Morrison and Quitely, *All-Star Superman*, 69, panel 7.
53. Eagleton, *On Evil*, 24.
54. Morrison and Quitely, *All-Star Superman*, 273.
55. Ibid., 275.
56. Ibid., 287, panel 1.
57. Jung, *Collected Works* 14, par. 760.
58. See *Nicomachean Ethics*, IV, in Jonathan Barnes, ed., *The Complete Works of Aristotle: The Revised Oxford Translation*, Bollingen Series 71, 2 vols. (Princeton: Princeton University Press, 1984).
59. See *Politics*, I, 2, in Barnes, ed., *The Complete Works of Aristotle*.
60. John Kenyon, *The History Men*, 2d ed. (Weidenfeld & Nicolson, 1993), 133.
61. See Terry Eagleton, *After Theory* (London: Penguin, 2003), 174–81.
62. Morrison and Quitely, *All-Star Superman*, 275, panel 2.
63. Umberto Eco includes the possible in the ambit of being: "*quod possibile est, ens est*," in *Kant and the Platypus: Essays on Language and Cognition*, trans. Alastair McEwen (London: Vintage, 2000), 12.
64. Morrison and Quitely, *All-Star Superman*, 240, panel 1.
65. Ibid., 280, panels 2–4.
66. See Schedel Luitjen's essay on Morrison's treatment of evil elsewhere in this volume.
67. For a pithy defence of the reality of human nature, see Terry Eagleton, *Why Marx Was Right* (New Haven: Yale University Press, 2011), 79–86; and for a magisterial example of philosophical anthropology, see P. M. S. Hacker, *Human Nature: The Categorial Framework* (Oxford: Wiley-Blackwell, 2010).
68. Mark Edmundson, *Literature Against Philosophy, Plato to Derrida: A Defence of Poetry* (Cambridge: Cambridge University Press, 1995), 192.

69. Ibid.

70. See Geoff Klock, "'It is with considerable difficulty...': The Revisionary Superhero Narrative, Phase Two," in *How to Read Superhero Comics and Why* (New York: Continuum, 2002), 77–97.

71. Douglas Wolk writes, "*Watchmen* systematically undermines the entire premise of adventure stories: not only that evil can be vanquished and that doing good can save the world but that 'good' and 'evil' are easy to apply. It upends the principles of heroic victory and heroic self-sacrifice, and at the end it looks like the saving of the world may not have been a good idea anyway," in *Reading Comics: How Graphic Novels Work and What They Mean* (Cambridge: Da Capo Press, 2007), 240. See also Singer, *Grant Morrison*, 52–3.

The Dark Knight and the Devil

Demons and Demonology in Batman, 2005–2013

SCHEDEL LUITJEN

A dark figure rises up from a pool of shadow, horns on his head and glowing, piercing eyes boring holes and striking terror into the hearts of men. This could equally describe two of the most prevalent figures in the popular psyche, one finding his origin in the pre–Christian past and one joining man's consciousness from the drawing board of a young man in the New York of 1939. In Grant Morrison's Batman *oeuvre*, the two come face to face, their stories intertwining across a canvas spanning centuries and light-years. Mortality, divinity, and death: these are some of the prevailing themes in Grant Morrison's Batman work in *Batman RIP* (2008), *Final Crisis* (2008–9), *The Return of Bruce Wayne* (2010), and *Batman, Incorporated* (2010–13), as the Dark Knight faces the self-proclaimed Devil, the God of Evil, and the Living Curse. These three enemies are drawn from the lore and themes of demonology, and are used as self-conscious references to historical concepts of the Devil. Weaving demonological themes from throughout Pagan and Christian history into these stories widens their meaning and places Batman in a cultural context that bridges times and cultures to create a Batman for all ages.

Part One: The Devil You Know

Doctor Simon Hurt is a dogged opponent of Batman, orchestrating massive conspiracies against the Caped Crusader from behind the scenes. He is the shadowy figure behind all crime, and he presents himself as though he were the Devil. This is not quite true, though, as a close reading of the literature demonstrates. Simon Hurt's first appearance in comics was in the story "Robin Dies at Dawn,"[1] though he is not mentioned by that name. He was a scientist who convinced Batman to take part in an isolation experiment, to determine how astronauts would cope with conditions in space. This event is formative, a turning point in Batman's psychological health, and this is an example of a technique which Grant Morrison uses over and over again to create an artificial sense of history and gravitas. By referencing a story written decades earlier and transposing his current thematic elements onto it, Morrison builds a feeling of the weight of a continuous presence of evil into the character of the Doctor.

Doctor Hurt is deeply involved in mind control and brainwashing throughout the work, from creating the psychologically fractured replacement Batmen from police officers in *Batman* #655–666, to helping Professor Pyg try to spread his Dollotron brainwashing virus throughout Gotham in *Batman and Robin* #14–16, to his deeply embedded mind control commands in the head of Batman. He is presented, in Morrison's retroactive continuity, as a government scientist working to control people in a manner similar to the CIA's "MK-Ultra" programs, well-documented[2] mid-twentieth century attempts to study the effects and effectiveness of various brainwashing techniques. It should be no surprise that the diabolical Doctor Hurt would be involved in such a thing, since conspiracy theories about continuing MK-Ultra and so-called Monarch Mind Control frequently feature devil-worship-like ceremonies in their depiction of the techniques used to break down a subject's personality. This, incidentally, fits perfectly with Morrison's usual use of conspiracy theory and alternative history themes in his works.

The next appearance of Doctor Hurt in continuity is in another work that predates the beginning of Morrison's *Batman* run in 2005. In Peter Milligan and Kieron Dwyer's story arc *Dark Knight, Dark City* (*Batman* #452–4 [1990]), the story is told of the summoning, in 1765, of "Barbathos," a bat-demon.[3] The summoning takes place in Gotham City and, according to the story, the demon became the spirit of the city, ultimately causing the events that drive Bruce Wayne to don the mantle of the Bat. Present at the summoning ceremony are several leading figures of pre–Revolutionary War Gotham. Grant Morrison, in another sleight of retroactive continuity, reveals in *Batman and Robin* #16 (2011) that Simon Hurt (under what is probably his true name, the avuncular ancestor of Batman, "Thomas Wayne") was also present at the summoning. Again, the insertion of the character into previous "in-continuity" events builds on his claims to devilhood, revealing a sort of omnipresence in the darkest events of the Batman history. The first three pages of *Batman and Robin* #16 are intertextually related to *Dark Knight, Dark City*, presenting near-exact repetition of dialogue from the earlier story. The ending of the summoning ceremony, however, is changed in Morrison's version. The original had the ceremony fail to take hold of "Barbathos" since the men did not kill their intended sacrificial victim; but in Morrison's version, Simon Hurt himself finishes the job and attains putative control over the demonic spirit.

The name "Barbatos" has its literary origin in a grimoire first printed in Johann Weyer's *Pseudomonarchia Daemonum* and reprinted with Reginald Scot's 1584 treatise *The Discoverie of Witchcraft*, an odd little book atypical of its time in that it denies the possibility of witchcraft. Supposedly in the interest of showing forth how ridiculous demonic magic is, Scot reproduces an entire book on demons and how to capture them in stones and other objects. Within this book is included the small encyclopedia of demons, in which there is this description of Barbatos:

> Barbatos, a great countie or earle, and also a duke, he appeareth in *Signo sagitarii sylvestris*, with foure kings, which bring companies and great troopes. He understandeth the singing of the birds, the barking of dogs, the lowing of bullocks, and the voice of all living creatures. He detecteth treasures hidden by magicians and inchanters, and is of the order of vertues, which in part beare rule: he governeth thirtie legions of divels by his authoritie.[4]

It would appear, thus, that the name is used by Milligan and Morrison more for the inclusion of the word "bat" in it than for the actual description of the demon's characteristics. The nature of this Barbatos and its retroactive alteration by Morrison in the context of the DC Comics universe will be addressed below. The important thing here is simply that Thomas Wayne/Simon Hurt believes it to be a diabolical spirit. He sees it as a giant bat made of shadows, with glowing eyes, which spouts confusing, jumbled dialogue. Hurt believes that the demon wishes him to finish the ceremony, both by consuming the heart of a giant bat and by killing a maiden named Dominique, the "Adapter incarnate," and saying that he will "bathe in all [her] blood."[5]

Whether the sacrifice worked or whether it was a hallucination taking place in the mind of Simon Hurt (as is implied when it is shown that, to Dominique, he seems to be talking to a blank wall rather than to Barbatos),[6] the experience is important in forming the character's mindset and ability to live for centuries without aging. Thomas Wayne/Simon Hurt is touched by this demon and believes himself to have become the herald of the Devil. The satanic imagery that pervades the ceremony underlines this connection and gives it a semblance of genuineness. The tapestry behind the intended victim, in both *Dark Knight, Dark City* and *Batman and Robin*, has at its center an inverted pentagram. The pentagram, or Solomon's Seal, has been for centuries associated with high ritual magic and the summoning of infernal entities.[7] Its use is generally in the context of a circumscribed shape, in many cases with protective names of God or archangels written at each point of the star. It appears in its inverted form in the comics, however, with two points up, representing the horns of the Devil. This reverses the sense of protective power in the symbol, representing diabolical intent and "the triumph of matter and duality over spirit and unity."[8] This symbolism of reversal as a sign of the demonic is continued in much of Doctor Hurt's portrayal. In the back matter of *Absolute Batman and Robin* (2013), Grant Morrison writes of Doctor Hurt as depicted on the cover of *Batman and Robin* #15: "Here the figures are flipped around, with left hands raised instead of right hands and a candelabra designed to hint at a trident or pitchfork shape, suggestive of the Devil."[9]

In spite of all this, Doctor Hurt never becomes more than the messenger of the demon Barbatos. This is continually reflected in the language and imagery of the books. First, the demon, at the summoning in *Batman and Robin* #16, calls Hurt "weapon in my hand,"[10] marking him not as a prince of spirits, but as a servant. Professor Pyg, in another scene, says, "RRRRNF! Bless the snail. The double is two, the deuce is snail horns. The snail is the Devil!"[11] The "double" refers to Doctor Hurt, who pretends to be another Thomas Wayne, namely, Bruce Wayne's father. This is also reflected in Barbatos's language, calling Doctor Hurt "Dark Twin."[12] Doctor Hurt, therefore, is the Deuce, the Devil's Horns, an accessory to Satan rather than the Devil himself. Similarly, Robin shows knowledge that the Doctor's claim to be the Devil is not true when he proclaims, "You're not the Devil! You're a man who lived too long. We know who you are!"[13]

At this point, Doctor Hurt shows evidence that he himself does not believe his own claims of devilhood. He is still attempting to call forth the diabolical source of his power: "The Ceremony of the Bat has begun again. As the sun shines black you and I will summon the spirit Barbatos to open this impenetrable box of ancient secrets."[14] Thus, the herald of the Devil returns to the Satanic ritual, this time seeking to offer Robin's soul as a sacrifice. Later, while attempting to trap Bruce Wayne in an inescapable box-like room in the Batcave, he proclaims: "*I am the Hole in Things! I bring Hell on Earth and to the world Debasement!*"[15] This echoes and reverses the well-known words of the angels in Luke 2:14, "Peace on Earth and to men good will."

Without his fabled demon, which has fallen at the hands of the Batman, Doctor Hurt escapes through the cave tunnels, out of the Batcave through the secret exit in the tomb of Bruce Wayne's parents. It may be well to note that, in *Dark Knight, Dark City*, Dominique, the girl who was to be sacrificed to raise Barbatos, "the devil-bat of the *Miagani* tribe, as summoned by ... Thomas Wayne and his cohorts in 1765,"[16] was also entombed there, adding special significance to Doctor Hurt's comeuppance in the following scene. This is another instance of Morrison intertwining old continuity elements into his current work and thereby adding to the weight of these events.

At the exit to the tomb, Doctor Hurt encounters the Joker, who causes him to split his skull open by slipping on a banana peel. Joker explains: "the banana represents the primal gag, the fall."[17] To the Joker, this is the Fall of Lucifer from Heaven, the expulsion of the sinful angels to Hell, represented in miniature as a joke. If Doctor Hurt would have himself be the Devil, the Joker would have him go to Hell. He explains further: "You've done this before, am I right? I can tell you already know how quickly everything you planned can just go to Hell? The Devil's in the details, right?"[18] He then proceeds to bury the gibbering Doctor Hurt alive. In this story, as in many others, the Joker represents Death, the true enemy of Batman. As Grant Morrison explains: "Wreathed in Satanic imagery, it only seemed right that the sinister Doctor Hurt should suffer Lucifer's fate and experience the Fall from Heaven one more time—in its most farcical form."[19] Driving the point home and complementing Professor Pyg's metaphor from earlier, the Clown Prince of Crime quips, "Joker trumps Deuce."[20]

Doctor Hurt, then, builds devilish imagery around himself not only in an attempt to aggrandize himself, but to drive his "subject," Bruce Wayne, to brainwashed madness, just as he had done earlier with the third replacement Police Batman. To the end, it is shown in the literature that his delusions of diabolical power are just that. Shortly before his defeat at the hands of Batman and the Joker, he sees a warped reflection of Batman in a glass pane and, believing it to be the demon he had attempted to summon, chokes out, "Barbatos. I live to be your weapon. Give me a sign."[21] The sign is a blow to the back of the head at the hand of Batman.

Through the constant diabolical imagery surrounding Doctor Hurt, his claims to devilhood remain believable and make him a compelling villain. Nonetheless, by the end of his story arc in *Batman and Robin*, he is seen to be more human than he would like to admit; not the "Hole in Things," but rather a man "contaminated by contact with a weapon from another world,"[22] as Batman states. That weapon was Barbatos, which turns out to be a living curse from a Platonic world of gods and demons, launched into Batman's life by the larger-than-life God of Evil, Darkseid.

Part Two: *The Devil You Don't*

In Part 6 of *Final Crisis*, the higher-dimensional being called Darkseid sends Batman spiraling through time, pursued by a demonic, living curse. In Grant Morrison's telling of the story, Darkseid is something more than the Devil of modern popular culture; his traits and actions show him to be drawn from an older conception of evil beings, from the Platonic Demonology of Late Antique source texts and Early Modern Christian writers. There are two main components to Morrison's presentation of Platonic Ideas: the demon god and the magic bullet.

When Grant Morrison "spent a year in Hell with Darkseid"[23] writing *Final Crisis*, he was meticulously crafting a picture of a god of Evil, a being which stops just short of being Platonic Evil incarnate. In Late Antiquity, the Neoplatonist philosophical movement produced several thinkers who, in the context of new interpretations based on the works of Plato, attempted to absorb the demonology of several cultures into one cohesive framework. Among them are Plotinus (*fl.* third century AD), his student Porphyrius (*fl.* late third century AD), Iamblichus (*fl.* third to fourth century AD), and Proclus (*fl.* fifth century AD), and most importantly to demonology, Apuleius (*fl.* second century AD).

One of the main points of interest derived from Plato's work was the belief that, beyond the physical universe, there is a world of *Ideas* or *Forms*, simpler and more perfect archetypes from which all the things in the experienced physical world derive their function and shape.[24] Forms exist in this higher realm, the World of Ideas, and they govern objects and realities in the lower realm, where humans live. Everything experienced is a shadow of the reality of the Forms; thus, a sword derives its sword-ness from a Sword Form, and love experienced for another person derives from Love the transcendent Form.

In Grant Morrison's interpretation of the New Gods, Jack Kirby's other-universe mythological characters, the Fourth World itself, the mysterious star-system where the New Gods reside, is the realm of Ideas or Forms. The Fourth World was itself an innovative creative shot in the arm to the structure of the DC Universe when it was conceptualized in the 1970s by "King of Comics" Jack Kirby. Although its influence on the mainstream DC titles was slow to develop, it has come to be an inseparable part of the tapestry of the DC Universe, producing arguably the only consistently formidable threat to the colorful champions of the Justice League, namely, Darkseid. In Kirby's works, there is a sense of transcendence and majesty to the Fourth World, such that even the less powerful of its characters, such as Mister Miracle, can only live among regular humans for a time before they are called back into the Wagnerian dramas of the intergalactic New Gods. In spite of the oft-glimpsed clues to the transcendence of the Fourth World, it is never made as clearly a representation of the Platonic Realm of Ideas in Kirby's work as it is in Morrison's. This is reflected in the language used when Batman enters Darkseid's infernal chamber: Batman says that he "stepped through that door into a bigger, simpler world. A world where the stakes were ultimate stakes, where each moment was heavy with the massive weight of unfolding myth..."[25]

To Neoplatonic philosophers, the Greek and Roman gods themselves were transcendent, corresponding to Forms of abstract concepts like Love for Aphrodite/Venus and Kingship or Rule for Zeus/Jupiter. The gods embodied the things over which they were said to rule. Batman, in *Batman* #702, explains that the New Gods are seen in the DC Universe in this Neoplatonic framework: "The New Gods are incredibly powerful living ideas from a kind of Platonic, archetypal world."[26]

Daemons in this Neoplatonic system, on the other hand, were intermediary beings, sometimes good and sometimes wicked, and who served occasionally as intermediaries between humans and the gods, often as semi-divine tricksters, and sometimes as righteous imposers of suffering upon a sinful mankind. Apuleius, a second-century Roman Neoplatonic writer, paints the picture that the daemons are subject to change and emotion, from which the more transcendent or true gods are free. Nonetheless, they use the same names as the gods and represent themselves as the rightful recipients of mankind's worship. These, says Apuleius, are the beings of whom Homer and Vergil wrote, the "masks" of the gods who aspire to godhood but are truly something lower.[27]

Which of these Neoplatonic beings is Darkseid, then? Is he a god or a daemon? If he is a god, he is the "God of Evil," an epithet liberally applied to him throughout DC Comics. What does this mean in a Platonic framework? What is Evil?

For the answer to that, it is best to turn to Augustine of Hippo, Saint and Bishop from the fifth century AD. Coming from a non–Christian Neoplatonic background, his thought patterns and modes of discourse reveal Plato's influence throughout his Christian work. He makes this explicit in his *Confessions*, wherein he notes the influence of "books of the Platonists"[28] on his philosophical formation before his conversion to Christianity.[29]

He was one of the Christian theologians who subscribed to the "despoiling the Egyptians" method of syncretistic theology, later called *prisca theologia*, wherein the belief was that ancient non–Christian philosophers such as Plato could have, due to their discipline and commitment to leading a virtuous life, happened upon truths about God in spite of their lack of a knowledge of Jesus. Thus Augustine sees things through a Platonic filter, and it is through this that he approaches the problem of evil in several of his works, including the tract *On Free Choice of Will*. In the course of the argument of this work, Augustine talks about the idea of evil, picking up a theme that he had explored less extensively in Book VII of the *Confessions*. God, in the Genesis narrative, states that the whole of Creation is good. Thus, anything fully evil must necessarily not exist, because God did not create anything evil and therefore did not create evil.[30] Any created thing, even the Devil, whom we perceive as being evil, must necessarily be by nature good, because he exists. What we refer to as evil is the failure to live up to potential for good. Evil is nonexistence, an uncreated non-entity, a lack rather than a separate principle:

> [W]hat is that which we call evil but the absence of good? In the bodies of animals, disease and wounds mean nothing but the absence of health; for when a cure is effected, that does not mean that the evils which were present—namely, the diseases and wounds—go away from the body and dwell elsewhere: they altogether cease to exist; for the wound or disease is not a substance, but a defect in the fleshly substance,—the flesh itself being a substance, and therefore something good, of which those evils—that is, privations of the good which we call health—are accidents. Just in the same way, what are called vices in the soul are nothing but privations of natural good.[31]

Evil, then, is not the opposite of good; it is a lack, a failing, a Hole in Things. Readers of Grant Morrison's work on Batman will be familiar with the concept of a Hole in Things. It shows up repeatedly in the issues surrounding and following *Final Crisis*, and its interpretations could be many. It is the trap into which Batman is thrown, the Omega Sanction, the Death that is Life; and it is the black hole where Darkseid's heart should be; the Black Hole at the end and beginning of Time; the hole created by Darkseid's fall backwards in time to his death.

"The hole in things is Darkseid-shaped," Batman says in *Batman #702*. "But it's only a hole. Darkseid is gone."[32] It is my argument that the hole is Darkseid-shaped because the hole was the essence of what Darkseid himself was trying to manifest. The black hole at his heart is evil, and Evil is non-being, non-existence, nothingness.

Darskeid does exist in the DC Universe (in fact, his frequent slogan is "Darkseid Is"), and therefore he cannot be Evil itself. Rather than being the "Tiger-Force at the core of all things"[33] that haunts men's dreams, he is just another demon aspiring to godhood. Under the Neoplatonic definition of gods and daemons, Darkseid falls under the latter category, moved by emotion and pettiness throughout his appearances in Jack Kirby's Fourth World saga and Grant Morrison's *Final Crisis*. It is not until Batman strikes him down and sends him spiraling into nonexistence that he creates the Hole in Things, the universal lack throughout time and space, which he himself had sought to be. Thus, he becomes "The Hole that remains when everything else has gone … the Emptiness shaped like God."[34]

Batman defeats the demon from space using a "magic bullet" made of Radion,[35] which Darkseid himself had brought to Earth from the Fourth World. Batman explains the use of the projectile: "It's a magic bullet, literally. An all-purpose *god-killing projectile* that can be loaded and fired over and over again from any gun ever invented. Essence of bullet."[36] This Radion bullet, then, is the Platonic Idea of a bullet, pairing the very ancient flavor of Platonic Types with a thoroughly modern invention, the bullet, and giving it a completely physical manifestation in the story, such that it can be held by Batman and kept in his utility belt for further study. Batman goes on, in a captioned excerpt from his journal: "It was the blueprint, the template for every bullet there had ever been. It was the bullet that killed JFK, Martin Luther King, John Lennon. Gandhi … Archduke Ferdinand … Thomas and Martha Wayne."[37] This connects the Essence of Bullet not only to the events of every war, but also to Bruce Wayne personally. The creation of Batman is dependent on a bullet, the bullet that killed his parents. Thus, the idea of Batman is predicated on this Idea of Bullet. In the concluding issue of *Batman, Incorporated*, Batman implies that it is against this evil that is emptiness he is fighting, and inside of which he operates.

Bruce Wayne says to Jim Gordon, "Two shots killed my father. I was ten years old. The third bullet left a smoking hole in my mother's new fur coat. It left a hole in me. A hole in everything."[38] These statements emphasize the relationship between Darkseid's bullet and the Hole in Things, which is not just evil but its negative effects, the loneliness and darkness which its tool, the bullet, leaves behind in its wake.

But Batman refuses to use guns or kill, because his parents were killed by a gunman's bullet. It is generally recognized that refusing to kill and use a gun is essential to the Batman legend. Morrison plays with this, having Batman use the Idea of Bullet to wound Darkseid mortally in *Final Crisis* #6. Batman says, before he fires the Radion Bullet: "I made a very solemn vow about firearms. But for you, I'm making a once-in-a-lifetime exception. A gun and a bullet, Darkseid. It was your idea."[39] "Idea" is here used in its two distinct senses, the ordinary everyday sense and the sense of the Platonic Idea. Batman understands that the Radion Bullet is the Platonic Idea of a bullet, and he places its derivation as being from Darkseid, the aspiring God of Evil. A bullet, to Batman, is something that could only arise from Evil. Batman therefore uses an Idea to kill an Idea. This clearly influences him when he decides, later on, to form Batman, Incorporated. He lays out its philosophy some time later: "Starting today, we fight ideas with better ideas. The idea of crime with the idea of Batman."[40] This is part of a major overarching theme of Morrison's *Batman* run: the replication and deification of Batman.

From the start of the run in *Batman* #655, the theme of the replication of Batman begins. Talia al Ghul creates her multiple Man-Bat soldiers; the Three Ghosts of Batman (the aforementioned Police Batman replacements) appear; the International Club of Heroes returns with its own cadre of Batmen to face the Black Glove; Batman is shown to have multiple Bat personae as the Batman of Zur-en-Arrh rises in *Batman RIP*; Darkseid creates a bevy of Bruce Waynes in *Final Crisis*; Batmen of past and future are revealed in *Time and the Batman*; Bruce Wayne fights as multiple Batman guises throughout time in *The Return of Bruce Wayne*; and Bruce Wayne creates Batman, Incorporated to replicate the Idea of Batman infinitely throughout the world, filling the Earth with Batmen to combat the super-terrorist organization Leviathan. All of this leads to the concept of the Idea of Batman being an Idea strong enough to overcome Death.

Death is the age-old enemy of Batman, and in Morrison's run this is played out over and over again, combining elements of Batman from every incarnation in every medium to create the ultimate Batman, the distilled Idea. More than villains, more even than crime, Death in all its forms is what Batman is constantly fighting against. Death took his parents, Death has taken his partners in crime-fighting, and he knows that Death will eventually come for him. Nonetheless, he fights on against it. The fact that this is an important, repeated theme in all of his Batman work demonstrates Morrison's integrative approach when it comes to Batman; the notion is one which is taken from what is probably the most loathed piece of Batman cinema ever produced, the visually beautiful but universally scorned *Batman and Robin* (1997). In it, the faithful butler Alfred confronts Bruce Wayne about his frustration and pain at the fact that he, Alfred, is not just sick, but dying:

> Death and chance stole your parents. But rather than become a victim, you have done everything in your power to control the fates. For what is Batman, if not an effort to master the chaos that sweeps our world? An attempt to control death, itself.[41]

This is Morrison's Batman, the Dark Knight who fights against Death at every turn. The Joker, grinning like a bleached skull, is usually a symbol of death in Batman comics, but in Morrison's comics he takes the back seat to the devilish Doctor Hurt and Darkseid, who both seek to lead Batman to his final adventure.

Even Talia al Ghul, formerly a love interest of the Batman and known by the epithet "Daughter of the Demon," ends her tenure in Morrison's Batman run by attempting to become Death, the destroyer of worlds. She creates Leviathan, the monolithic terrorist organization representing itself with the image of a serpent coiling around the world, a traditional symbol of Satan's power over the temporal world. She begins to wear a skull-mask and hood, evoking the Grim Reaper's traditional visual depiction, a walking Death, and seeking to destroy the earth with a "meta-bomb." It is no accident that the first major villain of *Batman, Incorporated* is Lord Death Man, a character from the Japanese Batman Manga of the 1960s, based on and, in Morrison's work, conflated with a character from 1966's *Batman* #180.

The essential transcendent persistence of the Batman Idea is expressed in his constant victory in the face of death. "Not everyone's going to survive it," as Batman says in *Batman, Incorporated*.[42] He has lost his parents, the second Robin, Jason Todd, and his son, Damian, to Death. Nonetheless, he continues on, unstoppable. His iterations may change, but the Idea stays the same and survives, unkillable. This is the meaning of the never-ending string of Batmen and Batman versions in the work: in *Batman, Incorporated (II)* #12, Batman attacks Death directly, incorporating aspects from several of his iterations. He is empowered by the Langstrom Atavistic Gene Regression serum with Man-Bat powers; he flies in a robotic suit acquired from his trusted ally Lucius Fox; and he wears the Suit of Sorrows, an unstoppable Bat-armor developed by an order of monks. Batman can be a being of nature, technology, or religion. He can also encompass all of them. Talia al Ghul, the "Devil's Daughter,"[43] expresses Death's fear in the face of this unstoppable Idea: "Why can't he admit defeat? ... Why won't he stop? ... MAKE HIM STOP!"[44]

In facing Death and the Devil, and making them shudder in fear, Batman shows himself to have become more than just an idea, as he tries to become in the film *Batman Begins* (2005); in Morrison's work, he has become an Idea in the Platonic sense, transcendent and immanent in all his iterations. As Dick Grayson says on Bruce Wayne's return from his presumed death: "Devil... meet Bat-God."[45] This profound statement on the one hand highlights the self-aware diabolical imagery of Doctor Hurt, while at the same time putting Batman into that context as himself being an Idea inherently more powerful than Doctor Hurt. As God will always trump the Devil, so Batman will always ultimately trump Doctor Hurt.

Part Three: The Voice of the Devil, a Living Curse

The rediscovery of Platonic philosophical texts and ideas in the fifteenth and sixteenth centuries added to the self-aware attitudes of Renaissance thinkers such as Marsilio Ficino and Giovanni Pico della Mirandola, and led to their reaching some conclusions that either could not have been, or simply were not, by earlier Neoplatonic thinkers. These new modes of thought eventually filtered into the conceptualizations behind the somewhat more practical and mundane field of exorcisms.

One of these new concepts is that angelic beings, instead of being sentient entities who happen to function occasionally as messengers for the Divine Will, are actually spiritual and sometimes physical manifestations of the message itself. They are the message they are delivering, embodied in a thinking, self-conscious being. This belief was consistent and sensible to Renaissance thinkers because of their worldview construct, wherein Creation itself is a speech from the voice of God, and human beings' lives are words or sentences in the *Logos*, or meaningful speech of God.[46]

In this conception, angels are embodiments and bringers of a divine message from God; their appearance, which is changeable according to their will, is simply manifested as a part of the message, in order to make the metaphor of their existence as recognizable and readable as possible to the recipient of the message, usually a human being.[47] Their body, if they have one, is thin, airy, and almost nonexistent.[48]

If angels are the good messages of God, bringing comfort, hope, warning, or Divine Retribution, then devils are warped metaphors, twisted and false statements, and evil tidings spoken by Satan to ensnare mankind. This conception of twisted speech's ability to warp reality is one of the bases for the belief in the efficacy of curses. Curses are spoken words that cause harm (physical or spiritual) to befall their targets.

Darkseid sends a living curse to hound Batman through a series of uncontrollable leaps into differing lives throughout history, the result of his Omega Beams.[49] This being is known as a "Hyper-Adapter," and it appears in several forms, from a Lovecraftian Cthulu-esque kraken monster to the aforementioned giant devil-bat, as it wraps around time with

Bruce and, arguably, becomes the spirit that inspires Batman's entire life's mission: inescapable, unstoppable, all-consuming. The hyper-adapter in bat form is interpreted as a manifestation of the aforementioned Barbatos, revealed in *The Return of Bruce Wayne* #3 to be the god of the American Indian bat-tribe, the Miagani. Under this name, the evil Dr. Hurt calls upon it as a demon, in the process becoming contaminated by the power of Darkseid and becoming immortal.[50]

This is not the first time Darkseid has used a Hyper-Adapter to construct false, depressing lives around someone. The Omega Adapter appears in Morrison's *Seven Soldiers*, a "Life Trap" built around Shilo Norman, the superhero known as Mister Miracle. After being exposed to the Adapter, Shilo is shown living through "the Life Trap. Each new existence more degraded than the last. More hopeless. More meaningless. Neverending."[51] The Omega Adapter explains its being:

> The trap that follows you wherever you go. That moves as you move, unseen and all around ... living oblivion! A weapon of Dark Side. Ever shifting, ever adapting, I am the prison you can never escape! Be born again and again in me! Suffocated in mortal clay![52]

The comic shows Norman being beaten nearly to death and burned, and implies that he is castrated, in one life. In the next, he is dead in a graveyard, then shot in the head. This curse is the most terrifying kind of trap, one of which the trapped person is unaware, a whole life conspiring to crush his spirit in the face of overwhelming perceived meaninglessness. Shilo Norman escapes because he is a mortal manifestation of Mister Miracle, the New God who embodies the Idea of Escape, Limitlessness.

Batman, meanwhile, faces the threat by absorbing it into his own fate. As is shown through *The Return of Bruce Wayne*, his life and his family are forged by the links of the Life Trap into becoming the Bruce Wayne he has always been. The death of his parents, the terror of the giant bat in the Batcave, all are manifestations of the trap that Darkseid has laid for Batman. Barbatos has forged the Batman legend as a trap for the man Bruce Wayne. This picks up on themes from the first "Barbatos" appearance in *Dark Knight, Dark City*: "You're born, and your history, your time, your place, is a mold into which you're thrown.... Does it make any difference if a few demons are behind it also?"[53] A "Demon," or in this case the "'Death-idea' that never tires, never stops,"[54] has pursued Batman to the end of time. Batman weakens it by absorbing its energy into himself, leading ultimately to Barbatos's doom at the hands of a time travel counter-trap.

This demonstrates again the unstoppable nature of the Batman: Bruce Wayne accepts the curse, accepts life as the Batman, but adapts to it, converting it into a strength rather than a weakness. As a man trapped by a god, bound by the words of the curse into the "box" of a lifetime of tragedy, Bruce Wayne takes hold of the trap and makes it his own. He traps the "Apokaliptian hunter-killer curse machine"[55] in a trap of his own, saving the universe by weakening the living curse and sending it in a time-loop to the beginning of time, where it is killed and absorbed into the Batman mythos. The life of Batman is conceived as a trap for Bruce Wayne, but he turns it into a trap for the curse itself. He absorbs the curse and uses it to transcend to ideahood.

In conclusion, this theme, then, is the reason for all of the devil imagery in all of Morrison's Batman work. The Devil, in his many forms—the diabolical doctor, the God of Evil, and the unstoppable living curse—is inserted thematically into the narrative as an enemy that never stops, that hounds humanity at every turn, attempting to turn human life into an inescapable pit of despair. Batman, representing the most transcendent version of Man, faces the Devil at every turn, and is ultimately shown to have been trapped from the beginning by these forces beyond humanity's control. Doctor Hurt has pursued Batman since the time of his ancestors, worked behind the scenes to warp his psyche and his life for years. Darkseid created the bullet that plunged young Bruce Wayne into the despairing life of a dark avenger. The Living Curse, Barbatos, haunted Bruce Wayne's family line from the time of the cavemen, hounding Batman to the end of time itself, investing the very cityscape with its wicked power and forcing history to create the wretched creature called Batman. Yet the consistent story of Batman as Humanity is not one of defeat. Batman, unable to escape from these powerful forces that force him into becoming the Caped Crusader, instead uses them to build the myth of the Batman ever larger until it has become an Idea strong enough to last forever. For the pit in which these diabolical forces chased him, the life they built around him as a trap, was in fact just what he needed to transcend himself and replicate his ideals until they were an integral part of the DC Universe.

The sum total of Batman's power to make tragedy into triumph and to build himself through these snares into a legend is expressed, fittingly, in the final issue of *Batman, Incorporated*: "I looked into that hole in things over and over again until it hurt… and you know what I found in there? Nothing… and a space big enough to hold everything."[56] The Hole in Things is the lack created by a gunman's bullet through the heart of Bruce Wayne's mother. The Hole in Things is the Evil that besets the world, calling out to man to "embrace Anti-Life and be whole."[57] The Hole in Things is the emptiness that called a man to fill his life with friends, partners, brothers, and to create an Idea powerful enough to protect those who would fall into the Hole and its despair. Wherever there is evil, the lack of good, there will be Batman to fill in the hole and keep mankind from plunging into it.

The Hole in Things is Batman-shaped.

Notes

1. Bill Finger and Sheldon Moldoff, *Batman* #156 (New York: DC Comics, 1963).
2. See for instance Colin Ross, *The CIA Doctors: Human Rights Violations by American Psychiatrists* (Richardson, TX: Manitou Communications, 2006).
3. See Peter Milligan and Kieron Dwyer, *Batman* #452–454 (New York: DC Comics, 1990).
4. Reginald Scot, *Discoverie of Witchcraft*, ed. Montague Summers (Mineola, NY: Dover, 1972), 218.
5. Grant Morrison *et al.*, *Absolute Batman and Robin: Batman Reborn* (New York: DC Comics, 2012), 385.
6. Ibid., 386.
7. While this term can also traditionally refer to a six-sided circumscribed star, it is popularly used for a five-sided one. It is used again by Leviathan as a brand for their infected cattle in Grant Morrison and Chris Burnham, *Batman, Incorporated* (2) #1 (New York: DC Comics, 2012).
8. As explained by Damian Wayne in Grant Morrison and Andy Kubert, *Batman* #666 (New York: DC Comics, 2007).
9. Morrison *et al.*, *Absolute Batman and Robin: Batman Reborn*, 463.
10. Ibid., 386.
11. Ibid., 368.
12. Ibid., 386.
13. Ibid., 373.
14. Ibid., 375.
15. Ibid. 399.
16. Ibid., 268.
17. Ibid., 64.
18. Ibid., 406.
19. Ibid., 476.
20. Ibid., 407.
21. Ibid., 403.
22. Ibid., 404.
23. Grant Morrison, in *Wizard Magazine* #216 (New York: Wizard Entertainment, 2009), 218.
24. Key proof texts include *Symposium* 211b, *Phaedrus* 247c, and *Timaeus* 52a.
25. Grant Morrison and Tony Daniel, *Batman* #702 (New York: DC Comics, 2010), 11–12.
26. Ibid., 12.
27. Apuleius takes up nearly all of his *On the God of Socrates* in building up a detailed picture of the Platonic cosmos and its beings on every level. The tract is a fascinating look at the mindset of pagan philosophers at the beginning of Late Antiquity.
28. Augustinus Hipponensis, *Confessiones* VII (IX) 13, my translation.
29. In the notes to Albert C. Outler's translation, he writes that scholars, while unsure

of which Platonists Augustine eventually read, believe that this reference may be to Plotinus's *Enneads*.

30. This notion is also expressed elsewhere in Augustine's works, such as *City of God* XI.9 and *Confessions* VII (V) 7.
31. Augustine of Hippo, *Enchiridion on Faith, Hope, and Love*, trans. J.F. Shaw (London: Religious Tract Society, 1885), 11.
32. Morrison and Daniel, *Batman* #702, 17.
33. Jack Kirby, *Forever People* #3 (New York: DC Comics, 1971), 21.
34. Grant Morrison and Chris Sprouse, *The Return of Bruce Wayne* #6 (New York: DC Comics, 2010), 26.
35. Radion is first introduced as a god-killing substance in Jack Kirby, *New Gods* #7 (New York: DC Comics, 1972), 4.
36. Morrison and Daniel, *Batman* #702, 4.
37. Ibid.
38. Morrison and Burnham, *Batman, Incorporated* (2) #13, 11.
39. Grant Morrison et al., *Final Crisis* #7 (New York: DC Comics, 2008), 26.
40. Grant Morrison and David Finch, *Batman: the Return* (New York: DC Comics, 2011), 13.
41. *Batman and Robin*, dir. Joel Schumacher (1997; Los Angeles: Warner Home Video, 2010).
42. Grant Morrison and Chris Burnham, *Batman, Incorporated* (1) #6 (New York: DC Comics, 2011), 10.
43. This appellation is applied to Talia by Grant Morrison in the title to *Batman, Incorporated* (2) #13.
44. Morrison and Burnham, *Batman, Incorporated* (2) #12, 1–3.
45. Morrison et al., *Absolute Batman and Robin*, 377.
46. See the works of Thomas Tropianus and Girolamo Menghi, and their explanation in Armando Maggi, *Satan's Rhetoric: A Study of Renaissance Demonology* (Chicago: University of Chicago Press, 2001). Incidentally, this makes Jesus as Word Incarnate (see John 1) the first known example of a "fiction-diver," diving (in the form of a created being) into the narrative he himself created.
47. See for examples and explanation Armando Maggi, *In the Company of Demons* (Chicago: University of Chicago Press, 2008), ix, x, 7, 8, 14, 21–23.
48. An idea present in Augustine's *On the Divination of Demons* and a staggering number of early modern demonological texts, but ultimately derived from Antony's speech to the monks in Athanasius, *Life of Antony*, 31.
49. Darkseid first used his Omega Beams to send people spiraling through time in Jack Kirby, *Forever People* #3 (New York: DC Comics, 1971).
50. "250 years ago, the hyper-adapter infected a human host. A pure strain of platonic evil," in Morrison and Sprouse, *The Return of Bruce Wayne* #6, 30.
51. Grant Morrison and Pasqual Ferry, *Seven Soldiers: Mister Miracle* #4 (New York: DC Comics, 2006), 11–12.
52. Ibid.
53. Milligan and Dwyer, *Batman* #454, 22.
54. Morrison and Sprouse, *The Return of Bruce Wayne* #6, 23.
55. Ibid., 4.
56. Morrison and Burnham, *Batman, Incorporated* (2) #13, 19–20.
57. Morrison and Daniel, *Batman* #702, 12.

"Our Father, Who Art in Gotham"

The Life, Death and Rebirth of Batman

NICHOLAS GALANTE

In the notes published with the fifteenth-anniversary edition of *Arkham Asylum: A Serious House on Serious Earth* (2004), Grant Morrison states that he believes "that people respond emotionally to deep mythical patterns whether or not they recognize or 'understand' them as such."[1] This is a tactic that he employs in most of his writing, relying on mythic and occult themes or situations to evoke powerful responses from his readers. Morrison's first major foray into the world of Gotham produced a powerfully symbolic text, a story fraught with dark psychological themes, strong overtones of the occult, and a heavy dose of religious symbolism. The mythic tone pervades not only *Arkham Asylum*, but the rest of Morrison's work on Batman as well, with a heavy emphasis on Batman's perpetual renewal through the cycle of life, death, and rebirth.

Batman, Tradition, and Myth

Traditionally, Batman has been primarily portrayed in one of two ways: as calculating, rational, and staggeringly intelligent (this persona will be called, for the sake of this argument, "the World's Greatest Detective") or as a darker, violent, and more vengeful figure (hereafter referred to as "the Dark Knight"). Over the course of Batman's more than seventy-year career, different writers have portrayed him with varying degrees of these personas, depending on the role they require him to perform. This could be argued to be an inherent aspect of the comic book medium: readers want Batman to change and develop, but at the same time he must not be allowed to age as an ordinary man. He must remain constant and changeless while somehow managing to grow and evolve as a character. By having Batman switch between these light and dark personalities, it provides an illusion of change while keeping him as a recognizable hero.

However, the significance of Batman's cycle of change/reconfiguration goes beyond a simple need to keep Batman interesting to readers. In Morrison's hands, the general cycle of alternation between Batman's identity as World's Greatest Detective and Dark Knight has deep religious and mythic symbolism. Morrison is well known for incorporating such symbolism into his writing, and has described superheroes as modern mythology on many occasions. His 2011 book *Supergods* alone contains a multitude of mythological references; and in its outro, Morrison even goes so far as to suggest that when theological writers like Giovanni Pico della Mirandola speak of "Cherubs and Seraphs and Thrones as our role models and intermediaries on the road to 'God' or 'cosmic consciousness,' we can just as easily call them superheroes."[2] Superheroes are modern gods, in Morrison's eyes at least, and the course that he has doomed Batman to repeat reflects this, as parallels to this course can be found in more than one religious tradition.

It could be argued that Batman's continuous cycle of death and rebirth places him in the archetype that Sir James Frazer famously called the Dying and Reviving God. While the accuracy of the title has been disputed since its debut in the late-nineteenth century, there can be no disputing the archetype's relevance to Morrison's Batman. In *The Golden Bough* (1890), Frazer describes the Dying and Reviving God as a rite intimately tied to the changing of the seasons, mimicking the life and death of vegetation. The worship of a Dying and Reviving God was intended "to ensure the vernal regeneration of plants and the multiplication of animals, which had seemed to be menaced by the inroads of winter,"[3] with the legend of Demeter and Persephone serving as the strongest example from Greek mythology. Persephone, as the bride of Hades, was compelled to spend one third of the year with her husband in the Underworld. The remainder of the year, she lived on the surface with her mother, the fertility goddess Demeter. Persephone's annual descent into the Underworld marked the start of winter (brought on by Demeter's sorrow), and her return brought her mother out of mourning and heralded the beginning of spring. Batman's appearances as the Dark Knight and his subsequent deaths parallel Persephone's time in the Underworld. The harsh, barren winter of Demeter's mourning is incarnated in the Dark Knight when Batman is at his most dangerous and unforgiving. The return of spring is shown in his rebirths as the World's Greatest Detective, his mind and senses sharp and renewed and ready for anything.

Alternatively, Batman's death and resurrection could come from the Hindu tradition of reincarnation. Krishna teaches Arjuna that "just as a person casts off worn-out garments and puts on others that are new, even so does the embodied soul cast off worn-out bodies and take on others that are new."[4] Though this describes a physical resurrection rather than a psychological one, the parallel remains. When Batman's mind becomes frayed and tattered and he finds himself nearing madness, the Dark Knight undergoes a symbolic death, only to be reincarnated as the World's Greatest Detective.

Finally, there remains a Christian parallel. My analysis of *Arkham Asylum* maintains that Morrison intends Batman to serve as a Christ figure, and the motif of death and resurrection certainly falls in line with that. After all, one of the most fundamental tenets of Christianity is that Christ dies and rises again. Batman's descent into madness can be seen as a tragic fall, mirroring Christ's own suffering in the days leading up to the crucifixion. Batman's mental anguish is an echo of Christ's scourging. Just as with Christ, the true power of Batman is seen not in his suffering, but in his resurrection. To quote Huston Smith:

> If Golgotha's cross had been the end, the goodness Christ embodied would have been tragically beautiful, but how significant? ... The resurrection completely reversed the cosmic status in which goodness had been left by the crucifixion. Instead of being pitiful it was victorious, triumphant over everything, even the end of all ends, death itself.[5]

As with Christ, it is in Batman's resurrection that his power is solidified. Over the course of his escapades, Batman finds himself dragged into a world of madness until he is almost as psychotic as the villains that he fights. If he had remained in the mad state that we see in *Arkham Asylum*, he would have remained as a tragic figure, but his significance would have been fleeting. Morrison's work on *Batman and Robin* post-*Final Crisis* (2008) made it clear that Batman can outlive Bruce Wayne. When Bruce was believed dead at Darkseid's hand, Dick Grayson assumed the role of Batman. What makes Bruce, the original Batman, an enduring figure is his ability to come back from the impossible, to conquer madness and death and the power of dark gods so as to resume his duties stronger and better than he was before his fall: therein lies the miracle.

While this chapter focuses primarily on the Christian and Messianic aspects of Morrison's portrayal of Batman, all three of the above interpretations have some degree of validity. It is by no means unheard of for Morrison to blend different traditions and influences to communicate his mythic tales. He has named tarot, religious mysticism, quantum physics, and surrealism as influences for *Arkham Asylum*, as well as the writings of Lewis Carroll, Carl Jung, and Aleister Crowley, just to name a few. Morrison sees myth and storytelling in everything, and his assertion that the Voodoo loa Legba is "known variously as Mercury, Thoth, Ganesh, Odin, or Ogma"[6] speaks of a belief that similar gods of different pantheons are actually the same god known by different names. Regardless of which tradition Morrison intends to evoke, it is clear that he means to invoke the mythic themes of life, death, and rebirth in his quest to prove that Batman and superheroes in general are part of a modern mythology.

World's Greatest Detective Versus the Dark Knight

When Morrison began his work on *Arkham Asylum* in the late 1980s, Batman had already been transformed. Writers like Frank Miller and Alan Moore solidified the darker, grittier, and more violent Dark Knight persona with *The Dark Knight Returns* (1986) and *The Killing Joke* (1988), respectively. *Arkham Asylum* was conceived as a direct response to a Batman that Morrison found to be "violent, driven, and borderline psychotic."[7]

Perhaps it is only natural that Morrison's first move is to send the psychotic Batman into the depths of the asylum. Batman expresses fear that entering the walls of Arkham will "be just like coming home,"[8] showing that even he suspects some degree of madness in himself. Morrison takes advantage of the inherently chaotic and illogical world of the asylum to toy with Batman's pre-existing roles, and to establish a dual nature for the Dark Knight.

The shadowy corridors of the asylum give rise to a darker, more sinister side of Batman. This is "the Batman his enemies experience and fear ... the Batman distilled to his essence—a vengeful, violent nightmare figure."[9] This "devil-eared shadow"[10] is the Batman of the 1980s, the side of Batman that does not hesitate to cripple Clayface with a kick or hurl Doctor Destiny down a flight of stairs. This is the side of Batman that belongs in the asylum with the murderers and psychopaths, the Batman that Morrison saw in *The Dark Knight Returns* and *The Killing Joke*.

Despite this, or rather because of it, Morrison takes great care to establish Batman's other side: that of the redeeming Christ figure. Even beyond *Arkham Asylum*, there are certain similarities between the Caped

Crusader and the Son of God. Batman, though an ordinary mortal, seems to possess supernatural powers, especially in the eyes of those he fights against. This echoes the Christian tenet that Jesus, though mortal, possessed the powers of the divine. Jesus preached peace and goodness and resistance to the forces of evil, and though Batman takes a more active approach, both men do battle against the forces of darkness. Finally, both men have a central theme of suffering and sacrifice to their characters. The fundamental teaching of Christianity is that Jesus suffered and died to save mankind. Bruce Wayne, constantly mourning the loss of his parents, puts his life on the line and sacrifices his own physical and mental well-being to protect the people of Gotham and make the world a better place.

Arkham Asylum serves to deepen this parallel. Following his entrance into the asylum, Batman has an initial confrontation with the Joker and undergoes a brief psychological examination from Dr. Adams. Shaken by the experience, he staggers away from the Joker's Feast of Fools and finds himself reliving the night of his parent's murder. In an effort to shock himself back to reality, Morrison envisioned a scene where Batman pricks his hand with a shard of glass. While he intended this to hearken back to the wounds of Christ, he was unprepared for the "unforgettable, apocalyptic bloodletting" that Dave McKean's art portrayed.[11] Batman inflicts agonizing pain upon himself, crippling his own hand so that he can continue the good fight for Gotham. Even the agonized cry of "Jesus," while a perfectly natural reaction to extreme pain, could be read as a degree of referential heavy-handedness on Morrison's part. If the reader's mind was not at the Crucifixion already, it is certainly there now.

During the battle with Killer Croc, Batman takes the spear from a statue of St. Michael the Archangel, gores Croc, and sends him crashing through the window. However, Croc's enormous bulk drives the butt of the spear into Batman's side, which, like the glass shard through Batman's hand, conjures up images of the Crucifixion, specifically of Longinus thrusting his lance through Christ's side. With a hole in his hand and a gash in his side, Batman requires only a wound to his foot to complete the set of stigmata. These nine pages, dark and violent and streaked with blood as the small, black figure of Batman combats the monstrous shape of Killer Croc, add another facet to the Messianic image of Batman. Indeed, the battle conjures up images of Revelation 12:

> And there was war in heaven: Michael and his angels fought against the dragon; and the dragon fought and his angels, And prevailed not; neither was their place found any more in heaven. And the great dragon was cast out, that old

serpent, called the Devil, and Satan, which deceiveth the whole world: he was cast out into the earth, and his angels were cast out with him.[12]

It is true that Batman is filling the role of Michael here and not of Christ, but it is perhaps worth noting that certain sects of Christianity (such as the Jehovah's Witnesses) believe the two to be one and the same. Regardless, Batman is once again playing the part of the redeemer, the defender of mankind, by doing battle with and quite literally casting to the earth the dragon portrayed by Killer Croc, whose very appearance has a certain dragon-like quality to it. Whether he is the archangel or the Messiah, Batman is the champion of goodness and sanity, protecting the world from evil and madness.

The most overt comparison between the Dark Knight and the Son of God is during Batman's encounter with Dr. Cavendish. Cavendish, who is revealed to be just as mad and murderous as any of his patients, believes Batman to be an incarnation of the Bat, the sinister apparition that drove Elizabeth Arkham mad and haunted her son until his dying day. When Cavendish insists that Batman is indeed the malevolent Bat, Batman merely bows his head and weakly says, "I ... I'm just a man" while a picture of Jesus hangs prominently behind him, inviting the comparison to be made.[13] It transforms Batman's simple statement, forcing the reader to look at the Dark Knight's insistence on his own humanity as something more than merely a denial of his identity as the Bat. With Christ's face staring from the background, this scene, like Batman's battle with Croc, becomes a re-enactment of a passage from the New Testament. When Jesus is arrested and brought before the high priest, the latter commands that Jesus confess to being the Son of God. Jesus responds by saying, "Thou hast said: nevertheless I say unto you, Hereafter shall ye see the Son of man sitting on the right hand of power."[14] Though he undeniably is something more, Jesus denies it, insisting that such an assertion is purely the invention of the high priest. He is not the Son of God, but rather the Son of Man, i.e. mortal. Batman's denial of being the supernatural Bat and insistence on his own humanity is a direct parallel to the scene depicted in Matthew 26. This parallel, though essential for Batman's function within the context of *Arkham Asylum*, can be extended beyond the narrative. Since Christianity teaches that Christ is the human incarnation of God, he acts as a bridge between the mortal and the divine, encompassing both while not wholly being either. Batman likewise bridges the gap between man and superman. He is undeniably mortal, but his abilities allow him to stand on equal footing with superhumans like Wonder Woman and Superman.

In addition to these Biblical re-enactments and the visual cues present, *Arkham Asylum*'s climax, in which Batman takes an axe and hacks a door to pieces, serves as a strong parallel to a significant (albeit non-canonical) act of Jesus: the Harrowing of Hell. Catholic teaching asserts that during the three days between the Crucifixion and the Resurrection, Jesus descended into Hell, confronted the Devil, tore down the gates of the infernal city and released the righteous souls that had been unfairly imprisoned within. Since medieval Christian dogma maintained that no souls could have entered Heaven before Christ's sacrifice, it was necessary for Jesus to harrow Hell, to set free "the shade of our first parent," along with the souls of Noah, Moses, Abraham, and many other prominent figures of the Old Testament.[15] Batman once again is figurative of Christ, descending into the Hell that is Arkham to battle the demons of insanity. Several characters are liberated from the walls of the asylum, but Batman's most significant act of liberation occurs in the last actions of the narrative. He returns Two-Face's trademark defaced coin, the means by which the latter makes all of his decisions. The tarot forgotten, the broken and uncertain Harvey Dent "straightens up, loses all the slackness of indecision, becomes himself again, made whole by the holy coin."[16] Two-Face commands the room in a heartbeat, declaring that Batman's fate will be decided by chance. If the coin lands with the scarred face up, Batman dies. Two-Face flips the coin, and no one questions his authority when he announces that Batman will go free. As the Joker escorts Batman from Arkham, Two-Face smiles at the coin, which McKean's illustration shows has landed scarred-side up.[17] Batman has not only freed Two-Face from the crippling uncertainty imposed upon him by Dr. Adams's tarot cards, but, for at least one moment, Two-Face has been freed even from his slavery to the coin. Batman has released Two-Face's soul from torment, and is rewarded with free passage through the gates of Hell.

Arkham Asylum, hence, serves as a resurrection of Batman's character. Morrison uses the madness of Arkham to break down Batman psychologically, and by his passage through Hell the borderline psychotic of the 1980s is reborn as a "super-confident zen warrior"[18] for the new decade. This rebirth is only the start of a course that Morrison sets Batman on. Throughout his subsequent work on Batman, Grant Morrison acknowledges the dual nature that he establishes in *Arkham Asylum*, and struggles to find balance between Batman's competent, rational side (the World's Greatest Detective) and his darker, more vengeful side (the Dark Knight). In his struggle for balance, Batman is forced to undergo symbolic deaths when the Dark Knight threatens to consume him, only to resurrect himself as the World's Greatest Detective.

The Many Struggles of the Batman

Nowhere is the capability of the World's Greatest Detective more apparent than in Morrison's 1990s work on *JLA*. Its "New World Order" story arc features the arrival of a group of alien superheroes calling themselves the Hyperclan. Within days, the Hyperclan earns the love and adoration of the entire world and turns the populace against the Justice League. When the League attempts to retaliate, the Hyperclan disables and captures them all, with the exception of Batman, who is left for dead in the flaming wreckage of the Batwing. While his comrades-in-arms are helpless captives, Batman deduces that the Hyperclan are, in reality, White Martians, and undertakes to destroy them.[19]

Despite their repeated insistence that Batman has no super powers, the White Martians are helpless as he dismantles them one by one. Protex, their leader, furiously reminds his comrades that Batman is "only one man,"[20] and yet that one man proves himself more capable than the superhumans that comprise the rest of the Justice League.

There could be no greater contrast to *Arkham Asylum*, where Batman became a haunted and nervous wreck after being subjected to the most basic psychological evaluation, than in *JLA*'s "Rock of Ages" story.[21] In an alternate future where Darkseid reigns, Batman is captured by master torturer, Desaad. After "eight years ... four of them in Desaad's psychofuge, experiencing all the physical and emotional pain of his victims,"[22] Batman triumphs in the battle of wills. Like St. Sixtus refusing, under torture, to renounce God and give up the location of the emperor's treasure,[23] Batman proves himself stronger than the most sadistic physical and psychological machinations of Apokolips's god of torture, and quietly assumes Desaad's mantle without Darkseid noticing. This shows a competence and capability unseen in and impossible for the unsure and half-mad Batman of *Arkham Asylum*.

However, the stability that Morrison gives the Caped Crusader does not last. Just as the pre–1980s Batman gave way to the violent Dark Knight of *The Killing Joke* (1988) and *The Dark Knight Returns* (1986), so does *JLA*'s World's Greatest Detective feel his darker side creeping back into play.

During the course of the "Batman and Son" storyline (2006–07), Bruce Wayne, though still very much playing the part of World's Greatest Detective, is beginning to lose himself in the cowl. "I thought I saw Killer Croc," he confesses to Alfred, "It's ... it's just a green raincoat."[24] Though Alfred waves this observation away with a joke ("I had a rather formidable nun down as the Penguin, sir"), it is clear that the pressures of being Batman are beginning to wear Bruce Wayne thin. When the famous international playboy is preparing for a party, Alfred is quick to point out the flaws in his bearing. Bruce is too tense, too defensive, and his voice bears traces of the Caped Crusader's menacing growl. "I have to learn to be myself?" Bruce cries, "This is insane."[25] Insane is the very word for it, as readers familiar with *Arkham Asylum* are aware of the consequences when Batman allows himself to slip too far into the Dark Knight persona.

The so-called "Three Ghosts of Batman" story likewise provides "cautionary tales, visions of what [Batman] might have become in other lives."[26] Though they manifest themselves as actual foes of the Caped Crusader, the ghosts function as spectral warnings of what Bruce Wayne might become if he ever strays too far from his core principles: a gun-toting murderer, a hulking brute, and a merciless destroyer. The ghosts (and the third one most of all) remain in the back of Batman's mind, haunting him.

The events of "The Black Glove" storyline (2007–8) further develop on Batman's encroaching insanity. The narrative is punctuated by mentions of Batman's training in Nanda Parbat, when he mastered Thögal, a meditative technique intended to simulate the sensation of dying. This instances Morrison's tendency toward heavy-handedness at work again, foreshadowing the inevitable death that looms in Batman's future. By repeatedly mentioning Thögal, Morrison makes it plain that Batman already has a thorough understanding of his own death. Like Odin, who "hung nine days and nights from the sacred tree Yggdrasil, gazing down into the immeasurable depths of Nifl-heim"[27] to gain knowledge of runes and the workings of the universe, Batman has knowledge of the cycle of life and death and no longer has fear of it. This adds to the superhuman persona that the Caped Crusader possesses. However, as is a central theme in the tales of Odin, knowledge comes at the cost of personal sacrifice. The Allfather deprived himself of happiness to learn the magic of runes, and the World's Greatest Detective gave up a piece of his sanity to learn the sensations of death, because "you don't just undergo a death and rebirth experience without consequences."[28]

It is in the final issue of the story arc, when Bruce and Jezebel are the targets of a kidnapping, that the World's Greatest Detective is pushed nearest to his breaking point. Even without his cape, he immediately assumes the persona of the Dark Knight, lurking in the shadows and taking out his would-be captors.[29] When a lightning bolt flashes through the sky, it illuminates a snarling, bestial figure that could be seen as an echo of the

Second Ghost, or even a reincarnation of the "violent, nightmare figure" of *Arkham Asylum*.

"When did I die?" is the repeated line during Batman's battle with the Third Ghost.[30] Though Batman does physically die for four minutes during his confrontation with the Third Ghost, his symbolic death is not yet at hand, inevitable though it be. As the title of *Batman* #669 proclaims, "The Dark Knight Must Die," especially if Batman is ever to return to being the World's Greatest Detective.

Just as in *Arkham Asylum*, the Dark Knight's death comes when Batman is as close to the precipice of madness as possible, this time in the story arc aptly named "Batman R.I.P." (2008). After his encounter with the Third Ghost, the Caped Crusader begins to see foes in every shadow. "This is how the Black Glove would work, isn't it?" Bruce wonders aloud to Jezebel Jet. "Wouldn't he try to isolate me, make me question my mission? Wouldn't he even use you as a weapon? Make you doubt me?"[31] His apparent paranoia proves justified, as mere moments later Jezebel herself utters the trigger word—Zur-En-Arrh—that causes Batman to collapse. "The Dark Knight is dead,"[32] Doctor Hurt declares with triumph, and indeed this is the case. The Batman that, over the course of the stories of "Batman and Son" and "The Black Glove," had drifted increasingly closer to his darker and more violent persona is dead. Unfortunately for Doctor Hurt, in the process of psychologically disabling Batman he unwittingly awakens the backup identity that Bruce Wayne implanted in his own subconscious, namely, the Batman of Zur-En-Arrh, a figure from the Batman comics of the 1950s that might have been forgotten had Grant Morrison not resurrected and transformed him into a part of "the story of what [Batman's] life might do to a man's mind."[33]

While the Batman of Zur-En-Arrh serves as a rebirth for the Caped Crusader, it is simultaneously the epitome of his symbolic death by showing just how far Batman can fall into himself. The Batman of Zur-En-Arrh is "what you get when you take Bruce out of the equation,"[34] which is an appropriate appraisal, given that the 1950s Batman of Zur-En-Arrh was an alien named Tlano whose only connection to the original Batman was that Tlano strove to imitate him.[35] This "real world"[36] version of the Batman of Zur-En-Arrh is a flamboyantly colored demon who does not hesitate to break a few heads with a baseball bat or a pipe. "You're looking at what's left of Batman," Doctor Hurt tells the other members of the Black Glove, "the last rags and tatters."[37] Doctor Hurt believes that he has broken Batman into a shell of his former self, when in fact he has done just the opposite. He has called this demon by name from the deepest parts of

Batman's psyche, a figure that knows next to nothing about his identity as Bruce Wayne and consequently has none of the hesitation or reasoning of his alter ego. The Batman of Zur-En-Arrh has only Bat-Mite to guide him, "the last fading echo of the voice of reason," and even that is forced to leave him when he crosses the threshold of Arkham.[38]

This part of "Batman R.I.P." is strongly reminiscent of *Arkham Asylum*, where a violent and psychotic Batman is forced into the confines of the insane asylum, leaving reason at the door, to do battle with his nemesis and rescue those imprisoned within. As mentioned earlier, the Harrowing of Hell parallel breaks down Batman's psyche, after which he is able to emerge confident and ready to face Gotham as the World's Greatest Detective reborn. Here, he descends again into Arkham, this time "dressed like a clown."[39] Batman's garish Zur-En-Arrh costume rivals any motley the Joker has ever worn, further denoting how close he is to losing all sanity and becoming more like the Clown Prince of Crime than ever before.

This is his rebirth, fully realized when the Black Glove swaps out his extravagant Zur-En-Arrh garb for the traditional black and grey cowl and buries him on the grounds of Arkham. Just as in *Arkham Asylum*, the Elizabeth Arkham Asylum for the Criminally Insane serves as the site of Batman's death and resurrection. The Caped Crusader literally rises from the grave here, attired once more in his iconic costume and ready to reprise his role as the World's Greatest Detective.

Unfortunately, with the apocalyptic *Final Crisis* on the horizon, Morrison cannot allow this period of hyper-competence to persist for very long. He must make Batman as broken and fragile as possible in order for him to play his part in the imminent war with Darkseid.

Batman Kills

In order to combat the dark New God of Apokolips, the entity that is perhaps the ultimate evil of the DC Universe (as explored by Schedel Luitjen in the previous chapter of this volume), Batman must be brought closer to the edge of the gulf of madness than ever before. Just when he is close to uncovering Darkseid's plot, the World's Greatest Detective is abducted by Darkseid's minions, Mokkari and Simyan, who imprison him and attempt to use his psyche to create an army of Batmen loyal to Darkseid. Their plan is to keep him powerless by forcing him to re-experience the most painful memories of his life, along with a few "what if" scenarios, such as Alfred's death or Thomas and Martha Wayne's survival. Like the White Martians in *JLA*'s "New World Order" or Desaad in *JLA*'s "Rock of Ages," Mokkari and Simyan underestimate the almost superhuman prowess of the mortal Batman. When Batman begins to fight against the psychological control of Mokkari's Lump, the half-formed clones deteriorate immediately. "The psycho-merge is killing these weaklings!" Mokkari cries in horror as his creations claw their own faces off, "How does Batman process this degree of stress?"[40] The meta-textual implications of this line are apparent, as this is a question that readers too have been asking for years. In *Supergods*, Morrison provides a succinct answer to Mokkari and anyone else who wishes to delve into the "why?" of Batman and superheroes in general: "the answer is obvious even to the smallest child: because it's not real."[41] Readers accept that superheroes (and Batman in particular) are better, faster, and stronger than mere mortals. Batman can process such an extreme degree of stress because he is Batman. It is what the readers expect from him.

The events of "Last Rites" suggest that even at his most competent and confident, Batman has not forgotten his past. The World's Greatest Detective still has his demons, and it is only when he is competent and rational that he is able to repress them. Even Morrison's hyper-confident Zen warrior is perpetually a hair's breadth from insanity.

The torture that Batman endures during "Last Rites" speeds up the "life" part of the cycle, preparing him for the final showdown with Darkseid at the climax of *Final Crisis*. Batman breaks free from Mokkari and Simyan and makes his way to Darkseid's throne room, wielding the same bullet that the dark god used to kill Orion. "I made a very solemn vow about firearms. But for you, I'm making a once-in-a-lifetime exception," Batman growls before shooting and mortally wounding the ruler of Apokolips.[42] Moments afterwards, the Caped Crusader is struck by Darkseid's Omega Sanction and apparently dies, making his once-in-a-lifetime exception his final act, at least in this life.

By breaking his cardinal rule, Batman has sacrificed a part of himself. In *Arkham Asylum* and "Batman R.I.P." Morrison portrayed the fearsome Dark Knight persona of Batman, a violent, bestial, and psychologically unhinged figure. Still, as close as Batman came to his breaking point, there was never an instance where he crossed it before now. Batman never kills, and, perhaps more importantly, "Batman doesn't use a gun."[43] By going against the fundamental tenet of his own code, Batman condemns himself to another symbolic death. A Batman that uses a gun cannot be allowed to exist.

Batman Forever

The cyclical nature of *Batman: The Return of Bruce Wayne* (2010) serves as a perfect embodiment of Morrison's struggle with Batman. The Omega Sanction causes the Caped Crusader to leap through history with no memory of his life as Bruce Wayne or his identity as Batman. Even without this knowledge, he still gravitates toward the symbol, taking a giant bat corpse from Vandal Savage in a prehistoric world and using it as a mantle in the raid on Savage's tribe. This inspires another tribe to adopt the name of "Bat-People." They take up residence in caves near what will become Gotham city, and incorporate bat imagery into almost every aspect of their lives, all the while worshipping the frayed and decaying cowl that Bruce Wayne brought with him to the dawn of history.

The circle is made complete in the final issue, when the hunter-killer virus that pursues Batman though time is contained in a time sphere and sent rocketing back to prehistory, where it transforms into a colossal bat and attacks Vandal Savage. Savage, of course, slays the bat and displays its corpse as a trophy, and the cycle repeats itself into infinity. Despite (and indeed because of) Darkseid's efforts to destroy him, Batman is visible throughout the history of the universe, a mythical figure that even time itself cannot wear away. The New God of death has made Batman immortal.

The Return of Bruce Wayne is Batman's "final adventure... and his new beginning," to quote the archivist at the end of time.[44] In this narrative, Morrison establishes Batman as a superhuman figure, a mythic hero that is ever-present and woven into the history of Gotham itself. Due in no small part to Batman's actions in the past, Wayne Manor:

> [...] sits on top of an immense maze of caves that's been associated with buried treasure and all kinds of romantic and deadly characters. Jeremy Coe, the frontiersman, the Black Pirate, the Hellerite sect and even the Bat-People.[45]

It even attracts the attention of the Black Glove for their worship of Barbatos, a demonic bat figure described as "the hunter, the finder of great treasure,"[46] which could refer to either Batman himself or the hunter-killer that stalks him. Regardless, Batman has made himself a permanent part of Gotham, ensuring that his legacy stretches from the dawn of the universe to the end of time (the archivists even sport small bat-like ears). When Doctor Hunter reveals that the archivists are "rebooting the universe... using the black hole to loop the timeline's end through its beginning,"[47] Batman's eternal presence is solidified. The cycle will always repeat.

However, *Batman, Incorporated* (2010–13) sees a new development for the Caped Crusader. Bruce Wayne publically endorses Batman, and announces his plans to financially back the fight against crime and turn the individual endeavors of the World's Greatest Detective into a global effort and enterprise. Batman proceeds to travel the world, tracking down crime fighters and recruiting them, turning them into the Batmen of their respective locales.

"What happened while you were away?" Selina Kyle a.k.a. Catwoman asks Bruce Wayne, "You decided one Batman wasn't enough?" To which Bruce replies, "I caught a glimpse of the big picture."[48] Bruce's sojourn through time has changed him and his perspective on Batman. Indeed, the last pages of *The Return of Bruce Wayne* present Batman's revelation:

> The gunshots left me alone. For years I was alone in the echoing dark of that well. But something else defined the exact moment Batman was born. The first truth of Batman ... the saving grace. I was never alone. I had help.[49]

Though he has always thought of himself as a solitary hunter, Bruce realizes that, through everything, there has always been someone willing to lend a hand, whether it be the Justice League, Robin, Nightwing, or even Alfred. After the Omega Sanction presents him with the daunting expanse of time itself, Bruce Wayne acknowledges his own shortcomings as a single man. For too long has he stretched himself too thin, trying to do the work of an army by himself, and perpetually hovering near insanity as a result. In order to correct that, he begins to recruit an actual army. "We're building a ghost," he declares, "a bogeyman too big to be clearly seen. Its edges indistinct, its full extent and purpose uncertain. A rumor. A terror made of shadows and flapping wings."[50] He establishes a network of Batmen that stretches to all the corners of the world. "Criminals used to be afraid because they didn't know where Batman was. Things are different now. Thanks to Batman Incorporated, I can tell you exactly where Batman is. Batman is everywhere."[51]

The hope, then, is that *Batman, Incorporated* has broken the cycle. Morrison presents this incarnation or iteration of Bruce Wayne not only as a man in full possession of his mental faculties, but as a man who acknowledges his own shortcomings. He is, after all, only a man, and for too long he has been trying to police the world on his own. Now that Bruce has acknowledged that Batman has always had help, and is furthermore encouraging and legitimizing said help, the cycle may be broken. This may be the balance between World's Greatest Detective and Dark Knight that Morrison has sought for over twenty years since *Arkham Asylum*. However, even Batman Incorporated cannot totally be free of the Dark Knight.

It would seem logical and even expected that Damian Wayne's murder, at the hands of the Heretic, an agent of Talia al Ghul and her global crime network, Leviathan, would overwhelm Batman with grief and cause him to slip into his Dark Knight persona. Batman's initial retaliation against the Heretic for Damian's death is what one would expect from a bereaved father: it is a brutal, bloody fistfight that nearly ends in the Caped Crusader's demise. Brute force will not prevail against the Heretic, who claims to be Batman, but "bigger. Faster. Younger. Stronger."[52] Though Batman makes his second assault on Wayne Tower snarling, red-eyed, and surrounded by a flock of bats, it is not the frenzied assault of a desperate and broken man. Criminals are, after all, "a superstitious, cowardly lot,"[53] and the howling Batman and his shrieking cloud of bats serve as theatrics to mask a carefully planned assault involving a powerful exoskeleton, an antidote to the Man-Bat serum, and, most importantly, the Suit of Sorrows.

The Suit of Sorrows, as the legend goes, "will destroy anyone who is not pure."[54] Though it bestows strength and agility and "protects its wearer from all harm,"[55] it also awakens a primal bloodlust that, if unchecked, will drive the wearer to genocidal rage. By employing the Suit of Sorrows, Batman, who for the entire story arc of *Batman, Incorporated* has been the World's Greatest Detective, willingly submits to the Dark Knight part of himself. He channels his grief for Damian's death into the power of the suit and uses it to defeat the Heretic. Still, when he is face-to-face with his son's killer, Batman relents. The fire fades from his eyes, he drops the broken Heretic, and announces to Nightwing and Knight that "it's over."[56] Even though he wears the Suit of Sorrows, and his enemy lies broken before him, Batman does not kill. This is the ultimate victory in the World's Greatest Detective/Dark Knight battle. Just as "Last Rites" hints that even the competent Batman is a hair's breadth from madness, the climax of *Batman, Incorporated* shows that even when driven onward by grief and the maddening bloodlust of the Suit of Sorrows, Batman can conquer the violent instincts of the Dark Knight.

In Morrison's final issue of *Batman, Incorporated*, Bruce Wayne tells Jim Gordon, "Batman died, Jim. That's what I heard."[57] Though the Dark Knight's appearance in *Batman, Incorporated* was brief, Bruce acknowledges that it still serves as Batman's symbolic death. When he returns to the Batcave and dons the cowl again, the reader can be sure that Gotham will once more be under the protective gaze of the World's Greatest Detective.

In conclusion, this perpetual cycle of life and death in Morrison's representations of Batman is what makes him a truly significant figure. The Caped Crusader is not a shining sun god like Superman. Batman is human, and like all humans he occasionally finds himself drawn into the darker parts of his own psyche, down into the infernal depths that hold the Joker, Two-Face, Clayface, and almost all of his most prominent adversaries. Yet, despite this, Gotham and the world can be sure that he will fight back against the madness, against the demons that plague him, so as to return to the light. He has done so for decades in the name of protecting his fellow men from burglars, terrorists, aliens, dark gods, and everything in between, and there is no doubt that he will continue to do so. As Jim Gordon reflects, "Batman always comes back, bigger and better, shiny and new. Batman never dies. It never ends. It probably never will."[58] In the end, Morrison makes it explicit that the cycle, like the universe in *The Return of Bruce Wayne*, like Talia's Oroboro in the final chapter of *Batman, Incorporated*, will continue itself into infinity.

Notes

1. Grant Morrison and Dave McKean, *Arkham Asylum: A Serious House on Serious Earth: 15th Anniversary Edition* (New York: DC Comics, 2004), 167.
2. Grant Morrison, *Supergods: What Masked Vigilantes, Miraculous Mutants, and A Sun God From Smallville Can Teach Us About Being Human* (New York: Spiegel & Grau, 2011), 414.
3. Sir James George Frazer, *The Golden Bough*, One Volume Abridged ed. (New York: MacMillan, 1963), 448.
4. S. Radhakrishnan, trans., *The Bhagavadgita* (New Delhi: HarperCollins, 1993), 108.
5. Huston Smith, *The Religions of Man* (New York: Harper & Row, 1986), 275.
6. Morrison, *Supergods*, 7.
7. Morrison and McKean, *Arkham Asylum*, 121.
8. Ibid., 10.
9. Ibid., 154
10. Will Brooker, *Batman Unmasked* (London: Continuum, 2000), 272.
11. Morrison and McKean, *Arkham Asylum*, 148.
12. Rev. 12:7–9 (King James Version).
13. Morrison and McKean, *Arkham Asylum*, 85.
14. Matt. 26:63–64 (KJV).
15. Dante Alighieri, *Inferno*, trans. Henry F. Cary (New York: P. F. Collier & Son, 1969), 18.
16. Morrison and McKean, *Arkham Asylum*, 180.
17. Ibid., 101.
18. Ibid., 182.
19. See Grant Morrison and Howard Porter, *JLA* #1–4 (New York: DC Comics, 1997).
20. Morrison and Porter, *JLA* #3, 21.
21. See Grant Morrison and Howard Porter, *JLA* #10–15 (New York: DC Comics, 1997–1998).
22. Morrison and Porter, *JLA* #13, 18.
23. Jacobus de Voragine, *The Golden Legend*, trans. Granger Ryan and Helmut Ripperger (Salem: Ayer Company, 1991), 439.

24. Grant Morrison and Andy Kubert, *Batman* #655 (New York: DC Comics, 2006), 14.
25. Ibid., 20.
26. Grant Morrison and Andy Kubert, *Batman* #665 (New York: DC Comics, 2007), 8.
27. H. A. Guerber, *Myths of the Norsemen* (New York: Dover, 1992), 33–34.
28. Grant Morrison and Ryan Benjamin, *Batman* #675 (New York: DC Comics, 2008), 12
29. Ibid., 18–19.
30. See Grant Morrison and Tony Daniel, *Batman* #673 (New York: DC Comics, 2008).
31. Grant Morrison and Tony Daniel, *Batman* #677 (New York: DC Comics, 2008), 15.
32. Grant Morrison and Tony Daniel, *Batman* #678 (New York: DC Comics, 2008), 19.
33. Grant Morrison, "Introduction," in Bill Finger *et al.*, *The Black Casebook* (New York: DC Comics, 2009), 4.
34. Grant Morrison and Tony Daniel, *Batman* #679 (New York: DC Comics, 2008), 19.
35. France Herron and Dick Sprang, *Batman* #113, in Finger *et al.*, *The Black Casebook*, 82–83.
36. Grant Morrison, "Introduction," in Finger *et al.*, *The Black Casebook*, 3.
37. Grant Morrison and Tony Daniel, *Batman* #680 (New York: DC Comics, 2008), 10.
38. Ibid., 9.
39. Ibid., 14.
40. Grant Morrison and Lee Garbett, *Batman* #683 (New York: DC Comics, 2008), 18.
41. Morrison, *Supergods*, 56.
42. Grant Morrison *et al.*, *Final Crisis* #6 (New York: DC Comics, 2009), 26.
43. Morrison and Daniel, *Batman* #680, 16.
44. Grant Morrison and Lee Garbett, *The Return of Bruce Wayne* #6 (New York: DC Comics, 2010), 5.
45. Grant Morrison and Ryan Sook, *The Return of Bruce Wayne* #5 (New York: DC Comics, 2010), 17.
46. Ibid., 29.
47. Morrison and Garbett, *The Return of Bruce Wayne* #6, 13.
48. Grant Morrison and Yanick Paquette, *Batman, Incorporated* (1) #1 (2011), 13.
49. Morrison and Garbett, *The Return of Bruce Wayne* #6, 31.
50. Grant Morrison and Chris Burnham, *Batman, Incorporated* (1) #6 (New York: DC Comics, 2011), 16.
51. Ibid., 3–4.
52. Grant Morrison and Chris Burnham, *Batman, Incorporated* (2) #9 (New York: DC Comics, 2013), 14.
53. Grant Morrison and Chris Burnham, *Batman, Incorporated* (2) #10 (New York: DC Comics, 2013), 18.
54. Peter Milligan and Dustin Nguyen, *Detective Comics* #842 (New York: DC Comics, 2008), 1.
55. Morrison and Burnham, *Batman, Incorporated* (2) #10, 3.
56. Grant Morrison and Chris Burnham, *Batman, Incorporated* (2) #12 (New York: DC Comics, 2013), 17.
57. Grant Morrison and Chris Burnham, *Batman, Incorporated* (2), #13 (New York: DC Comics, 2013), 18.
58. Ibid., 22.

Fallout Boys

Paranoia, Power and Control in Morrison's Cold War Superheroes

MUIREANN O'SULLIVAN

A shadow of paranoia and suspicion falls over much of Grant Morrison's literary landscape, yet it is the internalization and consequent manifestations of this shadow, as expressed through Morrison's versions of the superhero, which reveal most about the boundaries that shape his narratives.

Morrison himself is a product of the Cold War era, and so his work emerges following a period of aggravated international tension, exacerbated by the unrelenting threat of nuclear destruction during the author's formative years. As the young Morrison was exposed to a culture of conspiracy, his later versions of the superhero are not created out of a mere desire to entertain, but instead out of necessity, in response to an unyielding atmosphere of oppression where rebellion was driven underground. As the Cold War was a globally present concern, this inertia imposed by equally paralyzed authority resulted in a torrent of escapist literature.[1] Most pertinent, however, is the resulting satirical and reactionary literature that emerges specifically within British popular media as a consequence of this paranoid atmosphere.

The Cold War period in Britain saw "the emergence of 'the underground' and 'counter-culture'"[2] movement generated in direct response to ineffectual government attention towards individual concerns. Stuart Ward notes the trend of growing generational tension in this period. "From the late 1950s, changing tastes in popular British comedy had begun to generate an unprecedented appetite for mockery and ridicule of the manners, pretentions and pomposity of Britain's ruling elite—the so-called British 'establishment.'"[3] A more subtle movement known as the Satire Boom grew from this need to undermine authority in all its forms, yet contrary to this surreptitious method of undermining authority, Morrison's generation of writers are seen to be a particularly volatile offshoot of this movement, as they are part of a counter-cultural revolution reacting against stagnation in the Cold War era and the perceived values of the generation before. These are individuals "for whom the Fifties were a 'nightmare decade' of Cold War paranoia and sinister power without moral legitimacy—[who] posed a more serious challenge to the *status quo*."[4] It is my argument, then, that Morrison's idea of the superhero is directly influenced by this rebellious environment, and he, along with contemporaries such as Alan Moore and Neil Gaiman who heralded a new and more direct movement predicated by the post–Second World War Satire Boom, are combining this distinctly British phenomenon of subtle pre–50s downbeat satire with his own generation's brand of anti–Cold War volatility designed to undermine the establishment. Due to Morrison's immediate exposure to Cold War paranoia as part of his activist upbringing, much of the restraint often synonymous with this movement is disregarded in favor of a more direct style than that of previous writers, yet there are also layers of subtlety within his texts which add complexity to his work.

Timothy Callahan emphasizes the influence of Morrison's historical context, making itself apparent in the apocalyptic dread which permeates the author's work: "He grew up during the height of the Cold War and his parents were activists, and so the specter of the bomb was something that loomed large over his life and his creative career."[5] As a result, Morrison uses the comics form to articulate this sense of impending destruction, in order to create a more emotionally tangible forum in which to engage with and interrogate these fears. He illustrates for his readers the harsh reality of his formative years, saying:

> I just lived daily with the fact that my parents were fighting against "the Bomb." The minute that this thing happened we would be obliterated forever, and for me the big thing was discovering superhero comics, because suddenly in superhero comics here were people who could stop the bomb. You know, Superman could take an atom bomb hit on the chest and just smile and shake it off.[6]

Where Morrison's work diverges from his aforementioned contemporaries is primarily in his style of characterization; while Morrison also deals with classically British superheroes, he frequently focuses on firmly established American icons that are rarely exemplary of the quintessential British elements which set apart the work of Alan Moore and Neil Gaiman. Marc Singer observes:

> From his beginnings in the "ground level" comics of the 1970s to his most recent work for Vertigo, an imprint of industry giant DC Comics, Morrison has always sought to synthesize the various cultures of contemporary Anglo-

phone comics, alternating between corporate-owned superhero titles and creator-owned work in other genres.[7]

Consequently, he often imposes perceived British sensibilities on these icons, focusing on Batman's repression and imbuing him with traits not unlike British cultural touchstone James Bond. Morrison focuses on Bruce Wayne's almost neo-colonial endeavors with his single-handed privatization of international espionage in works such as *Batman, Incorporated*, (2011–13) yet also succeeds in delving into Wayne's fears as he attempts to consolidate his legacy as Batman. As a peak-human as opposed to a super-powered hero, Batman acts as an analogue for the interrogation of more individualistic social concerns, drawing attention to internalized reactions to external authority, a theme explored heavily in *Arkham Asylum: A Serious House on Serious Earth* (1989), which is occupied with the exploration of Batman's psyche. Morrison also deals with a wider scope of societal oppression in his treatment of Superman, and alludes to some of the more sinister machinations of the authoritarian Cold War British government with regard to nuclear threat, and the corrupt nature of authority figures such as Lex Luthor. As a result, when Morrison deals with Superman, he draws attention to his position as a patriarchal figure, for he is, in many ways, the ultimate authority, occupying a space between solar deity and embodying the pinnacle of human aspiration. Through these heroes, Morrison fosters a dialectic between the chaos of the Cold War era and the struggle to impose order in both the personal and social spheres, where Batman is used to address the internal conflict of the individual, and Superman to interrogate external versions of authority. In Morrison's later work, *Batman, Incorporated*, Batman attempts to emulate the omnipresence of Superman by franchising his own image, but finds that his human nature is an impediment to success, illustrating that Morrison espouses liberty without overly dominant ideals, even from a trusted, well-known authority figure. As Singer succinctly puts it, Morrison's works "promote political, economic, and artistic autonomy, while recognizing the consequences of unbridled individualism."[8]

He draws attention to the societal and, on occasion, inter-dimensional authoritarian structures which his narratives react against, and by this interaction they are consequently shaped. This revolution-inciting backdrop in turn influences the creation of Morrison's heroes, and this is apparent in Morrison's generation of original superheroes, as in his psychedelic magnum opus *The Invisibles* (1994–2000), which focuses on a collective of anarchistic vigilantes where "The only rule of the organization is disobedience."[9] In this chapter, I will reflect on Morrison's methods of questioning authoritarian strictures present in reality, with a particular focus on *All-Star Superman* (2005–8), *Arkham Asylum: A Serious House on Serious Earth*, and *Batman, Incorporated*. I will explore the varying forms of character depiction and moral alignment, while focusing on the actions of established, publisher-owned characters. Where Grant Morrison effectively generates his own super-powered entities to carry out this agenda, his re-imaginings of established cultural icons such as Batman reveal his dissatisfaction with the placement of absolute trust in authority. In this way, Morrison creates morally ambiguous narratives which reflect the precarious position of the vigilante hero, with the psychological instability of these heroes taking center-stage in many of his works. This is particularly palpable in *Arkham Asylum: A Serious House On Serious Earth*. He places emphasis on the volatile, unpredictable facets of individuals, who act impulsively in response to chaotic circumstances. These instances are symptomatic of a more subversive cultural movement, which while unfolding in a fantastical universe, has its genesis in Morrison's formative experiences of growing up against the uncertain backdrop of Cold War Britain. Morrison's rejection of convention, together with his evocation of authority, is always tinged by Cold War contexts and tropes, as evidenced by his exploration of childhood experiences in the documentary film *Talking with Gods* (2010).

In *Talking with Gods*, Morrison reveals that his childhood was marked by the constant threat of nuclear fallout. He recalls several occasions on which he aided his father in infiltrating military bases, journeys which would inform the main settings of *All-Star Superman*:

> My dad would go in, and he'd kick balls over fences and ... we'd pretend that his son was looking for his ball while he would take photographs of these underground nuclear bases.... They had things like they'd everyone's coffin, cardboard coffins piled up on the wall, and it was the idea that when the nuclear war came all the civil servants would have four minutes to rush to these hidden shelters, and from there they would sharpen their pencils and start the world up again—you know, it was insane.[10]

As Superman represents a safeguard against Morrison's fears of nuclear war, it is intriguing that an almost exact replica of this scenario is created in *All-Star Superman*, where the members of Project Cadmus are preparing for a day when Superman will be needed to protect them again. These are the civil servants whom Morrison spoke of, and so it seems that his concerns about covert governmental machinations are still alive and well. It appears that Leo Quintum, director of P.R.O.J.E.C.T., has always had a contingency plan in mind, as his first act on learning of Superman's impending demise is to use one of his employees, Agatha, to read Superman's genetic code in order to replicate it later. "I dedicated P.R.O.J.E.C.T. resources toward building a new race of superhumans in case ... in case anything ever happened to you."[11] In *Supergods*, Morrison writes about how nuclear war appeared to be an inexorable future of his youth, and the language he uses to describe the threat is reminiscent of a description of a comic book villain: "And the Bomb, always the Bomb, a grim and looming, raincoated lodger, liable to go off at any minute, killing everybody and everything."[12] The Bomb becomes an anthropomorphized entity, and by imbuing the Bomb with these characteristics and providing it with its own identity, Morrison not only makes his previously insurmountable, incorporeal fear fallible, but also creates a mold for the identity of its opposing force. He inserts the Bomb into his comics on several occasions, most notably in *Flex Mentallo* (1996), a heavily autobiographical work, and much like the superheroes of his youth, his heroes often triumph over it:

> The superheroes laughed at the Atom Bomb. Superman could walk on the surface of the sun and barely register a tan. ... In the shadow of cosmic destroyers like Anti-Matter Man or Galactus, the all-powerful Bomb seemed provincial in scale. ... My own world felt better already. I was beginning to understand something that gave me power over my fears.[13]

As representative of this version of the Cold War superhero espoused by Morrison, Superman then embodies the crucial force for stability in a period in history where stability was impossible due to the constant threat of nuclear attack. Morrison's retelling of this character's story, which is so heavily steeped in Cold War tropes and imagery, is then an attempt to address the tensions of the Cold War through interrogating a version of recent history which still looms large in science fiction and the superhero genre today.

Reinventing Superman

Superman is a pivotal influence on Morrison's work, and his reinvention of the character in *All-Star Superman* is arguably the most comprehensive in comic book history. Indeed, Callahan calls *All-Star Superman* "[t]he definitive Superman story."[14] As Superman himself is emblematic of the superhero genre as a whole, he is imbued with an authoritative status, rendering him, in Morrison's words, "the daddy of them all."[15] The paternal implications of this title transform Superman into a hero who could undermine the institutionalized authority of villains, whether it is manifested through the ultimate corporate businessman, Lex Luthor, or the megalomaniacal military general, Zod. Superman is repeatedly pitted against these and other manifestations of authority, and so it is unsurprising that in the opening pages of *All-Star Superman*, the eponymous protagonist finds himself squaring up against Morrison's primary childhood fear: that of the personified Bomb which explicitly states its intentions as a product of industrialized authority: "I'm a genetically modified suicide bomb in human form. Death, Courtesy of Lex Luthor!"[16] As a consequence of this encounter, we find that Superman's cells are "super saturated with solar radiation. Bursting from within."[17] His sacrifice is not in vain however, and Kal-El's subsequent journey toward a higher plane of existence is demonstrated through conversation with Jor-El, during which he occupies the space between life and death: "Matter, energy: these things cannot be created or destroyed... nor can consciousness Kal El of El."[18] Perhaps the most pivotal aspect of this experience is Jor El's ultimatum for Superman. He tells Kal-El, "Your body is undergoing a mutation, a conversion to solar radio consciousness."[19] Within this experience, Superman has the option to remain stagnant in his current form, or he may strike forward and "face down evil one last time,"[20] and so Superman takes the initiative, taking a dynamic approach to save the world. Superman then returns to Earth to vanquish Solaris, the tyrant sun, and stop Luthor. This journey is not a mere trial of the hero, but is one towards metamorphosis for Superman, and enhances his mythology, and the belief of others in him, instead of bringing that belief to an end with his death.

Superman secures his god-like status through his seeming destruction and transcendence of material form, graduating from super-powered alien to modern deity. Morrison acknowledges that while Superman is not a physical reality, he is an eidetic or ideological reality, and so as an idea, he becomes even more powerful: "It's not that I needed Superman to be 'real,' I just needed him to be more real than the Idea of the Bomb that ravaged my dreams."[21] As a result, Superman's mythology expands with Morrison's treatment of it, enabling Superman to become even more powerful in the face of nuclear destruction—he is as permanent as the sun. There is an eternal, timeless quality to Superman, as he does not age, and is adaptable to whatever new challenges are relevant to each new generation of readers. In *Talking with Gods*, Morrison acknowledges that the mythology of Superman seems to be all-encompassing:

> What's really interesting is the fact that these long-running universes have a weight, a reality of their own, which is, you know, bigger than mine. I wasn't alive when Superman was having his first adventures, I'll be dead and he'll still

be having adventures, so there's a certain element of that continuum we've created which is much more real than the one we live in.[22]

As Superman is a fictional character and by definition an impossibility in the real world, by showing him working to repair the sun, an ever-present guardian of Earth, supporting all life on it, Morrison is bringing Superman into the sphere of reality, holding him responsible for the survival of humanity, and by consequence making him real enough and believable enough to continue to guard against Morrison's old boyhood fears surrounding the Cold War now that he is an adult. Where a child accepts Superman without question, the adult Morrison needs to qualify this hero's status within human belief, and so he reclassifies him as an irrefutable constant who is capable of repairing the very celestial body on which all of human life is hinged, and this insistence that Superman could be a part of reality is consolidated further through creating opportunities for integration with real world events, such as those alluded to through Superman's Earth Q experiment. In a nutshell, then, Morrison works to make Superman as real and relevant as possible by using reference points from our world in order to deal with his own feelings of paranoia, and also make the global nuclear threat fade into the realm of fiction.

An extreme attention to detail is therefore required to facilitate belief, and this is expressed in Frank Quitely's disquieting art style which is so different from Dave McKean's ethereal shadows and intangible nightmares in *Arkham Asylum*. Indeed, *All-Star Superman* stands in sharp contrast to Grant Morrison's other offerings, instead jarring the reader with its harsh visuals. The stark radioactive spectrum of color, courtesy of colorist Jamie Grant, which appears in the opening pages sets the scene for the end of days, for the end of the solar system, and creates the perfect platform for a post-apocalyptic scenario. This recalls a version of Superman that a younger Morrison would have experienced, when Superman possessed all the qualities of a hero who would be capable of vanquishing the nightmarish reality around him. Morrison recalls his earliest memories of this iteration of the superhero, and its influence on his writing: "Before it was a Bomb, the Bomb was an Idea. Superman, however, was a Faster, Stronger, Better Idea."[23] This is the very reason why Superman is abhorred by Luthor in *All-Star Superman*, as he diminishes everything which Luthor esteems to be the pinnacle of human accomplishment, manifested by the atom bomb. As the pursuit of nuclear power is a promethean gesture on the part of humanity in attempting to harness the power of the sun, Superman is a further abomination in Luthor's eyes, for he stands as the uncorrupted manifestation of this endeavor: he is the sun made man. Superman is therefore the perfect hero to intercede with authority because through his steadfast, uncompromising morality, and consequent representation as "clean" energy, he exposes the inherent flaws of nuclear power in equally flawed, human hands, and its resulting capacity for harm.

In the mid–1930s, due to the continued rejection by publishers of Superman, creators Jerry Siegel and Joe Shuster were forced to redesign their character as a hero instead of a megalomaniacal villain, and so Superman is shaped as much by the cultural expectations of his time as by their own hands,[24] and is very much the archetypal hero defined in response to the requirements of a generation. Siegel and Shuster's original incarnation of Superman was very different to the one which was to eke out a place in the *Zeitgeist* of this generation and subsequent ones, appearing more as an early draft for Luthor, and a far cry from the omnipotent boy scout favored by legions of fans. On their initial pitch, Siegel and Shuster were informed that their character lacked the appeal which could make him popular to the masses, and had to significantly alter the character in order to become successful. As Les Daniels writes, "[Siegel's] first Superman, Bill Dunn, would be a megalomaniac ... Jerry Siegel's first Superman story features an ugly, evil Superman who seems completely different from the later incarnation that is so well known today."[25]

As Superman is shaped specifically to overcome Cold War issues, he becomes the ultimate vehicle for the destruction of authority, and the destruction of weaponry employed by these authorities, such as Luthor's human bombs. Morrison writes, "Superman is so indefatigable a product of the human imagination, such a perfectly designed emblem of our highest, kindest, wisest, toughest selves, that my Idea of the Bomb had no defense against him."[26] This idea is echoed through other characters' impressions of Superman, and in the opening pages of *All-Star Superman*, the resounding message is one of absolute faith, further establishing Superman's supremacy as an authoritative figure. At the Daily Planet offices, Lois Lane reveals her unwavering belief in the last son of Krypton: "I always write the Superman headlines before they happen, Steve."[27] Equally, parallels are drawn between Kal-El and Christ from the moment of his arrival. Jonathan Kent tells Clark the story of his life with the Kent family, emphasizing this religious connection: "A childless couple, blessed from above with a miracle boy from another world."[28] Jonathan also confesses, "I came right out here and I prayed.... Then one night, not long after, you came."[29] The character's similarity with the Christian idea of hypostatic union, where divinity and humanity are one, situates Superman in the theology of the real world, and means that for all Superman's destruction of authority, he operates in finite, pre-constructed spheres, at least where humanity is concerned.

This is true of the superhero genre as a whole according to Morrison, as he refers to the common ancestry of superheroes in mythology, where each hero is an avatar of particular qualities or concepts. He refers to this movement in *Supergods*: "Timely's big innovation, which was to serve the embryonic Marvel well and help to distinguish it from DC, was to come down from Olympus and give voice to the elements themselves by personifying the forces of nature as heroes."[30] By referencing this pantheon of heroes, Morrison draws attention to Superman's omnipotence, and further consolidates his position as an authority figure fuelled by human belief. The fact that Superman is in turn referenced and reproduced by other companies is also indicative of his importance and continued relevance as a cultural icon. On this point, Morrison notes, "Today every comics company has at least one, and sometimes several, characters who are direct analogues of Superman."[31]

As the enigmatic, omnipotent Man of Steel, hailing from an advanced civilization technologically and spatially light-years beyond the reach of Earth, Superman is more than equipped to destroy authority, or indeed opposition in any form, yet he operates within human-defined boundaries, deferring to the police force and even working with government programs such as Project Cadmus to achieve their goals. Superman avoids pursuing a solely authoritarian role as espoused by his Kryptonian peers Bar-El and Lilo, the first astronauts of the planet Krypton, who chastise him for not actively creating a new Krypton on Earth. Superman replies to their taunts: "What right do I have to impose my values on anyone?"[32] The Kryptonians argue that their physical prowess justifies their superiority, yet Superman refuses to align himself with this ideology, and so disregards the chance to become an infallible authority, instead embracing a role as a facilitator of human free will. Morrison refers to Superman's ongoing development in this role in his run on JLA, as when Wonder Woman asks, "When does intervention become domination?," Superman replies, "Humankind has to be allowed to climb to its own destiny. We can't carry them there."[33] In response to the Flash's further questioning of their purpose, Superman then adds that their function is one of facilitation rather than control. Their purpose is therefore: "To catch them if they fall."[34]

Superman embodies the renaissance of the superhero, as he merges god-like power with human moral sensibilities. Belief in the sun itself as a deity is a feature of ancient cultures the world over, and so the Kryptonians' powers are also rooted in the pagan beliefs of the ancestors of the people they are attempting to subsume. By re-appropriating this power instead of disregarding it, Superman assumes the position of savior, yet he does not eradicate free will in the process. Similarly, Superman succeeds in vanquishing the tyrant sun Solaris, and the symbolic implications of his victory are immense.[35] In returning to the sun, which has long been a symbol of human belief, he vows to reform it from the inside with his sacrifice, as he merges with the sun, and attempts to revolutionize the solar power from its core. This metaphor is a powerful one, illustrating his reformation of the authoritarian foundations of Christianity, which are evoked by comparisons surrounding his birth, and it is no coincidence that this religion also draws heavily on Roman Mithraism. Superman therefore literally reforms religion and becomes a new authority figure, disregarding unnecessary authoritarian-based conflict in favor of ensuring the continued prosperity of humanity as a whole. Superman thus transcends the authoritarian power of religion, and reforms the beliefs of humanity in a purer form as he does with nuclear power, and so all look skyward, awaiting his return. In this way, Morrison creates a Superman who represents not punishment or exclusion, but instead is a beacon of hope for the future.

Equally, we learn that the tyrant sun Solaris will reform and become a weapon for good in the future, suggesting that Superman will succeed in his endeavors. Lex Luthor is portrayed to be "tampering with the sun,"[36] and as he does so he is literally playing with fire, as the sun becomes a metaphor for power and its propensity for corruption. Morrison's incarnation of Superman is designed not only to save society and lead it away from the destructive powers of radiation, as the sun is almost destroyed, but also to subvert the personification of nuclear disaster, which is Solaris, by capturing the tyrant sun to provide an opportunity for positive change. He tells the destructive creature, "rehabilitation begins here Solaris,"[37] and undertakes the herculean task of repairing the existing sun. In doing so, Superman saves humanity, and directly influences the future that the human race is journeying toward. In his re-appropriation of power and the steps he takes to harness it for the good of humanity, Superman therefore is changing the nature of humanity's future, and facilitating its development instead of purposefully controlling it. In aid of this, he then leaves, avoiding the potential dictatorship his presence and status as an omnipotent being threatens, thus allowing humanity to forge their own path instead of having one chosen for them by Superman. He even conducts the Earth Q experiment as he wishes to study a "world without Superman,"[38] and in doing so, he creates the world as we know it, and so, one that is capable of functioning without him.

All-Star Superman serves as an allegory for the detrimental nature of both an excess of power and more specifically, nuclear destructive power, and so it is only when Superman chooses to adopt a new role and go through personal reform that balance is restored. He is experiencing the deleterious side-effects of an over-abundance of power through exposure to massive levels of radiation and consequently, must undergo change to survive. While Superman represents the messiah-hero with omnipotent powers in an authoritative role, Morrison's Superman is a facilitator as opposed to an incontrovertible tyrant, and representations of Solaris, his own illness, and the mutated Lex Luthor are analogues for the dangers of flying too close to the sun, and attempting to subjugate humanity through force.

As Morrison has arrived at this version of Superman as an unwavering constant through evoking images of the sun and pantheon of immortal gods, his incarnation of the Dark Knight from over a decade before as a mentally unstable, potentially impotent human authority figure illustrates his changing views on what should constitute an effective authority figure. By virtue of his omnipotence, Superman is inherently closer to dictator than democratic leader, and so Morrison naturally explores versions of a less assured, more flexible, and altogether more human authority figure in *Arkham Asylum: A Serious House on Serious Earth*. This version of Batman who stumbles through Arkham Asylum, confronting aspects of his fractured psyche, is undergoing a different kind of metamorphosis, which involves a much more convoluted and challenging set of circumstances marked by internal dialogue and critical self-evaluation as a result of said chaos. This is an existential crisis, heavily influenced by Morrison's experiences of Cold War paranoia. As the following section will show, the Batman of *Arkham Asylum* is attempting to mediate the chaos both around him and within him, in order to prevent the destruction of Gotham; a destruction which could easily result from the citizens' rising levels of paranoia before war even begins.

The Politics of Arkham Asylum

Morrison's *Arkham Asylum* portrays a Batman in a precarious mental state, and even more precarious surroundings, framed by a narrative layered with Jungian and occultist symbolism, yet Batman does not overcome chaos and restore order, but instead embraces his inherent frenetic nature in order to combat chaotic surroundings. McKean's impressionistic artwork with its allusions to vague shapes and ambiguous shadows acutely resembles the Rorschach psychoanalytical technique popularized in the 1960s, and it is intriguing to note that this same technique is employed by the Joker in the story itself in an attempt to reveal the root of Batman's neuroses. Where Batman represents the internal effects of paranoia, the Joker is a further manifestation of this paranoid Cold War atmosphere, as he uses a technique of the period which is also rooted in chaotic imagery to infiltrate Batman's psyche further, and overwhelm him entirely, rendering him ineffective and undermining him as an authority figure. As both Luthor and the Joker evoke chaos in these texts and threaten their respective nemeses, both Superman and Batman must navigate this chaos successfully in order to bring balance. However, due to Batman's status as a mortal hero, he must confront his own human fears if he is to reconcile with them and be an effective defender of Gotham.

While a disparity between different versions of this hero is compounded by a dual identity, that of "Bruce Wayne the millionaire playboy,"[39] and Batman, the "Dark Knight,"[40] the psychological instability of the character takes precedence in this text over themes of international espionage synonymous with Morrison's later Batman tales. The earliest incarnation of Batman in particular was notorious not only for his unconventional brutality as a superhero, but also for his portrayal as an unyielding opposing force in the face of the actions of frenzied villains. "He was a grim figure in his first years, casually killing criminals."[41] This rigid form of authority is absolute, but inherently flawed when compared with the authority of Superman; the nature of his character is built on a dichotomy, and his position as an authority is ambiguous, as he has been presented in a variety of opposing characterizations. In contrast to the absolute resolve of his literary antecedent, Morrison presents to us a Batman who is irresolute in action, and shaped more by trauma, repression and the malevolent endeavor of his enemies than by a desire to facilitate the well-being of mankind. Here, he is a victim of Cold War anxiety, and finds himself inept in the face of chaos. It seems that the character he embodied in his genesis has been superseded in a modern context, where Batman's most insidious foe may arguably be himself, and as a figure of authority, he no longer has the desire or ability to smite his enemies with the same vigor. This characterization of Batman is molded through Morrison's use of Cold War spy tropes, and consequently this version of Batman epitomizes many aspects of the male Cold War action hero. In discussing the film heroes of the Cold War period, Susan Jeffords refers to a "sequence of what they call vigilante films, in which a larger-than-life superhuman hero battles alone against an increasingly deteriorating society in which the only recourse from crime, violence and corruption is the determined individual who acts on his own principles and commitments."[42] This accurately describes the Batman that Morrison portrays in *Batman, Incorporated*; one who is self-assured and resolute in action. He plans to overturn corruption through privatization of a code of conduct among his fellow superheroes by having them undertake his mantle and adhere to his rules concerning morality. However, Morrison recounts the character arc of the protagonist in *Arkham Asylum* as Batman is forced to confront and come to terms with the paranoia and insanity around him, before developing into a fully-fledged action hero who commands respect.

At the beginning of *Arkham Asylum*, however, Batman is presented as a two-dimensional, uptight, and overly macho version of the classic Cold War action hero, yet this version of the character is quickly deconstructed through the actions of the Joker, who satirizes this characterization of Batman through his own gender fluidity and overtly sexual behavior. In doing so, the Joker is used not only as an instrument to expose the stereotype which Batman initially embodies in this incarnation, but also is the impetus for the transformation of Batman into the sort of hero which Morrison believes could be capable of negotiating the paranoid atmosphere of the Asylum, and perhaps would be better adapted to life in the Cold War period. In addition, Morrison also draws attention to the culture of homosexual panic palpable during the Cold War period through Batman's interactions with the Joker, who behaves in a flamboyant manner, much to the abhorrence of Bruce Wayne. The Joker exposes Batman's homophobia as he chastises him. "Loosen up, tight ass!"[43] Elaine Tyler May notes that paranoia had infiltrated every facet of American society during the Cold War, and that "the most severe censure was reserved not only for those suspected of ties to the Communist Party, but also for gay men and lesbians, who faced harsh repression and official homophobia."[44] By acting so aggressively toward Batman and breaking down his resolve, the Joker successfully begins a chain of events which bear an unusual resemblance to the treatment program undertaken by Dr. Adams for Two-Face, where she effectively destroys his personality and autonomy through experimental treatment. "Sometimes we have to pull down in order to rebuild, Batman."[45] This entire story arc for Two-Face may be seen as an allegory for the Joker's equally experimental world view, where he embraces the use of mayhem to break down society and destroy order; an order which Batman maintains to a fault through utilizing rigid and unchanging methods. Batman opposes this experimental conduct in every way, as he strives to maintain the status quo of Gotham City through actively reinforcing a system which is constantly failing him. By placing villains in Arkham Asylum he continuously perpetuates the cycle of villainy as these criminals will, and do, inevitably break out. In crime-fighting, Batman simply packs away the overflow without ever dealing directly with the problem; an approach which echoes his repression of his own psyche. As a consequence of the Joker's actions then, Batman is released from his usual constraints in order to confront his psyche in the Asylum, proving his potential to be more than a frozen stereotype which is incapable of change. This Batman could, presumably, withstand pressure much more effectively than the one presented to the audience at the beginning of the narrative.

Jeffords also refers to portrayals of Batman in film which reveal his conflicted nature as a consequence of his divided psyche. "Batman is confident, muscular, invulnerable, decisive, and strong. Bruce Wayne is uncertain, isolated, and vulnerable because of the early death of his parents. He is slight and retiring."[46] Morrison's decision to focus on the mental volatility of the superhero reveals a response to an already unstable culture, as superheroes themselves are often created as a consequence of chaotic circumstances. In this respect, Batman is no exception, but Batman's status as a superhero is unusual in that he possesses no supernatural or mutative traits, but rather an indomitable strength of will and resolve in response to chaotic factors in his own life, including profound loss beyond his control and childhood trauma. This loss of control further emphasizes his status as a representation of the Cold War viewpoint, and so Batman becomes a potential cautionary tale; he must move forward or be overcome by the chaos around him. Batman's power comes from his success in operating both within and outside the social structures of his world, as Bruce Wayne negotiates the highly ordered world of corporate business, where Batman is a vigilante on the fringes of civilized society. He is an individual who operates within his own resources, and his wealth as Bruce Wayne and his athletic prowess as Batman form the cornerstones of his persona, but also arguably represent the utmost definition of success as defined within the boundaries of hegemonic masculinity.

Consequently a portrayal of an incapable, irresolute Batman is extremely effective, as it conflicts with these ideals and distances Batman's persona from the rigid definitions usually associated with him. As the Joker pretends to stab a young woman at Arkham Asylum while on the phone with Batman in the opening pages of the graphic novel,[47] the fact that Batman screams in anguish in response is indicative of his paralysis: "Batman screams with murderous but quite impotent rage."[48]

Batman's interactions with his enemies who inhabit the asylum are equally revelatory. Morrison writes that "the Joker has not only invaded Batman's precious personal space, but he has done so in an overt and threatening sexual manner."[49] This heralds a concatenation of events which are beyond Batman's control, and so the text becomes a vehicle for the paranoia and powerlessness which were to be expressed again many years later in *All-Star Superman*. Batman is emasculated and incapacitated, and it seems throughout the text that he has lost his ability to maintain his own sanity under pressure. As Batman seems little more than a collection of fears, he is a direct manifestation of Morrison's past. In the same way that Superman embodies a hopeful tomorrow, Batman then encapsulates the unrelenting fear and dread of Morrison's youth.

Considering that Batman was inspired by *The Bat Whispers*,[50] where the chief protagonist known as "the Bat"[51] was a cold-blooded killer, the Batman who attempts to survive Arkham Asylum is more vulnerable than his pulp-influenced predecessor. The opening pages contain images of icaronycteris, an ancient form of the modern bat, and this is indicative of Batman's need to reconnect with a more primal form of himself in order to successfully navigate the myriad darkened tunnels of Arkham, where ambiguity is rife and the lines between chaos and order are often blurred.[52] He must therefore conversely embrace the strengths of his dark side to re-establish his own sanity, and function as an effective authoritative figure in the face of paranoia and uncertainty, worthy of the faith of others. This Batman is therefore essentially preparing himself for an atmosphere reminiscent of the Cold War, and must adapt in order to survive. Morrison alludes to occultist Aleister Crowley to emphasize the importance of the animalistic instincts that the bat affords Batman. As Morrison notes in the introduction to the book, "The knight upon this quest has to rely on the three lower senses: touch, taste and smell."[53] In order to successfully navigate this chaotic landscape and resolve the inherent insanity of his reality, Batman must delve into his own subconscious, and question the stability of his own sanity.

Douglas Wolk proposes that Batman is already extremely unstable before he enters the asylum, and that being a hero has come with a heavy cost: "Batman … has pushed himself to the edge of being greater-than human … he's a benign psycho but barely functional as a person."[54] This is expressed through his journey in the asylum, as he comes face to face with the Jungian projections of his psyche which manifest as the various villains inhabiting Arkham Asylum, each representing an element of his fractured mind and reflecting a distorted sense of self. As he is uncertain about even his own identity, he is incapable of being a unified ideal like Superman, and therefore cannot be an effective authority figure.

While duality is synonymous with the superhero genre, in Batman's case it is more difficult than usual to discern which side of the character is its true representation. Jason Bainbridge remarks, "the true Bruce Wayne is the brooding face beneath the cowl of Batman."[55] However as long as Bruce Wayne cultivates Batman, he will be isolated, yet paradoxically, if he were to relinquish his title, he would be unable to protect those with whom he did manage to form relationships: "His whole life has been torn between his desire to reveal himself and his desire to conceal himself."[56] It seems that the longer Batman maintains his facade, the more ambiguous his true identity becomes. "Even Bruce Wayne, while being a real person who becomes the Batman to avenge his parents' deaths, becomes a performance."[57] Batman is unable to define his own identity as independent from his childhood fears, and so he creates a shield based on childhood fears in order to navigate adult life. In this regard, Morrison is arguably similar, as he utilizes superheroes to mediate his worldview. As Wendy Doniger observes, "Putting on a mask gets us closer to one self and farther from another."[58] The Joker takes advantage of this, and identifies the mask as a sign of weakness: "That is his real face. And I want to go much deeper than that."[59] As the character of Batman is created out of fear, and is a composite of all the villains he faces, he will not be an effective authority figure until he embraces all facets of his being, just as Morrison confronts Cold War tropes and the all-pervasive fear which must have often dominated his childhood landscape. For Batman, through doing so, he can first control and rationalize his fears, so that they cannot become insurmountable through the manipulations of his enemies, and Morrison uses this harrowing and surreal experience in the asylum to create a more capable Batman at the close; one who has not conquered his fear through force, but one who has accepted this fear as a part of himself and his reality.

The Authoritarian Batman

Batman disregards this idea in Morrison's most recent reimagining of the character in *Batman, Incorporated*, and instead of destroying his current model of justice in favor of reform, he franchises his image and his methodologies, by creating an even more rigid structure of authority with no room for deviation or change. Where the Joker is mercurial, dynamic and changeable, Batman is unyielding to a fault, and as it appears that this rigidity may have made his mind brittle, the entire organization is threatened. By opposing chaos with forceful order, this version of Batman therefore negates the lessons learned by the Batman of *Arkham Asylum*, and chooses instead to retreat deeper into the persona he has created. The copies of himself that he creates on an international scale then act as magnifications of his current projections, making the instability at his core all the more apparent, while he refuses to acknowledge it.

At the beginning of the series, Batman sets out on a mission to recruit the aptly named Mr. Unknown for his international crime-fighting organization. He says, "Mr. Unknown is the man I came here to recruit. I hoped he'd appreciate that I'd worked out his secret identity."[60] Due to Batman's considerable resources, he claims to have discovered Mr. Unknown's identity, yet he chooses to refer to him almost exclusively by his anonymous moniker, and as Batman later discovers that his information on the true identity of Mr. Unknown is inaccurate, this illustrates his lack of interest in, or regard for, the identity and humanity of those he will be subsuming under his own mantle. Just as Bruce Wayne is superseded by the superego he has created, individuals recruited by Batman simply become carbon copies, devoid of their own personality or judgment. "But I'm here to train a Japanese Batman,"[61] Bruce protests to Selina Kyle, and proceeds to reject potential additions to the Batman franchise based on the slightest justification. He immediately dismisses the highly skilled Mr. Unknown based on his decision to use a gun, as this choice conflicts with Wayne's moral code and everything Batman has come to represent: "You used a gun. Rule Number One: No guns. My people have to be better than that."[62] As Batman is human, he can never replicate the omnipresence of Superman, though he does try to extend his reach through the above endeavors, and he also similarly attempts to produce stalwart morals which have become synonymous with the character in order to lead by example. However, due to Batman's status as a human, he carries the inherent potential for corruption, and he cannot, whether purposefully or subconsciously, attempt to perfectly emulate Superman's example.

In order to align himself further with Superman's omnipotence Batman continuously refers to Bruce Wayne in the third person, and in doing so there is an indication that he is distancing himself from his humanity. His flawed ideologies are reflected in his enemies as in *Arkham Asylum*, and as Lord Death Man sets about destroying the identity of the original Mr. Unknown by removing any immediately identifiable features such as his fingers and face, this is indicative of a disregard for individuality shared by both villain and hero. Equally, Lord Death Man exclaims, "I am the headmaster!,"[63] perhaps alluding to the word "headsman" as another word for executioner, while also referencing the normalization of authoritarian social strictures. One panel later, Selina Kyle's phrasing is significant as she warns Batman of becoming a totalitarian figure of authority: "One mistake and you're all judge, jury and executioner."[64] However, not all are amenable to Batman's assimilative plans, and El Gaucho responds negatively to Wayne's proposal: "As for 'Batman Incorporated,' I'm grateful and flattered that you came all this way, but El Gaucho is his own man, Batman. Not an employee."[65]

At the close of *Batman, Incorporated*'s run, Batman achieves that which he has always admired in Superman: the immortality of his legacy, and the omnipresent reach he would be unable to maintain as one man; however this has come at a terrible cost to his humanity. When Damian Wayne (his son with Talia al Ghul) is killed, it proves there is no room for heirs, or those who would deviate from Batman's strict code of behavior, as these are contaminants. Any legacy of Batman's must be a facsimile of the Bruce Wayne who has gone before. Batman refuses to allow Damian to become the future Batman, as he fears an apocalyptic scenario which would culminate in the destruction of Gotham by nuclear catastrophe: "I had a dream of a future Batman who sold his soul to the devil and destroyed Gotham. Your mother is manipulating events to mold you into that Batman, her agent.... But you can't be Robin. You can never be Batman."[66] As the nuclear bomb and the destruction which would accompany it are as strong a presence in Batman's field of vision as they are in Morrison's, he imposes strict rules on his son, and as the imposition of these rules leaves no margin for negotiation. Damian makes the decision to aid his father's cause, though this time he is without Batman's backup. Consequently, when Damian is forced to diverge from Batman's code, it results in his death: "I promised my father I wouldn't ever kill anyone ever again."[67] Damian dies because of his father's flaws, though these are not always negative, as he is selfless, stubborn, and above all, human. Talia al Ghul is in many ways the expression of Batman's Jungian shadow in this series, as her international terrorist organization known as Leviathan mirrors Batman's privatization of superheroes at Batman, Incorporated; and so her actions warn of the dangers of corruption, and the danger of the absolute control which Batman craves.

In fact, as a result of Damian's death, Batman realizes that true heroism cannot be manufactured or replaced, and so he abolishes his plans for a complete infiltration of society by means of robotic versions of himself: "These were going to be family robots—a Batman in every home."[68]

Unfortunately, Ra's al Ghul has other plans, and demonstrates the potential for corruption already present in Batman's plans for global pervasion, as he approaches the cloned children of Batman and instructs them to "Rise."[69]

In this society, entropy is the natural state, and the constant struggle between rigid order and moral flexibility has implications for the future of the human race in Morrison's versions of the universe. As the Joker is referred to by psychiatrists as the next stage of human evolution, or "More suited to urban life at the end of the Twentieth Century,"[70] it seems that a balance between both sides of the spectrum must be maintained in order to create this new universe which Morrison's characters are moving towards. The Joker and Batman occupy extremes, with one being dynamic and unpredictable and the other static and unyielding to a fault. The Joker is therefore sometimes "a mischievous clown, others a psychopathic killer..... He creates himself each day."[71] The Joker's parting shot to Batman as he leaves Arkham is therefore all the more poignant: "Enjoy yourself out there. In the Asylum."[72] This sentiment is echoed in *Batman, Incorporated*, as Jackanapes warns, "It's a madhouse out there."[73] Batman is therefore unable to instigate a new authority as he is unable to address his own fears; he never deviates from his strict, self-imposed moral code, and this is developed in response to a perpetually paranoid atmosphere. Batman chooses to retreat into his superhero persona instead of dealing with his flawed human self, and so he cannot hope to mediate the concerns of humanity, as he distances himself from them and uses his most primal fear to ward off the insanity which paradoxically seeks to claim him. "Bruce Wayne would only have become conflicted and mentally unstable if he had NOT put on his scary bat-suit."[74] Wayne is therefore concerned that when he walks through the gates of Arkham, "It'll be just like coming home."[75] In this way, through his treatment of Batman, Morrison addresses the importance of remembering one's humanity in the face of war, and so Batman's story becomes an allegory for the dangers of allowing altruistic intentions to become absolute tyranny in response to extreme circumstances.

In conclusion, Morrison's versions of these established superheroes offer new models of authority capable of confronting the paranoid landscape of his youth. As these heroes are capable of defending humanity against the terrors of the Cold War period, they consequently foster contemplation of a brighter future in place of a perpetually panic-stricken atmosphere where the future is uncertain, and optimism seems impossible. The models portrayed by Morrison are not dictatorships, and while there are boundaries these models are without restriction. As Morrison tells us in *Supergods*, "We love our superheroes because they refuse to give up on us. We can analyze them out of existence, kill them, ban them, mock them, and still they return, patiently reminding us of who we are and what we wish we could be."[76] These heroes are devoid of absolute judgment, and never seem to relinquish their hope of redemption for the human race, instead focusing on enabling humanity to glimpse a potential future that we could not visualize without their assistance. While Superman is the guardian who represents the pinnacle of human achievement, as well as embodying stability and order, Batman represents an equally inspiring talisman against Cold War concerns: the meta-human striving to maintain his sanity and cultivate hope for others in spite of horrific circumstances and limited resources. The facilitation of humanity's development and transformation is indicative of Morrison's overarching theme of metamorphosis, as his characters transcend not only the dangers of their respective times, but also the comic books themselves. Consequently, it seems that humanity must first navigate the asylum in its path before our heroes can lead us to enlightenment. Batman is a primal reminder of the fear from Morrison's tension-filled past that drives us forward, and Superman emerges as a beacon of hope for humanity to strive towards in the future. Jor-El's parting words to Kal-El in *All-Star Superman* are, thus, all the more poignant: "You have given them an ideal to aspire to, embodied their highest aspirations. They will race and stumble and fall and crawl and curse, and finally, they will join you in the sun Kal-El."[77]

Notes

1. Andrew Hammond, *British Fiction and the Cold War* (London: Palgrave Macmillan, 2013), 8.
2. Humphrey Carpenter, *A Great, Silly Grin: The British Satire Boom of The 1960s* (Cambridge: Da Capo Press, 2003), 309.
3. Stuart Ward, "'No Nation Could Be Broker': The Satire Boom and the Demise of Britain's World Role," in *British Culture and the End of Empire* (Manchester: Manchester University Press, 2001), 91.
4. Ian MacDonald, *Revolution in the Head: The Beatles' Records and the Sixties* (London: Vintage, 2008), 5.
5. *Grant Morrison: Talking with Gods*, directed by Patrick Meaney (New York: Sequart, Respect! Films, 2010), DVD.
6. *Grant Morrison: Talking with Gods*.
7. Marc Singer, *Grant Morrison: Combining the Worlds of Contemporary Comics* (Jackson: University Press of Mississippi, 2012), 3.
8. Singer, *Grant Morrison*, 4.
9. Grant Morrison and Jill Thompson, *The Invisibles* 1 #5 (New York: DC/Vertigo: 1995), 3.
10. *Grant Morrison: Talking with Gods*.

11. Grant Morrison and Frank Quitely, *All-Star Superman* (New York: DC Comics, 2005–2008), 1.22
12. Grant Morrison, "Introduction," in *Supergods: What Masked Vigilantes, Miraculous Mutants, and a Sun God from Smallville Can Teach Us About Being Human* (New York: Spiegel & Grau, 2011), Kindle edition.
13. Ibid.
14. *Grant Morrison: Talking with Gods*.
15. Ibid.
16. Morrison and Quitely, *All-Star Superman*, 1.10.
17. Ibid., 1.21.
18. Ibid., 2.275.
19. Ibid.
20. Ibid.
21. "Introduction," in Morrison, *Supergods*.
22. *Grant Morrison: Talking with Gods*.
23. "Introduction," in Morrison, *Supergods*.
24. Ibid., chap. 1.
25. Les Daniels, *Superman: The Complete History: The Life and Times of the Man of Steel* (San Francisco: Chronicle, 2004), 13–14.
26. "Introduction," in Morrison, *Supergods*.
27. Morrison and Quitely, *All-Star Superman*, 1.12.
28. Ibid., 1.130.
29. Ibid., 1.129.
30. "Chapter 2: Lightning's Child," in Morrison, *Supergods*.
31. Ibid.
32. Morrison and Quitely, *All-Star Superman*, 2.207.
33. Grant Morrison and Howard Porter, *JLA* #4 (New York: DC Comics, 1997), 19.
34. Ibid.
35. Morrison and Quitely, *All-Star Superman*, 2.267.
36. Ibid., 1.13.
37. Ibid., 2.266.
38. Ibid., 2.230.
39. Jason Bainbridge, "Worlds Within Worlds," in *The Contemporary Comic Book Superhero*, ed. Angela Ndalianis (New York: Routledge, 2009), 71.
40. Henry Jenkins, "Just Men in Tights," in *The Contemporary Comic Book Superhero*, ed. Ndalianis, 19.
41. Les Daniels, *Batman: The Complete History* (New York: Chronicle, 2004), 31.
42. Susan Jeffords, *Hard Bodies: Hollywood Masculinity in the Reagan Era* (Brunswick: Rutgers University Press, 1993), 17.
43. Grant Morrison and Dave McKean, *Arkham Asylum: A Serious House on Serious Earth: 15th Anniversary Edition* (New York: DC Comics, 2004), 14.
44. Elaine Tyler May, *Homeward Bound: American Families in the Cold War Era* (New York: Basic Books, 2008), 19.
45. Morrison and McKean, *Arkham Asylum-A Serious House on Serious Earth*, 19.
46. Jeffords, *Hard Bodies*, 97.
47. Morrison and McKean, *Arkham Asylum*, 6.
48. Ibid., 7.
49. Ibid., 14.
50. Daniels, *Batman: The Complete History*, 20.
51. Ibid.
52. Sue Cartledge, "Fossil Bat Flew While Deaf: 52 Million-Year-Old Bat Could Fly But Not Echolocate," American Museum of Natural History, http://www.suite101.com/content/fossil-bat-flew-while-deaf-a44696#ixzz1L8SaCO21 (accessed February 2, 2014).
53. Morrison and McKean, *Arkham Asylum*, 1.
54. Douglas Wolk, *Reading Comics: How Graphic Novels Work and What They Mean* (Cambridge: Da Capo Press, 2007), 97.

55. Bainbridge, "Worlds Within Worlds," 71.
56. R. D. Laing, *The Divided Self* (London: Routledge, 1999), 38.
57. Bainbridge, "Worlds Within Worlds," 71.
58. Scott Bukatman, "Secret Identity Politics," in *The Contemporary Comic Book Superhero*, ed. Ndalianis, 114.
59. Morrison and McKean, *Arkham Asylum*, 22.
60. Grant Morrison and Yanick Paquette, *Batman, Incorporated* (1) #1 (New York: DC Comics, 2011), 15.
61. Ibid., 13.
62. Grant Morrison and Yanick Paquette, *Batman, Incorporated* (1) #2 (New York: DC Comics, 2011), 9.
63. Ibid., 12.
64. Ibid., 13.
65. Grant Morrison and Yanick Paquette, *Batman, Incorporated* (1) #3 (New York: DC Comics, 2011), 15.
66. Grant Morrison and Chris Burnham, *Batman, Incorporated* (2) #5 (New York: DC Comics, 2013), 18.
67. Grant Morrison and Chris Burnham, *Batman, Incorporated* (2) #8 (New York: DC Comics, 2013), 18.
68. Grant Morrison and Chris Burnham, *Batman, Incorporated* (2) #10 (New York: DC Comics, 2013), 9.
69. Grant Morrison and Chris Burnham, *Batman, Incorporated* (2) #13 (New York: DC Comics, 2013), 24.
70. Morrison and McKean, *Arkham Asylum*, 20.
71. Ibid., 21.
72. Ibid., 65.
73. Morrison and Burnham, *Batman, Incorporated* (2) #5, 11.
74. Morrison and McKean, *Arkham Asylum*, 5.
75. Ibid., 8.
76. "Epilogue (Outro)," in Morrison, *Supergods*.
77. Morrison and Quitely, *All-Star Superman*, 278.

"Morrison Inc." and Themes of Benevolent Capitalism

Emmet O'Cuana

> You ask me what my real feelings are so that you can follow them. Nothing was as tactful as that part of your letter, but it will be with the greatest difficulty that I shall reply to your question. First, as a man of letters, the obligation I am under to work each day, either for one party or for the other, establishes a mobility in my opinions which is reflected in my innermost thoughts. Do I really want to fathom them? They favor no party and are a mixture of them all. ... What am I? An aristocrat or a democrat? You tell me, if you please ... for I am unable to judge.—Marquis de Sade, "Letter to Gaufridy"[1]

Grant Morrison's career has seen him progress from cult author to mainstream comic auteur. It is his balance between the weird and the marketable that has ensured his continuing popularity, but also his work's intellectual heft. In this chapter, I will address his alteration of comic book superheroes to corporate icons within the fictional universes they inhabit, as well as their being commercially solvent comic book properties for mainstream American publishers Marvel Comics and DC. His heroes in *The Invisibles* (1994–2000), *New X-Men* (2001–4), and *Batman, Incorporated* (2011–13) do not simply fight crime—they change society.

Managing the Media

In an interview with Grant Morrison published in the *New Statesman* in September 2012, journalist Laura Sneddon states, "*The Invisibles* regularly makes any list of anarchist reading material."[2] It was an impression actively courted by the outré comic series, which opens with a full-bleed image of hooligan Scouser Dane McGowan flinging a Molotov cocktail into the air. The distinctive cover design of Rian Hughes, showing an Andy Warhol silk-screen-print-style grenade in pastel colors, hinted beautifully at the larger themes of the book—underground culture as a fashion statement—but also served as a promise: *The Invisibles* would realize the revolutionary rhetoric of the 1960s that had collapsed into lazy hedonism and was left exhausted by the corporate excess of the 1980s. By the same token, the book reversed reader expectations with its rejection of violence, concluding with a utopian future where the Invisibles have exchanged anarchism for a benevolent corporate structure.[3]

The letters page of *The Invisibles* #1 included a huckster-style rant from Morrison that resembled a manifesto:

> This is the comic I've wanted to write all my life—a comic about everything: action, philosophy, paranoia, sex, magic, biography, travel, drugs, religion, UFOs... you can make your own list. And when it reaches its conclusion, somewhere down the line, I promise to reveal who runs the world, why our lives are the way they are and exactly what happens to us when we die.[4]

Morrison managed this perception of himself as a counterculture guru for the duration of the series, exciting his readership with impromptu lectures on chaos magick, contact with aliens and even updates on his personal life. His sincerity and the clearly personal nature of *The Invisibles*—which did indeed set out to be a comic about everything that he was interested in—became an essential marketing tool for Morrison. Issue by issue, rant by rant, with each publicity stunt—including the infamous "wankathon" event of *The Invisibles* #16—he was building a community of fellow travellers, following Timothy Leary's apocryphal dictum, "find the others."[5]

The upswing of the internet in the mid–1990s greatly facilitated online discussions of what *The Invisibles* really meant. Stories about the weird and wonderful Scotsman proliferated.[6] He began to model his appearance on his original character the punk-terrorist-shaman King Mob. Morrison has proven himself to be a fascinating interviewee in both the mainstream press and online fan sites, always quick with a memorable quip, helping to position him as a highly visible presence both within the insular comics community and the wider pop culture spectrum.

In essence, Morrison has provided fellow creators with a master class on how to transform oneself into a brand. Not only has the author of a countercultural series about drug-taking terrorists gone on to become the trusted steward of clean-living, all–American icons such as Superman and Batman, but he has since been the subject of a documentary,[7] and in 2012 enjoyed the attentions of a personalized convention, MorrisonCon, held on the weekend of 28 September at the Hard Rock Hotel in Los Angeles. A new generation of creators such as Matt Fraction, Kieron Gillen, Gerard Way, and Jonathan Hickman have entered the comics industry by following his blueprint, combining varied content in their writing with more media-savvy publicity skills. What Morrison taught them was to be hip, sexy, weird, but most importantly, visible.

Morrison's rise to the status of media darling enjoyed a spike in 1990 with a frothing-at-the-mouth article published in *The Sun* under the headline "'DEATH TO MAGGIE' BOOK SPARKS TORY UPROAR,"[8] an overt attempt to stir controversy over the publication of *St. Swithin's Day* (1989–90). The comic itself is about a disturbed young man travelling to London, apparently with the intention of assassinating Margaret Thatcher. As controversy-bait the story could not have done better, with the book achieving a rare second print run for publisher Trident Comics. The article in *The Sun*, was accompanied by a photograph of a fuming Sir Teddy Taylor, who described the comic as "blasphemous," and continued: "I am astonished and appalled. This is in the worst possible taste—utterly despicable."[9] Morrison, the target of this tabloid ire, only appeared at the end of the piece. Following on from a paragraph with the disingenuous header "PSYCHO" in reference to his characterization of Batman, there is a bemused note to Morrison's response: "I do not think anyone needs to shoot Mrs. Thatcher. She is on her way out of government because of the Poll Tax."[10] Trident Comics embraced the controversy—going so far as to sell copies at a Poll Tax demonstration held during the weekend of the first Glasgow Comic Art Convention (GlasCAC), as well as t-shirts quoting Taylor's line, "Blasphemous!" After this incident, Morrison became more adept at handling the press.

The irony is of course that *The Sun's* attack was a pointless exercise in controversy. *St. Swithin's Day* mocks and parodies the very notion of a political assassination. The nameless protagonist identifies himself as "Neurotic Boy Outsider" and carries a copy of J.D. Salinger's *The Catcher In The Rye* on his person, because it is famously associated with well-known killers such as Mark David Chapman and John Hinckley.[11] Despite the apoplexy of Teddy Taylor or the gleeful enthusiasm of the Poll Tax protesters who bought the comic in Glasgow, Morrison had adopted a point of view that while critical of the then government in power, also reduced the empty revolutionary rhetoric of the time to an absurdity. Morrison would prove to be a far too canny operator to be easily pigeonholed as an anarchist rebel, or Thatcher-era class traitor.

The Third Way

The future Prime Minister of the United Kingdom, Tony Blair, who came into his own during the pre-millennial years of the 1990s, was also notable for avoiding an established ideological position, instead aiming for a "Third Way." Liberal philosopher Isaiah Berlin, while lying on his deathbed in 1997, received a letter from the New Labour party leader with the following appeal to provide insight on this concept:

> As you say, the origins of the Left lie in opposition to arbitrary authority, intolerance and hierarchy. The values remain as strong as ever, but no longer have a ready-made vehicle to take them forward. ... [T]here remains action, too, to devolve political power and to build a more egalitarian community.[12]

Here Blair desperately tries to convince an icon of liberal thought that the political Left could adapt to the realities of twentieth-century capitalism, by piggy-backing its values onto the traditional economic mechanisms of the Right. Morrison, being only seven years his junior, is a peer of Blair's and demonstrates a similar fascination with the idea of a Third Way; of working within the System—that concept so hated by revolutionary ideologues—to effect the positive changes in society that outmoded socialist policies were unable to achieve.

While *The Invisibles* does open with the imagery of revolution, it concludes with the members of the terrorist cell adopting the methods of a twenty-first-century corporation. They sell enlightenment to the citizens of 2012 in a convenient inhaler, New Revolution Inc.! (which happens to feature as a logo Rian Hughes's cover image of the pastel-colored grenade from *The Invisibles* #1). In keeping with his practice of promoting the book as a personal dialogue with the readership, Morrison claimed his views on politics, society, marketing, and capitalism had shifted during its writing.[13]

Yet before he started writing *The Invisibles*, he had already presented a similar progression of ideas in *St. Swithin's Day* with its mocking parody of the radicalized angry young man, and in *Zenith* (1987–2000), in which, as Marc Singer observes, a Tory politician "is not only the voice of conscience but also the voice of maturity."[14] Morrison's work therefore offers a consistently disenchanted perspective on post–Soviet Marxist radicalism. Clearly, then, his subversion of his own countercultural cachet and a fascination with corporate iconography, is a theme within his work that predates both *The Invisibles* and continues to feature as part of his subsequent stewardship of multimedia icons for major superhero comics publishers DC and Marvel. *The Invisibles* is a story about sympathetic terrorists slowly coming around to the idea of adopting corporate techniques to change the world. It was an opportunity for Morrison to make his intentions overt—a position summarized neatly within his essay "Pop Magic!":

For every McDonalds you blow up, "they" will build two. Instead of slapping a wad of Semtex between the Happy Meals and the plastic tray, work your way up through the ranks, take over the board of Directors and turn the company into an international laughing stock. You will learn a great deal about magic on the way. Then move on to take over Disney, Nintendo, anyone you fancy. What if "The System" isn't our enemy at all? What if instead it's our playground? The natural environments into which we pop magicians are born? Our jungle, ocean and ice floe [...] to bargain with and dance around and transform, as best we can, into poetry?[15]

The corporation in this view was best suited to become the model for a genuinely progressive movement that could affect positive change. He has since defined it as a living entity, with Hexus the Living Corporation in *Marvel Boy* (2000–01)[16] one clear example from his fiction, as well as in an interview with Brother Yawn from Barbelith.com, ascribing daemonic traits to it.[17] "Pop Magic" gives us McDonalds the company instantly recognizable by its logo, which in Morrison's view is a sigil. Appropriately when he took over *New X-Men* the comic's title itself became a reversible symbol and the characters rejected costumes for a branded "X" uniform.[18]

How to Sell a Revolution

Ironized perspectives on revolution within film and advertising utilize the "sexiness" of the revolutionary figure. The appropriation of such imagery for corporate ends strips the image of its counter-cultural content but retains its appeal to concepts of "freedom" on a purely superficial level. Perhaps the most telling example of this trend within Morrison's own work comes in *New X-Men* with the apotheosis of genocidal mutant terrorist Magneto into a Che Guevara-style t-shirt-icon martyr. This also serves as a commentary on the superficial aspect of "champagne socialist" rhetoric and the anti–State posturing observed by Morrison during his upbringing,[19] with the romanticism of Guevara excusing his terrorist actions.[20] Magneto, in Morrison's hands, is more popular for his prospective mutant followers as an empty symbol, into which revolutionary and utopian desires may be projected, than the man himself ever was.[21] The "real" Magneto is a disillusioning figure for those mutants not convinced of Xavier's lectures on tolerance. He is old, embittered, addicted to the drug Kick and ultimately fails to change society in any concrete way beyond causing further suffering and destruction.

In 2001's *New X-Men Annual* Morrison introduced a new character named Xorn, seemingly a soulful healer rescued from a bleak prison run by corrupt Chinese officials.²² Years later, he was unmasked as Magneto, in a move that shocked fans of the series.²³ How could this gentle figure be a mass murderer? Yet the phenomenon of a villain rebranding himself as a healer is not as outlandish as we might think, as Slavoj Žižek presents this real-life example that is not a million miles away from the riddle of Xorn:

> When Radovan Karadžić, the leader of the Bosnian Serbs accused of organizing ethnic cleansing, was arrested, it was discovered that in his last years as a fugitive he had been "hiding in plain sight" as a spiritual healer, taking part in forums and lectures attended by several hundred people, and contributing articles to the *Zdrav Život* (Healthy Life) magazine.²⁴

Žižek locates in the invented persona of "Dragan Dabić," the identity taken by Karadžić, a key to the atrocities committed by his former self. Only someone who can see the world in such dualistic terms—black and white, healthy and sick, virtuous and sinful—can appeal to such rarefied ideological concepts to justify crimes against the masses. Empathy with others is discarded in favor of dogmatic principles that give rise to violence. Žižek's "hiding in plain sight" calls attention to how the context of that dualism shifted the perception of the same man. In a similar way, Morrison makes the tragic character of Magneto doubly so—a victim of the Holocaust who then adopts the blood and thunder idealism of the Nazis, preaching to an entirely invented mutant nation. In this regard, Alain Badiou's definition of fascism comes to mind, namely, the corruption of romanticism to violent ends, "the total destruction of law in favor of a special conception of desire for an entirely particular object."²⁵ Karadžić, Guevara and Magneto all share this same trait, the ability to reduce the destructive reality of human conflict to an attractive image or persona. The business of revolution lies in convincing the downtrodden to exchange one boss for another and Magneto, the post-human savior of mutantkind, is actually just another member of a very old club. He is the quintessential revolutionary-turned-dictator.

Morrison's creative arc on *New X-Men* commenced with the destruction of the nation of Genosha, which was Magneto's previous fiefdom; then, in "Planet X," he presents himself to the "liberated" mutants of New York following his takeover of the city and is taken aback to discover they preferred the heroic martyr from counter-cultural t-shirt and poster designs.²⁶ Even his faithful followers, teenage mutants enrolled at Xavier's school complain that they miss Xorn, which sends Magneto into a rage. He insists that the persona was a fiction, but as Žižek has observed with Karadžić/Dabić, there was more of him in Xorn than he would like to admit.

Morrison's run on *New X-Men* concludes with the overt rejection of both Magneto and Xavier's ideological positions. They have become so fixated on the oppositional character of their views that the world has left them behind. Xavier preached peaceful co-existence between humanity and mutants, but his dream never accounted for mutant fashions or sprawling ghettos. Magneto sees himself as a revolutionary leader, but the teenagers of Xavier's School prefer him as a martyr.[27] These two characters are unable to adapt because they are more defined by their enmity than any dream of a better future. Their very personalities have become mere symptoms of their ideological conflict. During Žižek's discussion of "Dr Dabić," he points out the following aphorism quoted favorably by the fictional guru: "He who cannot agree with his enemies is controlled by them."[28]

The early storylines in *New X-Men* appeared to be suggesting a genuine turn to the utopian. Talk of secondary mutations,[29] mutant fashion[30] and Charles Xavier "coming out"[31] as a mutant promised a genuine break from the endless cycle of costumed comic book violence in the title. Magneto the primary antagonist was thought to be dead, the destruction of Genosha[32] an event that ended an era just as the Fall of the Berlin Wall had. Morrison's cruel joke is to reveal that this narrative progression is untenable. In his dying moments Magneto prophesies that he will return and the final storyline in the run "Here Comes Tomorrow"[33] reveals that the future will bring yet another version of Chris Claremont and John Byrne's *Days of Future Past* (1980).[34] Even at the end of the world though, the X-Men logo continues to survive, appearing on Tom Skylark's uniform. Morrison has framed superhero conflict as an exercise in perpetual branding.

Billion-Dollar Batmen

Morrison would also have success with *Batman, Incorporated*, which married the concept of a corporate takeover to superhero battles. The notion of using superhero identities as a familiar brand to facilitate the changing of the world predates Morrison's transformation of the Batman concept. For example, both Alan Moore's *Miracleman* (1982–89) and *Watchmen* (1986–87) as well as Joe Casey's *Wildcats* (2000) had presented superheroes tackling politics as well as corporate culture. In *Miracleman*, Moore has the eponymous superhero—a knockoff of Fawcett's Captain Marvel—seize control of the country from a bewildered Prime Minister Margaret Thatcher.[35] There is a winking air of wish-fulfillment to this scene between the economic champion of 1980's Britain and a Nietzschean superman who has a plan to "save the world":

MIRACLEMAN. ... After that, the world economy must be restructured. Broken down into more manageable units.

THATCHER. No, no, no! This is all quite preposterous. We can never allow this kind of interference with the market.

MIRACLEMAN. Allow?[36]

The threat of a superhuman who chooses not to obey society's conventions is made abundantly clear. Moore would further develop and refine this theme for his next ground-breaking work, this time for DC.

In *Watchmen*, the superhuman Dr. Manhattan props up the administration of President Richard Nixon, having single-handedly won the Vietnam War. His presence acts as a convincing nuclear deterrent. His powers have also led to advances in technology providing the United States with clean energy.[37] Joe Casey's take on this kind of story begins in *Wildcats* #12. The android superhero Spartan redefines himself as a "corporate crusader." He calls a press conference to dedicate the HALO Corporation (which previously served as a front for the Wildcats) as a research and technological advancement organization: "HALO will diligently strive to serve the world in only the most positive ways. That is our mission... to effect necessary change that will advance a common world culture."[38] Independently of one another, Moore and Casey produced works that spelled out just how the existence of superheroes would necessitate the changing of the status quo—trickle-down superheroics.

Morrison's *Batman, Incorporated*, by contrast, was able to avail of a far larger canvas and far more iconic characters than Moore or Casey's books. His story revolved around a genuinely global organization bankrolled by Bruce Wayne. Wayne's strategy is to execute socially progressive crime-fighting measures across the world through the franchising of the Bat-brand, applying the model of a corporation to the work of a superhero. Batman's alter ego, Bruce Wayne, never had to hide behind a mask. Morrison portrays him in *Batman and Robin* (2009–10) realizing he only had to announce himself as the chief shareholder in the Bat:

Some of you may have wondered.... How does a man like Batman afford to constantly update his crime-fighting technology? Where does his money come from? Well, the answer is me. I've been financing Batman in secret for years.[39]

Batman, Incorporated provided Morrison with the opportunity to transform the lone vigilante of Gotham City into a genuine corporate icon, officially endorsed and sponsored by Wayne Enterprises. Over the course of two volumes—broken up by the publishing line relaunch of DC Comics in 2011—Batman recruited an army of Bat-heroes, opening franchises in England, France, Argentina, Australia and Japan.

Batman, Incorporated #0 contains a line that sums up the redefinition of the character: "The first truth of Batman. The saving grace. I was never alone."[40] Wayne has been surrounded by allies from the very beginning. The lone avenger image does not take account of Batman's relationships with Alfred Pennyworth, Commissioner Gordon, or the various Robins—and then there are the superhero teams of which he is a member: the Justice League of America and the Outsiders. By corporatizing this network, as well as the international heroes inspired by his example, Batman makes official his previously established myriad partnerships. Like the McDonalds logo of "Pop Magic," the Bat iconography is recognized around the world. In franchising it, Wayne is able to control events on a scale unimaginable when he contented himself to prowling the rooftops of Gotham at night.

However, the events of *Batman, Incorporated* lead to an escalation of enemy action, with Wayne Enterprises targeted by the forces of rival organization Leviathan, a criminal empire headed by Talia al Ghul. As Batman announces his intention to create an organization to change the future, the reader is made privy to his vision of the Leviathan logo eclipsing the Bat symbol.[41] While Batman strives to prevent this nightmarish vision of the future taking place,[42] Talia dismisses his efforts as being an indulgence that will achieve nothing: "Leviathan—an empty, arbitrary suggestion of vague promises and unformed ideas like the Bat."[43] The series ends on an ambiguous note, with Morrison concluding that the idea of Batman will continue, that it will perpetuate itself: "All I really need to know is this: Batman always comes back, bigger and better, shiny and new. Batman never dies. It never ends. It probably never will."[44] Morrison goes so far as to reveal the Bat itself to be both a corporate intellectual property—after all the publisher takes its name from Detective Comics itself—and, as alluded to in his discussion with Brother Yawn, a daemonic force. In *Batman: The Return of Bruce Wayne* (2010) it is a diabolical force that has haunted the Wayne family for generations.[45] The suggestion is that change is impossible. The status quo is reasserted by issue #13 with Batman, Incorporated disbanded, although the final page makes clear that an army of cloned antagonists wait for future writers to pit against Batman if they so choose. The secretive Kathy Kane, the former Batwoman who debuted in *Detective Comics* #233 (1956),[46] appears in this final issue to advise Batman, "Stick to what you do best."[47]

Batman, Incorporated is the concluding part of a "benevolent capitalist" trilogy for Morrison. The second is *New X-Men*, discussed above, where the mutant superheroes turn themselves into a global franchise, using corporate branding to become recognizable to the public, instead of mimicking the behavior of terrorist cells. The first is *The Invisibles*, also discussed above, which had the billionaire Mason Lang bankroll the subversive activity of King Mob and his team of cool anarchists. The character of Lang is a clear analogue for Morrison's Bruce Wayne, with Mob uttering this endorsement of Lang: "You are Batman."[48] However, over the years Morrison's Third Way, the corporate structure adapted for progressive ends instead of pointless superhero vigilantism, has become tarnished. Mason Lang changes the world, but Charles Xavier and Bruce Wayne are left with failed investments. Both *New X-Men* and *Batman, Incorporated* end in the same manner, the characters returning to where they were before Morrison began writing them. There is a conservationist instinct at work here: Morrison recognizes that he is a temporary author of these characters, introducing fresh perspectives to comic book morality fables.[49]

Supergods and Comics History

There is a story related about Bob Kane, the creator of Batman now largely known to have been "assisted" by both writer Bill Finger in his conception of the character, as well as a growing number of uncredited others down through the years.[50] During Jerry Siegel and Joe Shuster's negotiations with National[51]—the precursor to DC Comics—the two made an approach to Kane, inviting him to join them in a move designed to force the publisher to accede to their demands for more earnings and control over their intellectual property. As a gambit it made a lot of sense—no doubt the company would have balked at losing both Superman and Batman. Kane, however, saw a different opportunity and approached National to inform them of the move, thereby ensuring his own sweetheart deal in the process and handicapping Siegel and Shuster, whose estates continue to this day to dispute the ownership of Superman. In Bruce Scivally's *Billion Dollar Batman*, he describes how Kane himself alluded to these events in his autobiography:

> Kane relates that after an "important artist"—no doubt he was referring to both Siegel and Shuster—lost a lawsuit with National, Kane joined Editor Whitney Ellsworth for a drink at the local bar. "It was January," wrote Kane, "and I said, 'Whit, it looks like it's going to be a very cold winter for so-and-so.' He touched my martini glass with his hand and answered sardonically, 'I'm not cold, are you?' Somehow in that terse remark, Whit summed up the self-preservationist philosophy of most people, and that is: 'Better him than me.'"[52]

In Morrison's memoir-cum-industry history of comics, *Supergods* (2011), he touches on the dodgy deals and subsequent hardship suffered by the likes of Siegel and Shuster. Instead of addressing the issue of creator rights as framed by Will Eisner, who was as much a businessman as an artist,[53] or the plainly exploitative practices of both established publishers and those that occasioned a moonlight flit, Morrison describes the period as giving rise to a folk art.[54] Perhaps the damning assessment of the treatment of creators casts too dark a pall over the industry, and he wishes to refocus attention on the imaginative potential of these fantastical characters, and so chooses to ignore the real-world impact of shoddy business practices in favor of magic realist descriptions of the industry, portrayed as the birthing ground of twentieth-century monomyths.

This notion of a transcendent, beatific comics universe invested the titles with a radical sense of meaning. Morrison realized this concept through an overarching storyline from his work on *JLA* to *All-Star Superman*, establishing that our world is a fiction existing within the fictional universe of DC Comics with Superman as our own personal demiurge.[55] It too was cleverly tied to Morrison's own authorship. Morrison's talk of neo-myths and Superman as a deity redefines the iconic comic book property as a benevolent presence, a source of positive ideas: "Actually, it's as if he's more real than we are. We writers come and go, generations of artists leave their interpretations, and yet something persists, something that is always Superman."[56] Accordingly, the thousands of invisible hands that have paved the way for the elevation of Superman to pop culture icon since Siegel and Shuster were merely functions of his existence. There is a bizarre hint of the language of sacrifice to this unusual philosophy. This post-modern religious mystery language is suggestive of deliberately avoiding the documented realities of cutthroat business practices towards creators. The comingling of comics history and autobiography, with an uncritical assessment of his then employers DC, undercuts *Supergods*. The book becomes hagiographic instead of a genuinely insightful work into a genre of comics Morrison is clearly passionate about.

As Above, So Below: Depictions of Authority in The Filth *and* All-Star Superman

While Morrison's *The Filth* (2002–2003) is commonly referred to as a companion piece to *The Invisibles*, a comparison can be made with *All-Star Superman*. Both books are treatises by Morrison on the nature of authority. Both are also troubled by the exploitative history of the comic industry. Finally, both are ultimately hopeful tales, although some readers of *The Filth*, having endured pages of depictions of rape, death and perversion, might have a hard time stomaching that claim. Nonetheless, both *The Filth* and *All-Star Superman* end on a note of hopeful expectation towards the future.

It is no accident that Siegel and Shuster initially conceived of their character Superman as a villain.[57] Power naturally is equated with authority and the heroes of the pulps were often rogues and misfits. Therefore "The Reign of the Superman" is a story where that power needs to be challenged by ordinary men and women, or, as luck would have it, by divine intervention.[58] To reverse the model and have the Superman finally become a less violent, and more sympathetic, character was a fascinating innovation. The cover to anthology title *Action Comics* #1 (1938) presents the now heroic Superman lifting a car above his head as bystanders flee in a panic. Still implicit in the character is his capacity to be superhumanly violent, but the cover star is now a "Champion of the Oppressed." In his first adventure he rescues a woman from death-row and punishes a murderous wife-beater. In a 2011 interview with *Rolling Stone* Morrison described this as Superman's socialist period.[59]

More recently, the 2013 film *Man of Steel* directed by Zack Snyder focused excessively on the character's capacity for destruction. As the medium of film can now depict spectacular scenes of violence, audiences were treated to Superman and his Kryptonian opponents trashing the town of Smallville, as well as collapsing the towering buildings of Metropolis resulting in presumably thousands of deaths. The feats of Weisinger's Superman seem positively quaint in comparison to the devastating might of the "hero" of *Man of Steel*, though admittedly the film does carry an echo of Siegel's pulp nihilism from "The Reign of the Superman." Snyder, however, has produced a work stripped of any hint of wish-fulfillment, its protagonist capable of incredible acts of violence for the purpose of allowing modern cinematic technology to depict it in detail. The box office success of *Man of Steel* points to a public willing to embrace the film as a showcase for its incredible special effects. The story of an all-powerful alien who was happy to live among humans, to serve the greater good instead of rule over them, is in the past. *Man of Steel* ends with Superman destroying a military satellite to demonstrate that he cannot be controlled. He is happy to be above human society and its laws.

For *All-Star Superman* Morrison set himself the challenge of celebrating the history of the character with an homage to his classic depiction as a benevolent god-man on Earth, who is then confronted with the prospect of his own death. Superman becomes determined to ensure that there is a legacy left behind him that will keep his message of hope alive. Clones, alternate-selves, flawed contemporaries, even Lex Luthor himself—Superman turns to each of them in the hope that they are worthy to take his place. Might does make right where Superman is concerned—he genuinely is a benevolent god, and this is made explicit in the final issue when he saves the world by entering the sun itself. The final page[60] even promises a continuing Superman franchise, realized in Morrison's earlier series, *DC One Million*.[61]

The Filth, on the other hand, depicts authority in a more negative light. In the comic, the Filth is an organization that defends reality, known as Status Q, from threats such as contamination from anti-persons, dangerous ideas, and rogue fictions. The form that this protection takes is framed strictly in scatological terms—the Filth are the people who deal with the shit ordinary people refuse to handle. Their organization models itself on the structure of a hand, the philosophy based around the image of "social hygiene." As one character notes, "Ours is the hand that wipes the arse of the world, remember?"[62] Their vehicles resemble garbage trucks and their uniforms fetish suits which emphasizes their concern with the baser aspects of human nature. Greg Feely is the nominal hero, a middle-aged bachelor who is introduced buying cat-food for his beloved pet Tony and pornography for himself.[63] Then a woman named Miami Nil appears in his home and reveals that Feely is in fact an agent of an organization called the Filth and actually named Ned Slade. Feely is a "parapersona" created to allow Slade to retire from his work as an enforcer of Status Q. Now they need him to return to track down the dangerous psychopath Spartacus Hughes.

Attempts to bring him back into the fold are frustrated by his attachment to the Feely persona, and in particular his concern for his dying cat.[64] His fellow agents are perpetually annoyed by this, as there are greater issues at hand—such as threats to the nature of reality itself. *The Filth* initially appears to be a satire of the Nanny State, with his fellow agents actively resenting the ordinary people Feely prefers to live among. The preservation of life is a low priority. The callousness of the agents of the Filth is mirrored by the self-absorbed selfishness of Feely and his neighbors, who are quick to accuse the unassuming bachelor on their street of being a pedophile.

As in *All-Star Superman*, the main concern of the series is that someone has to protect the world—from itself if need be. At its heart, this is a story about the sacrifices made by those in authority. There is no "Third Way" in *The Filth*, no subversion of the system to progressive ends. Instead Morrison gives us Feely-as-Christ and a final page suggestive of an impossible utopia. The two worlds of Feely/Slade appear to have merged. Feely heals a bed-ridden man named Bernard with his own blood, dripping from a stigmata-like wound on his palm. A town center is transformed by wild flowers growing out of bins. A mother passes by wheeling a bee hive in a pram down a path. Feely's embracing of his authoritarian and rebellious personas has transformed everything around him. This achieves the gnosis described in the famous Hermetic phrase "as above, so below." The series presents an unlikely tribute to the notion of a loving authority, hidden in and amongst the trash. The popular hatred for politicians, police—the "filth"—is rooted in society's resentment of those in power, yet there is also a tacit acknowledgement that while these are dirty jobs, someone's got to do them. Greg Feely, in turn, is forced to endure his own rejection and degradation at the hands of his neighbors before he realizes his higher purpose. Ultimately, Feely is revealed to have been a member of a conspiracy attempting to dismantle the Hand, and so he was brainwashed and transformed into their agent Ned Slade.[65] The ending hinges on Feely himself taking on the job of changing the world, by becoming an unassuming messiah.

The relentless depictions of rape, death and decrepitude are introduced by Morrison as confronting images that the reader must endure to earn the utopian finale. Both *New X-Men* and *Batman, Incorporated* have plots motivated by visions of a nightmarish future. *The Filth*, however, exists in a nightmarish present.[66] Its horror and scatology speak to the compromised perspective of absolute authority. Feely only manages to bring about the book's happy ending, and save the world, after having seen reality from both the point of view of the rebellious conspiracy he was a member of, as well as the Ned Slade persona that was forced upon him. He is transformed into a decentered being, leaving his individuality behind.

In conclusion, the rejection of the binary connotations of individualism can be found throughout Morrison's work. From the subversion of conflict in *The Invisibles* to the competing ideologies of *New X-Men* playing out *ad infinitum* and Batman embracing his nature as a corporate icon. *Supergods* blithely passes over the poorly negotiated contracts of creators, instead emphasizing how their contributions to an ongoing canon of comics will outlive them. Superman becomes a godhead and Feely the host for intelligent I-Life that rewrites the world. Arguably Morrison's attraction to the notion of a commercial comic book character becoming a mystical transcendental idea is positioned to excuse corporations trampling on creators' rights. The narrative of a wronged individual fighting the system has the poetry of myth, but like all revolutionary figures there is a suspicion that they are tilting at windmills. This is also a rich source of inspiration for Morrison in navigating the straits between creativity and commercial gain. Ultimately, like de Sade or Feely, Morrison has embraced the contradiction of experiencing both sides and choosing neither.

NOTES

1. Marquis de Sade, "Letter to Gaufridy" (January 5, 1791), quoted in George Bataille, *Literature and Evil* (London: Penguin, 1957).
2. Laura Sneddon, "Grant Morrison: Why I'm stepping away from superheroes," *New Statesman*, September 15, 2012, http://www.newstatesman.com/blogs/voices/2012/09/grant-morrison-gay-batman-superheroes-wonder-woman.
3. Cover to *The Invisibles* #1, in Grant Morrison et al., *The Invisibles* (New York: DC Comics/Vertigo, 2002), 1.7.
4. In Grant Morrison and Steve Yeowell, *The Invisibles* #1 (New York: DC Comics/Vertigo, 1994).
5. For more on the "wankathon," see Grant Morrison's account, quoted in Patrick Meaney, *Our Sentence Is Up* (Edwardsville, IL: Sequart, 2010), 302; "Who knows what you might learn from taking a chance on conversation with a stranger? Everyone carries a piece of the puzzle. Nobody comes into your life by mere coincidence. Trust your instincts. Do the unexpected. Find the others"—popular quotation attributed to Timothy Leary.
6. The fan community at Barbelith.com have kindly put together an extensive list at http://www.barbelith.com/topic/23861.
7. *Grant Morrison: Talking with Gods*, dir. Patrick Meaney (New York: Sequart, Respect! Films, 2010), DVD.
8. Ian Brandes, "Death to Maggie: Book Sparks Tory Uproar," *The Sun*, March 19, 1990.
9. Ibid.
10. Ibid.
11. Grant Morrison and Paul Grist, *St. Swithins Day* #1 (Leicester: Trident Comics, April 1990).
12. Tony Blair to Isaiah Berlin, October 23, 1997, in "Letters to Berlin," in *The Isaiah Berlin Virtual Library*, http://berlin.wolf.ox.ac.uk/letterstoberlin.html.
13. "*The Invisibles* comes to the conclusion that the bad guys are us. And as I say in *The Invisibles*, are there any years when there are no policemen born? I began to question everything about the counterculture I belonged to, why they kicked police horses in the streets, and why they smashed buildings, and what they were actually achieving? Or were they just part of a bigger system that used these checks and balances in order to propel itself forward through the stages of its mega-development?" Grant Morrison, "One Nervous System's Passage Through Time," interview by Jay Babcock, *Arthur* 12 (September 2004), http://arthurmag.com/2007/02/01/interview-with-grant-morrison-from-the-pages-of-arthur-magazine/.
14. Marc Singer, *Grant Morrison: Combining the Worlds of Contemporary Comics* (Jackson: University Press of Mississippi, 2012), 50.
15. Grant Morrison, "Pop Magic!" in *Book of Lies: The Disinformation Guide to Magick and the Occult*, ed. Richard Metzger (New York: Disinformation, 2011), 25.
16. Grant Morrison and J. G. Jones, *Marvel Boy* #3 (New York: Marvel, 2000).
17. "Suddenly I thought, 'What the Hell is Disney?' Walt Disney's dead now but Disney

persists as a concept and people who were born after the death of Walt Disney grow up and assume positions within Disney. What are they assuming positions within? It's in this really devotional way too. What makes you grow up to wear a Mickey Mouse head and go round scaring children? Or 'I'm going to end up on the Board of Directors of Disney?' Why, why do these things occur? So I was just seeing them as in the way the Demons in the old Grimoires were seen which was kinda aggregates of power to which people could adhere themselves to or join in cultish fashion so I began to think I could talk to them like that and use ceremonial magic methods to talk to corporations and found there were ways of doing it—that's why I'm wearing a suit—this is my magical garb for this working. That's why we evoked gmWORD Ltd. They're very powerful, ravenous weird things—corporations, strange to deal with." Grant Morrison, "Interview with an Umpire," interview by Brother Yawn, September 2, 2002, archived in http://www.barbelith.com/old/interviews/interview_1.shtml.

18. Grant Morrison and Frank Quitely, *New X-Men* #114 (New York: Marvel Comics, July 2001).

19. Morrison says that his father was "arrested during the antinuclear protest marches of the sixties. He was a working-class World War II veteran who'd swapped his bayonet for a Campaign for Nuclear Disarmament badge and became a pacifist 'Spy for Peace' in the Committee of 100. Already the world of my childhood was one of proliferating Cold War acronyms and code names," in Grant Morrison, *Supergods: Our World in the Age of the Superhero* (London: Random House eBooks, 2012), Kindle edition, location 127.

20. Here is an instance of Guevara excusing himself: "At the risk of seeming ridiculous, let me say that the true revolutionary is guided by great feelings of love. It is impossible to think of a genuine revolutionary lacking this quality. Perhaps it is one of the great dramas of the leader that he or she must combine a passionate spirit with a cold intelligence and make painful decisions without flinching. Our vanguard revolutionaries must idealize this love of the people, of the most sacred causes, and make it one and indivisible. They cannot descend, with small doses of daily affection, to the level where ordinary people put their love into practice." Quoted in Slavoj Žižek, *Living in the End Times* (London: Verso, 2011), Kindle edition, location 108.

21. Grant Morrison and Phil Jimenez, *New X-Men* #149 (New York: Marvel Comics, 2003).

22. Grant Morrison and Leinil Francis Yu, *New X-Men Annual: 2001* (New York: Marvel Comics, September 2001), 1.

23. Grant Morrison and Phil Jimenez, *New X-Men* #147 (New York: Marvel Comics, October 2003).

24. Žižek, *Living in the End Times*, 94.

25. Alain Badiou, *Philosophy for Militants*, trans. Bruno Bosteels (London: Verso, 2012), Kindle edition, location 73.

26. Morrison and Jimenez, *New X-Men* #149.

27. Grant Morrison and Frank Quitely, *New X-Men* #135 (New York: Marvel Comics, 2003).

28. Žižek, *Living in the End Times*, 95.

29. Grant Morrison and Frank Quitely, *New X-Men* #114 (New York: Marvel Comics, 2001).

30. Grant Morrison and Keron Grant, *New X-Men* #134 (New York: Marvel Comics, 2003).

31. Grant Morrison and Frank Quitely, *New X-Men* #116 (New York: Marvel Comics, 2001).

32. Morrison and Quitely, *New X-Men* #114.

33. Grant Morrison and Marc Silvestri, *New X-Men* #151 (New York: Marvel Comics, 2004).

34. Chris Claremont and John Byrne, *Uncanny X-Men* #141 (New York: Marvel Comics, 1980).

35. Alan Moore and John Totleben, *Miracleman* #16 (Forestville, CA: Eclipse Comics, 1989).

36. Ibid., 6.
37. Alan Moore and Dave Gibbons, *Watchmen* #1–12 (New York: DC Comics, 1986–7).
38. Joe Casey and Sean Phillips, *Wildcats* #12 (San Diego: WildStorm, 2000).
39. Grant Morrison et al., *Batman and Robin* #16 (New York: DC Comics, 2010).
40. Grant Morrison, Chris Burnham, and Frazer Irving, *Batman, Incorporated* (2) #0 (New York: DC Comics, 2012), 3.
41. Ibid.
42. Grant Morrison and Andy Kubert, *Batman* #666 (New York: DC Comics, 2007).
43. Grant Morrison and Chris Burnham, *Batman, Incorporated* (2) #13 (New York: DC Comics, 2013), 4.
44. Ibid., 22.
45. Grant Morrison et al., *Batman: The Return of Bruce Wayne* #1–6 (New York: DC Comics, 2010).
46. Edmond Hamilton, Sheldon Moldoff, and Stan Kaye, *Detective Comics* #233 (New York: DC Comics, 1956).
47. Ibid., 18.
48. *The Invisibles* #22, in Grant Morrison et al., *The Invisibles* (New York: DC Comics/Vertigo, 1999), vol. 2.
49. Morrison, *Supergods*, 406.
50. Bruce Scivally, *Billion Dollar Batman* (Wilmette, IL: Henry Gray, 2011) Kindle edition, location 442.
51. Ibid.
52. Ibid.
53. Michael Schumacher, *A Dreamer's Life In Comics* (New York: Bloomsbury, 2010), 173.
54. Morrison, *Supergods*, 361.
55. The "infant universe" named Qwewq, which first appeared in Morrison's "Rock of Ages" storyline in *JLA* #10–15, returns in his *JLA Classified* #1–3 and *Seven Soldiers* maxiseries, before appearing in *All-Star Superman* #10, where Morrison reveals that it hosts a version of our Earth created by Superman himself.
56. Morrison, *Supergods*, 406.
57. Gerard Jones, *Men of Tomorrow: Geeks, Gangsters and the Birth of the Comic Book* (New York: Basic Books, 2005), Kindle edition, 82, location 1141.
58. Ibid., 84, 1166.
59. Brian Hiatt, "Grant Morrison: Psychedelic Superhero," *Rolling Stone*, September 2011.
60. Grant Morrison and Frank Quitely, *All-Star Superman* #12 (New York: DC Comics, 2008), 23.
61. Grant Morrison et al., *DC One Million* (New York: DC Comics, 1998).
62. Grant Morrison and Chris Weston, *The Filth* (New York: DC Comics/Vertigo, 2003), 35.
63. Ibid., 9.
64. Ibid., 23.
65. Ibid., 254.
66. See Grant Morrison and Marc Silvestri, *New X-Men* #151–154 (New York: Marvel Comics, 2004); Morrison and Kubert, *Batman* #666; and Grant Morrison and Chris Burnham, *Batman, Incorporated* (2) #5 (New York: DC Comics, 2013).

Bibliography

Primary Sources

General

Alighieri, Dante. *Inferno*. Translated by Henry F. Cary. New York: P. F. Collier & Son, 1969.
Amis, Kingsley. "City Ways." In *What Became of Jane Austen? And Other Questions*, 134-40. London: Penguin, 1980.
Angus, Ian, and Peter Davison, eds. *The Complete Works of George Orwell, vol. 12, A Patriot After All, 1940–1941*. London: Secker & Warburg, 2000.
Augustine of Hippo. *Enchiridion on Faith, Hope, and Love*. Translated by J. F. Shaw. London: Religious Tract Society, 1885.
Barrie, J. M. *Peter Pan and Peter Pan in Kensington Gardens*. Ware: Wordsworth Editions, 2007.
Baym, Nina, ed. *The Norton Anthology of American Literature*, vol. B, *1820–1865*, 7th ed. New York: Norton, 2007.
Blake, William. "Auguries of Innocence" (c.1803). In *Blake: The Complete Poems*. Edited by W. H. Stevenson, 3d ed. Harlow: Pearson Education, 2007.
Boethius. *The Consolation of Philosophy*. Translated by S. J. Tester. Cambridge: Harvard University Press, 1973.
Borges, Jorge Luis. "Partial Magic in the Quixote." Translated by James E. Irby. In *Labyrinths: Selected Stories and Other Writings*, edited by Donald A. Yates and James E. Irby, 193–196. New York: New Directions, 1964.
Carroll, Lewis. *Alice's Adventures in Wonderland*. London: The Folio Press, 1961.
Chopra, Deepak. *The Seven Spiritual Laws of Superheroes*. New York: HarperOne, 2011.
Crowley, Aleister. "The Holograph Manuscript of Liber AL vel Legis" (1904). U.S. Grand Lodge Ordo Templis Orientis. Accessed July 17, 2013. http://lib.oto-usa.org/libri/liber 0031.html?num=1.
Hesse, Hermann. *Demian*. Translated by W. J. Strachan. London: Peter Owen, 2006.
Horace. *Satires, Epistles and Ars Poetica*. Translated by H. R. Fairclough. Rev. ed. London: Heinemann, 1929.
King, Stephen. *Stephen King's Danse Macabre*. London: Fontana, 1985.
Lincoln, Abraham. "First Inaugural Address of Abraham Lincoln" (speech). March 4, 1861. Yale Law School: The Avalon Project. Accessed 27 October 2013. http://avalon.law.yale.edu/19th_century/lincoln1.asp.
Longinus. *On the Sublime*. Translated by H. L. Havell. London: Macmillan, 1890.
Lovecraft, H. P., and August Derleth. *The Lurker at the Threshold*. Sauk City, WI: Arkham House, 1945.
MacNeice, Louis. "Snow." In *Collected Poems of Louis MacNeice*. Edited by E. R. Dodds, 30. London: Faber & Faber, 1965.
Marlowe, Christopher. *Doctor Faustus* (1604 text). In *The Complete Plays*. Edited by Mark Thornton Burnett. London: J.M. Dent, 1999.
McKenna, Terence. "Alien Dreamtime with Terence McKenna" (speech). Transmission Theater, San Francisco, February 27, 1993. Deoxy/Video. Accessed July 10, 2013. http://deoxy.org/t_adt.htm.

Morrison, Grant. "Introduction." In Finger et al., The Black Casebook, 4–6.
_____. "The Paperverse." Crack!Comics. December 7, 2003. Archived in http://www.crackcomicks.com/the_paperverse.htm.
_____. "Pop Magic!" In Book of Lies: The Disinformation Guide to Magick and the Occult. Edited by Richard Metzger, 16–25. New York: Disinformation, 2011.
_____. "The Status Quorum." Crack!Comics. December 7, 2003. Archived in http://www.crackcomicks.com/the_status_quorum.htm.
_____. Supergods: Our World in the Age of the Superhero. London: Jonathan Cape, 2011.
_____. Supergods: Our World in the Age of the Superhero. London: Random House ebooks, 2012. Kindle Edition.
_____. Supergods: What Masked Vigilantes, Miraculous Mutants, and a Sun God from Smallville Can Teach Us About Being Human. New York: Spiegel & Grau, 2011.
Pico della Mirandola, Giovanni. Oration on the Dignity of Man. Edited and translated by Francesco Borghesi, Michael Papio and Massimo Riva. Cambridge: Cambridge University Press, 2012.
Pope, Alexander. Martin Scriblerus' Peri Bathous, or, The Art of Sinking in Poetry. Richmond: Oneworld Classics, 2009.
Radhakrishnan, S., trans. The Bhagavadgita. New Delhi: HarperCollins, 1993.
Schumacher, Joel, dir. Batman and Robin. Los Angeles: Warner Home Video, 1997; 2010. DVD.
Scot, Reginald. Discoverie of Witchcraft. Edited by Montague Summers. Mineola, NY: Dover, 1972.
Seuss, Dr. (Theodor Geiss). On Beyond Zebra. New York: Random House, 1955.
Shakespeare, William. Shakespeare's Sonnets. Edited by Katherine Duncan-Jones. Rev. ed. London: Bloomsbury, 2010.
Sidney, Sir Philip. The Defence of Poesy, in The Major Works, ed. Katherine Duncan-Jones, 212–50. Oxford: Oxford University Press, 2002.
Thoreau, Henry David. "Resistance to Civil Government." In Baym, The Norton Anthology of American Literature, 1857–72.
_____. Walden. In Baym, The Norton Anthology of American Literature, 1872–2046.
Tzara, Tristan. Seven Dada Manifestos and Lampisteries. Translated by Barbara Wright. London: Calder, 1977; rpt., New York: Riverrun Press, 1981.
Whitman, Walt. "Song of Myself." In Leaves of Grass: Reader's Edition, edited by Harold W. Blodgett and Sculley Bradley, 28–89. London: University of London Press, 1965.

Interviews

Morrison, Grant. "Grant Morrison: Master and Commander" (part 4). Interview by Jonathan Ellis. Popimage. http://www.popimage.com/content/grant20044.html. Accessed February 11, 2014.
_____. "Grant Morrison: Why I'm stepping away from superheroes." Interview by Laura Sneddon. New Statesman. September 15, 2012. Archived in http://www.newstatesman.com/blogs/voices/2012/09/grant-morrison-gay-batman-superheroes-wonder-woman.
_____. "Grant Morrison Tells All About Batman and Robin." Interview by Graeme McMillan. io9www. January 7, 2009. http://io9.com/5301435/grant-morrison-tells-all-about-batman-and-robin.
_____. "A Healing Inoculation of Grime: Grant Morrison on The Filth." Interview by Matt Brady. Crack!Comics. July 12, 2003. Archived in http://www.crackcomicks.com/the_filth_questions.htm.
_____. Interview by Daniel Epstein. Suicide Girls. February 27, 2005. Archived in https://suicidegirls.com/girls/anderswolleck/blog/2679166/grant-morrison/.
_____. Interview by Daniel Robert Epstein. Suicide Girls. March 4, 2005. Archived in http://suicidegirls.com/interviews/Grant%20Morrison/.
_____. Interview by Dylan Ratigan. The Dylan Ratigan Show. MSNBC. July 28, 2011.
_____. "Interview with an Umpire." Interview by Brother Yawn. September 2, 2002. Barbelith Webzine. Archived in http://www.barbelith.com/old/interviews/interview_1.shtml.

———. "Magic, Fiction Suits, and Putting Buddy Through Hell…: Grant Morrison on Animal Man." Interview by Matt Brady. *Newsarama*. June 7, 2001. Archived in https://sites.google.com/site/deepspacetransmissions/interviews-1/2000–2005/newsarama--grant-morrison-on-animal-man.
———. "One Nervous System's Passage Through Time." Interview by Jay Babcock. *Arthur* 12 (September 2004). Archived in http://arthurmag.com/2007/02/01/interview-with-grant-morrison-from-the-pages-of-arthur-magazine.

Comics (Single Issue)

Casey, Joe, Sean Phillips, Wildstorm FX, and Richard Starkings. *Wildcats* #12. San Diego: WildStorm, 2000.
Claremont, Chris, John Byrne, Terry Austin, Glynis Wein, and Tom Orzechowski. *Uncanny X-Men* #141. New York: Marvel Comics, 1980.
Ellis, Warren, John Cassaday, Laura DePuy, David Baron, and Ryan Cline. *Planetary* #7. La Jolla, CA: Wildstorm Productions, 2000.
Finger, Bill, Sheldon Moldoff, and Charles Paris. *Batman* #156. New York: DC Comics, 1963.
Fox, Gardner, Carmine Infantino, Joe Giella, and Carl Gafford. *The Flash* #123. New York: DC Comics, 1961.
Hamilton, Edmond, Sheldon Moldoff, and Stan Kaye. *Detective Comics* #233. New York: DC Comics, 1956.
Haney, Bob, Neal Adams, Jim Aparo, Dick Giordano, and Nick Cardy. *The Brave and the Bold* #102. New York: DC Comics, 1972.
Kanigher, Robert, Carmine Infantino, and Joe Kubert. *Showcase* #4. New York: DC Comics, 1956.
Kirby, Jack, Vince Colletta, and John Costanza. *Forever People* #3. New York: DC Comics, 1971.
Kirby, Jack, Mike Royer, and Ben Oda. *New Gods* #7. New York: DC Comics, 1972.
Milligan, Peter, Kieron Dwyer, Dennis Janke, Adrienne Roy, and John Costanza. *Batman* #454. New York: DC Comics, 1990.
Milligan, Peter, Dustin Nguyen, Derek Fridolfs, John Kalisz, and Sal Cipriano. *Detective Comics* #842. New York: DC Comics, 2008.
Moore, Alan, John Totleben, Sam Parsons, and Wayne Truman. *Miracleman* #16. Forestville, CA: Eclipse Comics, 1989.
Morrison, Grant. *Near Myths* #2–5. Edinburgh: Galaxy Media, 1978–1980.
Morrison, Grant, Andy Kubert, Jesse Delperdang, Dave Stewart, and Nick J. Napolitano. *Batman* #655. New York: DC Comics, 2006.
———. *Batman* #656. New York: DC Comics, 2006.
Morrison, Grant, Andy Kubert, Jesse Delperdang, Guy Major, and Jared K. Fletcher. *Batman* #665. New York: DC Comics, 2007.
———. *Batman* #666. New York: DC Comics, 2007.
Morrison, Grant, Chaz Truog, Doug Hazlewood, Tatjana Wood, John Constanza, and Brian Bolland. *Animal Man* #5. New York: DC Comics, 1988.
———. *Animal Man* #25. New York: DC Comics, 1990.
———. *Animal Man* #26. New York: DC Comics, 1990.
Morrison, Grant, Chris Burnham, Frazer Irving, and Pat Brosseau. *Batman, Incorporated* (2) #0. New York: DC Comics, 2012.
Morrison, Grant, Chris Burnham, Jason Masters, Andrei Bressan, Nathan Fairbairn, and Dave Sharpe. *Batman, Incorporated* (2), #10. New York: DC Comics, 2013.
Morrison, Grant, Chris Burnham, Jason Masters, Nathan Fairbairn, Hi-Fi Design, and Dave Sharpe. *Batman, Incorporated* (2), #9. New York: DC Comics, 2013.
Morrison, Grant, Chris Burnham, Nathan Fairbairn, and Dave Sharpe. *Batman, Incorporated* (2) #5. New York: DC Comics, 2013.
Morrison, Grant, Chris Burnham, Nathan Fairbairn, and Dave Sharpe. *Batman, Incorporated* (2) #12. New York: DC Comics, 2013.

Morrison, Grant, Chris Burnham, Nathan Fairbairn, and Dave Sharpe. *Batman, Incorporated* (2) #13. New York: DC Comics, 2013.
Morrison, Grant, Chris Burnham, Nathan Fairbairn, and Pat Brosseau. *Batman, Incorporated* (1) #6. New York: DC Comics, 2011.
Morrison, Grant, Chris Burnham, Nathan Fairbairn, and Pat Brosseau. *Batman, Incorporated* (2) #1. New York: DC Comics, 2012.
Morrison, Grant, Chris Weston, Gary Erskine, Matt Hollingsworth, Clem Robins, and Carlos Segura. *The Filth* #1. New York: DC/Vertigo, 2002.
_____. *The Filth* #2. New York: DC/Vertigo, 2002.
_____. *The Filth* #9. New York: DC/Vertigo, 2003.
_____. *The Filth* #10. New York: DC/Vertigo, 2003.
_____. *The Filth* #11. New York: DC/Vertigo, 2003.
_____. *The Filth* #12. New York: DC/Vertigo, 2003.
_____. *The Filth* #13. New York: DC/Vertigo, 2003.
Morrison, Grant, Chris Weston, Ray Kryssing, Daniel Vozzo, Todd Klein, and Brian Bolland. *The Invisibles* 2 #20. New York: DC/Vertigo, 1998.
Morrison, Grant, David Finch, Matt Benning, Ryan Winn, Peter Steigerwald, Dave Sharpe, and Scott Williams. *Batman: The Return*. New York: DC Comics, 2011.
Morrison, Grant, Doug Mahnke, John Kalisz, and Phil Balsman. *Seven Soldiers: Frankenstein* #1. New York: DC Comics, 2006.
Morrison, Grant, Doug Mahnke, Tom Nguyen, Drew Geraci, Christian Alamy, Norm Rapmund, et al., *Final Crisis* #7. New York: DC Comics, 2009.
Morrison, Grant, Ethan Van Sciver, Prentiss Rollins, Richard Starkings, Saida Temofonte, Frank Quitely, and Tim Townsend. *New X-Men* #117. New York: Marvel Comics, 2001.
Morrison, Grant, Frank Quitely, Hi-Fi Design, and Saida Temofonte. *New X-Men* #116. New York: Marvel Comics, 2001.
Morrison, Grant, Frank Quitely, Hi-Fi Design and Saida Temofonte. *New X-Men* #121. New York: Marvel Comics, 2002.
Morrison, Grant, Frank Quitely, Jamie Grant, and Travis Lanham. *All-Star Superman* #12. New York: DC Comics, 2008.
Morrison, Grant, Frank Quitely, John Stokes, Daniel Vozzo, Todd Klein, and Brian Bolland. *The Invisibles* 3 #1. New York: DC/Vertigo, 2000.
Morrison, Grant, Frank Quitely, Peter Doherty, and Ellie De Ville. *Flex Mentallo, Man of Muscle Mystery* #1–4. New York: DC/Vertigo, 1996.
Morrison, Grant, Frank Quitely, Tim Townsend, Brian Haberlin, and Saida Temofonte. *New X-Men* #114. New York: Marvel Comics, 2001.
Morrison, Grant, Frank Quitely, Tim Townsend, Chuck Chuckry, Richard Starkings, and Saida Temofonte. *New X-Men* #135. New York: Marvel Comics, 2003.
Morrison, Grant, Frazer Irving, Cameron Stewart, Chris Burnham, Alex Sinclair, Pat Brosseau, and Frank Quitely. *Batman and Robin* #16. New York: DC Comics, 2010.
Morrison, Grant, Freddie E. Williams II, Pascal Williams, Dave McCraig, and Phil Balsman. *Seven Soldiers: Mister Miracle* #4. New York: DC Comics, 2006.
Morrison, Grant, Howard Porter, John Dell, Pat Garrahy, and Ken Lopez. *JLA* #3. New York: DC Comics, 1997.
_____. *JLA* #4. New York: DC Comics, 1997.
_____. *JLA* #13. New York: DC Comics, 1998.
Morrison, Grant, J. G. Jones, Carlos Pacheco, Doug Mahnke, Marco Rudy, Christian Alamy, Jesús Merino, Alex Sinclair, Pete Pantazis, and Rob Clark. *Final Crisis* #6. New York: DC Comics, 2009.
Morrison, Grant, J. G. Jones, Matt Milla, Richard Starkings, and Wes Abbot. *Marvel Boy* #3. New York: Marvel, 2000.
Morrison, Grant, Jill Thompson, Daniel Vozzo, Clem Robins, and Sean Phillips. *The Invisibles* 1 #13. New York: DC/Vertigo, 1995.
Morrison, Grant, Jill Thompson, Dennis Cramer, Daniel Vozzo, Clem Robins, and Sean Phillips. *The Invisibles* 1 #5. New York: DC/Vertigo, 1995.

Grant, Kelley Jones, Mark McKenna, Daniel Vozzo, John Workman, and Simon Bisley. *Doom Patrol* #36. New York: DC Comics 1990.
Morrison, Grant, Keron Grant, Norm Rapmund, Chris Chuckry, Richard Starkings, and Saida Temofonte. *New X-Men* #134. New York: Marvel Comics, 2003.
Morrison, Grant, Lee Garbett, Trevor Scott, Guy Major, and Jared K. Fletcher. *Batman* #683. New York: DC Comics, 2008.
Morrison, Grant, Leinil Francis Yu, Gerry Alanguilan, Hi-Fi Design, Richard Starkings and Saida Temofonte. *New X-Men Annual*: 2001. New York: Marvel Comics, 2001.
Morrison, Grant, Marc Silvestri, Matt Banning, Joe Weems, Billy Tan, Steve Firchow, and Russ Wooton. *New X-Men* #151. New York: Marvel Comics, 2004.
Morrison, Grant, Marc Silvestri, Joe Weems, Billy Tan, Steve Firchow, Matt Milla, John Starr, and Chris Eliopoulos. *New X-Men* #152. New York: Marvel Comics, 2004.
Morrison, Grant, and Paul Grist. *St. Swithins Day* #1. Leicester: Trident Comics, April 1990.
Morrison, Grant, Pere Pérez, Lee Garbett, Alejandro Sicat, Walden Wong, Guy Major, and Jared K. Fletcher. *The Return of Bruce Wayne* #6. New York: DC Comics, 2010.
Morrison, Grant, Philip Bond, Daniel Vozzo, Todd Klein, and Brian Bolland. *The Invisibles* 3 #12. New York: DC/Vertigo, 2000.
Morrison, Grant, Philip Bond, David Hahn, and Todd Klein. *Vimanarama!* #3. New York: DC/Vertigo, 2005.
Morrison, Grant, Phil Jimenez, Andy Lanning, Chuck Chuckry, and Russ Wooton. *New X-Men* #147. New York: Marvel Comics, 2003.
Morrison, Grant, Phil Jimenez, John Stokes, Daniel Vozzo, Clem Robins, and Sean Phillips. *The Invisibles* 1 #17. New York: DC/Vertigo, 1996.
_____. *The Invisibles* 1 #18. New York: DC/Vertigo, 1996.
_____. *The Invisibles* 1 #19. New York: DC/Vertigo, 1996.
Morrison, Grant, Phil Jimenez, John Stokes, Daniel Vozzo, Todd Klein, and Brian Bolland. *The Invisibles* 2 #1. New York: DC/Vertigo, 1997.
_____. *The Invisibles* 2 #13. New York: DC/Vertigo, 1998.
Morrison, Grant, Richard Case, John Nyberg, Daniel Vozzo, John Workman, and Simon Bisley. *Doom Patrol* #27. New York: DC Comics, 1989.
_____. *Doom Patrol* #28. New York: DC Comics, 1989.
_____. *Doom Patrol* #29. New York: DC Comics, 1990.
Morrison, Grant, Richard Case, Scott Hanna, Michele Wolfman, John Workman, and Carlos Garzon. *Doom Patrol* #20. New York: DC Comics, 1989.
Morrison, Grant, Ryan Benjamin, Saleem Crawford, Guy Major, and Sal Cipriano. *Batman* #675. New York: DC Comics, 2008.
Morrison, Grant, Ryan Sook, Mick Gray, Nathan Eyring, and Dave Stewart. *Seven Soldiers: Zatanna* #4. New York: DC Comics, 2005.
Morrison, Grant, Ryan Sook, Pere Pérez, Mick Gray, Jose Villarrubia, Jared K. Fletcher, and Travis Lanham. *The Return of Bruce Wayne* #5. New York: DC Comics, 2010.
Morrison, Grant, Simone Bianchi, Dave Stewart, and Rob Leigh. *Seven Soldiers: Shining Knight* #2. New York: DC Comics, 2005.
Morrison, Grant, Sean Phillips, Jay Stephens, Daniel Vozzo, Todd Klein, and Brian Bolland. *The Invisibles* 3 #6. New York: DC/Vertigo, 1999.
_____. *The Invisibles* 3 #5. New York: DC/Vertigo, 2000.
Morrison, Grant, Steve Yeowell, Daniel Vozzo, Clem Robins, and Sean Phillips. *The Invisibles* 1 #1. New York: DC/Vertigo, 1994.
_____. *The Invisibles* 1 #2. New York: DC/Vertigo, 1994.
Morrison, Grant, Steve Yeowell, Daniel Vozzo, Todd Klein, and Brian Bolland. *The Invisibles* 3 #4. New York: DC/Vertigo, 2000.
_____. *The Invisibles* 3 #2. New York: DC/Vertigo, 2000.
_____. *New X-Men* #149. New York: Marvel Comics, 2003.
Morrison, Grant, and Tony O'Donnell. *Abraxas*. In *Sunrise* #1–2. Middlesex: Harrier Comics, 1987.
Morrison, Grant, Tony S. Daniel, Ian Hannin, and Travis Lanham. *Batman* #702. New York: DC Comics, 2010.

Morrison, Grant, Yanick Paquette, Chris Burnham, Lichael Lacombe, Scott Clark, Cameron Stewart, et al., *Batman, Incorporated*, 2 vols. New York: DC Comics, 2012–13.

Secondary Sources

Ault, Donald. "'Cutting Up' Again Part II: Lacan on Barks on Lacan." In *Comics & Culture: Analytical and Theoretical Approaches to Comics*. Edited by Anne Magnussen and Hans-Christian Christiansen, 123–140. Copenhagen: Museum Tusculanum Press, 2000.
Badiou, Alain. *Philosophy for Militants*. Translated by Bruno Bosteels. London: Verso, 2012. Kindle Edition.
Bainbridge, Jason. "Worlds Within Worlds." In Ndalianis, *The Contemporary Comic Book Superhero*, 64–86.
Bandura, Albert. "The Stormy Decade: Fact or Fiction?" *Psychology in the Schools* 1, no. 3 (1964): 224–31.
Barnes, Jonathan, ed. *The Complete Works of Aristotle: The Revised Oxford Translation*. Bollingen Series 71. 2 vols. Princeton: Princeton University Press, 1984.
Barthes, Roland. *Image, Music, Text*. Edited and translated by Richard Howard. London: Fontana, 1977.
Bartky, Sandra Lee. *Femininity and Domination: Studies in the Phenomenology of Oppression*. New York: Routledge, 1990.
Bataille, George. *Literature and Evil*. London: Penguin, 1957.
Blair, Tony, to Isaiah Berlin, October 23, 1997. In "Letters to Berlin." *The Isaiah Berlin Virtual Library*. Archived in http://berlin.wolf.ox.ac.uk/letterstoberlin.html.
Bloom, Harold, et al., *Deconstruction and Criticism*. New York: Continuum, 1995.
Brandes, Ian. "Death to Maggie: Book Sparks Tory Uproar." *The Sun*, March 19, 1990.
Brooker, Will. *Batman Unmasked*. London: Continuum, 2000.
Brown, Jeffrey A. *Black Superheroes, Milestone Comics, and Their Fans*. Jackson: University Press of Mississippi, 2001.
Bukatman, Scott. *Matters of Gravity: Special Effects and Supermen in the 20th Century*. Durham: Duke University Press, 2003.
———. "Secret Identity Politics." In Ndalianis, *The Contemporary Comic Book Superhero*, 109–25.
Burke, Sean. *The Death and Return of the Author: Criticism and Subjectivity in Barthes, Foucault, and Derrida*. Edinburgh: Edinburgh University Press, 2010.
Butler, Judith. *Bodies That Matter: On the Discursive Limits of "Sex."* New York: Routledge, 1993.
———. *Gender Trouble: Feminism and the Subversion of Identity*. New York: Routledge, 1999.
Callahan, Timothy. *Grant Morrison: The Early Years*. Edwardsville, IL: Sequart, 2007.
———. *Grant Morrison: The Early Years*. Edwardsville, IL: Sequart, 2012. Kindle Edition.
Carpenter, Humphrey. *A Great, Silly Grin: The British Satire Boom of the 1960s*. Cambridge: Da Capo Press, 2003.
Cartledge, Sue. "Fossil Bat Flew While Deaf: 52 Million-Year-Old Bat Could Fly But Not Echolocate." *American Museum of Natural History*. Accessed February 2014. http://www.suite101.com/content/fossil-bat-flew-while-deaf-a44696#ixzz1L8SaCO21.
Chomsky, Noam. *Aspects of the Theory of Syntax*. Cambridge: Massachusetts Institute of Technology, 1965.
Coe, Jonathan. "Sinking Giggling into the Sea." *London Review of Books* 35, no. 14 (2013): 30–31.
Connor, Steve. "The Shame of Being a Man." *Textual Practice* 15, no. 2 (2001): 211–30.
Cook, Roy T. "Canonicity and Normativity in Massive Serialized Collaborative Fiction." *The Journal of Aesthetics and Art Criticism* 71, no. 3 (2013): 271–6.
———. "Do Comics Require Pictures? Or Why *Batman* #663 Is a Comic." *The Journal of Aesthetics and Art Criticism* 69, no. 3 (2011): 285–296.

Coughlan, David. "The Naked Hero and Model Man: Costumed Identity in Comic Book Narratives." In *Heroes of Film, Comics and American Culture: Essays on Real and Fictional Defenders of Home*, edited by Lisa M. DeTora, 234–52. Jefferson, NC: McFarland, 2009.
Crangle, Sara, and Peter Nicholls, eds. *On Bathos: Literature, Art and Music*. London: Continuum, 2010.
Daniels, Les. *Superman: The Complete History: The Life and Times of the Man of Steel*. San Francisco: Chronicle, 2004.
_____. *Batman: The Complete History*. New York: Chronicle, 2004.
Dennett, Daniel C. *Consciousness Explained*. London: Penguin, 1993.
Derrida, Jacques. *Dissemination*. Translated by Barbara Johnson. London: Continuum, 2004.
De Voragine, Jacobus. *The Golden Legend*. Translated by Granger Ryan and Helmut Ripperger. Salem, MA: Ayer, 1991.
Dickens, Gregory. "Review: Flex Mentallo." *Popimage*. Accessed July 17, 2013. http://www.popimage.com/profile/morrison/012501flexrev.html.
Dyer, Richard. "The White Man's Muscles." In *The Masculinity Studies Reader*, edited by Rachel Adams and David Savran, 286–314. Oxford: Blackwell, 2002.
Eagleton, Terry. *After Theory*. London: Penguin, 2003.
_____. *On Evil*. New Haven: Yale University Press, 2010.
_____. *Reason, Faith, and Revolution*. New Haven: Yale University Press, 2009.
_____. *Why Marx Was Right*. New Haven: Yale University Press, 2011.
Easthope, Antony. *What a Man's Gotta Do: The Masculine Myth in Popular Culture*. New York: Routledge, 1990.
Eckert, Penelope. "Language And Adolescent Peer Groups." *Journal of Language and Social Psychology* 22, no.1 (March 2003): 112–18.
Eco, Umberto. *Kant and the Platypus: Essays on Language and Cognition*. Translated by Alastair McEwen. London: Vintage, 2000.
_____. "The Myth of Superman." *Diacritics* 2, no. 1 (1972): 14–22.
Edmundson, Mark. *Literature Against Philosophy, Plato to Derrida: A Defence of Poetry*. Cambridge: Cambridge University Press, 1995.
Eisner, Will. *Comics and Sequential Art*. Tamarac, FL: Poorhouse Press, 1985.
Eliot, T. S. "*Ulysses*, Order, and Myth." *The Dial* 75, no. 5 (Nov 1923): 480–83.
Eriksen, Thomas Hylland. *Small Places, Large Issues: An Introduction To Social and Cultural Anthropology*, 3d ed. Milton Keynes: Cram101, 2012.
Fink, Bruce. *The Lacanian Subject: Between Language and Jouissance*. Princeton: Princeton University Press, 1995.
Frazer, Sir James George. *The Golden Bough*. New York: Macmillan, 1963.
Genette, Gerard. *Narrative Discourse: An Essay in Method*. Ithaca: Cornell University Press, 1972.
Gillespie, Jim, dir. *Halfway to Paradise—Grant Morrison*. Glasgow: Big Star in a Wee Picture, 1988.
Greenblatt, Stephen. *Renaissance Self-Fashioning from More to Shakespeare*. Chicago: University of Chicago Press, 1980.
Groensteen, Thierry. "The Monstrator, The Recitant and The Shadow of The Narrator." *European Comic Art* 3, no. 1 (2010): 1–21.
_____. *The System of Comics*. Translated by Bart Beaty and Nick Nguyen. Jackson: University Press of Mississippi, 2009.
Guerber, H. A. *Myths of the Norsemen*. New York: Dover, 1992
Hacker, P. M. S. *Human Nature: The Categorial Framework*. Oxford: Wiley-Blackwell, 2010.
Hamilton, Charles (Frank Richards). "Frank Richards Replies to George Orwell, May 1940." In Angus and Davison, *A Patriot After All*, 79–85.
Hammond, Andrew. *British Fiction and the Cold War*. London: Palgrave Macmillan, 2013.
Harris, Jonathan Gil. *Foreign Bodies and the Body Politic: Discourses of Social Pathology in Early Modern England*. Cambridge: Cambridge University Press, 1998.
Harvey, A. D. "The Body Politic: Anatomy of a Metaphor." *Contemporary Review* 275, no. 1603 (1999): 85–93.

Bibliography

Hatfield, Charles, Jeet Heer, and Kent Worcester, eds. *The Superhero Reader*. Jackson: University Press of Mississippi, 2013.
Hauser, Marc D., Noam Chomsky, and W. Tecumseh Fitch, "The Faculty of Language: What Is It, Who Has It, and How Did It Evolve?" *Science* 298, no. 5598 (2002): 1569–1579.
Hayman, Ronald. *A Life of Jung*. London: Bloomsbury, 1999.
Healy, Margaret. *Fictions of Disease in Early Modern England: Bodies, Plagues and Politics*. Houndsmills, Basingstoke: Palgrave, 2001.
Hiatt, Brian. "Grant Morrison: Psychedelic Superhero." *Rolling Stone*, September 2011.
Hofstadter, Douglas. *Godel, Escher, Bach: An Eternal Golden Braid*. London: Penguin, 1979.
_____. *I Am a Strange Loop*. New York: Basic Books, 2007.
Holland, Catherine A. *The Body Politic: Foundings, Citizenship, and Difference in the American Political Imagination*. New York: Routledge, 2001.
Jeffords, Susan. *Hard Bodies: Hollywood Masculinity in the Reagan Era*. New Brunswick: Rutgers University Press, 1994.
Jenkins, Henry. "Just Men in Tights." In Ndalianis, *The Contemporary Comic Book Superhero*, 16–43.
Jones, Gerard. *Men of Tomorrow: Geeks, Gangsters and the Birth of the Comic Book*. New York: Basic Books, 2005. Kindle edition.
Jung, C. G. *Collected Works*. Edited by Herbert Read, Michael Fordham, and Gerald Adler. Translated by R. F. C. Hull. 20 vols. London: Princeton University Press, 1959–79.
_____. *Modern Man in Search of a Soul*. Translated by W. F. Dell and C. F. Baynes. London: Routledge and Kegan Paul, 1961.
Kenyon, John. *The History Men*, 2d ed. Weidenfeld & Nicolson, 1993.
Kerby, Anthony Paul. *Narrative and the Self*. Bloomington: Indiana University Press, 1991.
Kim, J. S. "Research and the Reading Wars." In *When Research Matters: How Scholarship Influences Education Policy*, edited by F. M. Hess, 89–111. Cambridge: Harvard Education Press, 2008.
Klock, Geoff. *How to Read Superhero Comics and Why*. New York: Continuum, 2002.
Kristeva, Julia. *Powers of Horror: An Essay on Abjection*. New York: Columbia University Press, 1982.
Lacan, Jacques. *Joyce and the Sinthome: The Seminar of Jacques Lacan, Book XXIII*. Translated by Luke Thurston. Unpublished manuscript, 1975–1976.
_____. *The Psychoses: The Seminar of Jacques Lacan, Book III* (1955–1956). Translated by Russell Grigg. London: Routledge, 1993.
Laing, R. D. *The Divided Self*. London: Routledge, 1999.
Lendrum, Rob. "The Super Black Macho, One Baaad Mutha: Black Superhero Masculinity in 1970s Mainstream Comic Books." *Extrapolation* 46, no. 3 (2005): 360–72.
Lewis, Helen Block. "Shame and the Narcissistic Personality." In *The Many Faces of Shame*, edited by Donald L. Nathanson, 93–132. New York: Guilford Press, 1987.
MacDonald, Ian. *Revolution in the Head: The Beatles' Records and the Sixties*. London: Vintage, 2008.
MacKinnon, Kenneth. *Uneasy Pleasures: The Male as Erotic Object*. London: Cygnus Arts, 1997.
Maggi, Armando. *In the Company of Demons*. Chicago: University of Chicago Press, 2008.
Mandelbrot, Benoît, *The Fractal Geometry of Nature*. New York: W.H. Freeman & Co., 1982.
Maynard, Patrick. *Drawing Distinctions: The Varieties of Graphic Expression*. Ithaca: Cornell University Press, 2005.
McAfee, Noëlle. *Julia Kristeva*. New York: Routledge, 2004.
McCloud, Scott. *Understanding Comics*. New York: Kitchen Sink, 1993.
_____. *Understanding Comics: The Invisible Art*. New York: Harper Perennial, 1994.
Meaney, Patrick, dir. *Grant Morrison: Talking with Gods*. New York: Respect! Films, 2010.
_____. *Our Sentence Is Up: Seeing Grant's Morrison's The Invisibles*. Edwardsville, IL: Sequart, 2010. Kindle edition.

Miller, J. Hillis. "The Critic as Host." In Harold Bloom et al., *Deconstruction and Criticism*, 217–53.
Miller, Jacques-Alain. "Teachings of the Case Presentation." In *Returning to Freud: Clinical Psychoanalysis in the School of Lacan*, edited and translated by Stuart Schneiderman, 42–52. New Haven: Yale University Press, 1980.
Murray, Christopher. "Invisible Symmetries: Superheroes, Grant Morrison and Isaiah Berlin's Two Concepts of Liberty." *Studies in Comics* 4.2 (2013): 277–306.
_____. "More Space Combat! An Interview with Grant Morrison." *Studies in Comics* 4.2 (2013): 219–34.
_____. "Subverting the Sublime: Romantic Ideology in the Comics of Grant Morrison." In *Sub/versions: Cultural Status, Genre and Critique*, edited by Pauline MacPherson, Christopher Murray, Gordon Spark and Kevin Corstophine, 34–51. Newcastle: Cambridge Scholars, 2008.
Ndalianis, Angela, ed. *The Contemporary Comic Book Superhero*. New York: Routledge, 2009.
Neighly, Patrick, and Kereth Cowe-Spigai. *Anarchy for the Masses: The Disinfomation Guide to the Invisibles*. New York: Mad Yak Press, 2003.
Nicholl, Charles. *The Chemical Theatre*. London: Routledge & Kegan Paul, 1980.
Orwell, George. "Boys' Weeklies." In Angus and Davison, *A Patriot After All*, 57–78.
Rauch, Stephen. "We Have All Been Sentenced: Language as a Means of Control in Grant Morrison's *The Invisibles*." *International Journal of Comic Art* 6, no. 2 (2004): 350–63.
Robertson, Robin. *C. G. Jung and the Archetypes of the Collective Unconscious*. New York: Peter Lang, 1987.
_____. *Introducing Jungian Psychology*. Dublin: New Leaf, 1992.
Ross, Colin. *The CIA Doctors: Human Rights Violations by American Psychiatrists*. Richardson, TX: Manitou Communications, 2006.
Ryan, Marie-Laure. *Narrative as Virtual Reality: Immersion and Interactivity in Literature and Electronic Media*. Baltimore: Johns Hopkins University Press, 2001.
Schumacher, Michael. *A Dreamer's Life in Comics*. New York: Bloomsbury, 2010.
Scivally, Bruce. *Billion Dollar Batman*. Wilmette, IL: Henry Gray, 2011. Kindle edition.
Segal, Lynne. "Back to the Boys? Temptations of the Good Gender Theorist." *Textual Practice* 15, no. 2 (2001): 231–50.
_____. *Slow Motion: Changing Masculinities, Changing Men*. London: Virago, 1990.
Segal, Robert A. *Jung on Mythology*. Princeton: Princeton University Press, 1998.
Sharp, Daryl. *Personality Types: Jung's Model of Typology*. Toronto: Inner City Books, 1987.
Short, Robert. *Dada and Surrealism*. London: Octopus Books, 1980.
Singer, Marc. *Grant Morrison: Combining the Worlds of Contemporary Comics*. Jackson: University Press of Mississippi, 2012.
Smith, Huston. *The Religions of Man*. New York: Harper & Row, 1986.
Sonne, Paul and Alistair Macdonald. "In the Longest-Running Joke in Politics, Life Imitates Farce." *The Wall Street Journal*. May 6, 2010.
Stevens, Anthony. *On Jung*, 2d ed. London: Penguin, 1999.
Streib, Heinz. "Magical Feeling and Thinking in Childhood and Adolescence: A Developmental Perspective." *British Journal of Religious Education* 16, no. 2 (1994): 70–81.
Sutherland, Keston. "What is Bathos?" In Crangle and Nicholls, *On Bathos*, 7–26.
Thacker, Eugene. "*Nomos, Nosos* and *Bios*." In "Biopolitics," edited by Melinda Cooper, Andrew Goffey, and Anna Munster. *Culture Machine* 7, Special Issue (2005), http://www.culturemachine.net/index.php/cm/article/view/25/32.
Theweleit, Klaus. *Male Fantasies 2, Male Bodies: Psychoanalyzing the White Terror*. Translated by Erica Carter and Chris Turner with Stephen Conway. Cambridge: Polity Press, 1989.
Thomas, Calvin. *Male Matters: Masculinity, Anxiety, and the Male Body on the Line*. Urbana: University of Illinois Press, 1996.
_____. *Masculinity, Psychoanalysis, Straight Queer Theory: Essays on Abjection in Literature, Mass Culture, and Film*. New York: Palgrave Macmillan, 2008.

Tunnell, Michael O., and James S. Jacobs. "Using 'Real' Books: Research Findings on Literature Based Reading Instruction." *The Reading Teacher* 42, no. 7 (1989): 470–7.
Turner, E. S. *Boys Will Be Boys*. London: Penguin, 1975.
Tyler May, Elaine. *Homeward Bound: American Families in the Cold War Era*. New York: Basic Books, 2008.
Verhaeghe, Paul. *On Being Normal and Other Disorders: A Manual for Clinical Psychodiagnostics*. Translated by Sigi Jottkandt. London: Karnak, 2008.
Von Franz, Marie-Louise, and James Hillman. *Lectures on Jung's Typology*. Woodstock, CT: Spring Publications, 1998.
Walker, Steven F. *Jung and the Jungians on Myth*. New York: Garland, 1995.
Waller, Alison. *Constructing Adolescence in Fantastic Realism*. London: Routledge, 2011.
Walton, Kendall L. *Mimesis as Make-Believe: On the Foundations of the Representational Arts*. Cambridge: Harvard University Press, 1990; rpt., 1993.
Ward, Stuart. *British Culture and the End of Empire*. Manchester: Manchester University Press, 2001.
Wertham, Fredric. *Seduction of the Innocent*. London: Museum Press, 1955.
Wittgenstein, Ludwig. *On Certainty*. Edited by G. E. M. Anscombe and G. H. von Wright. Translated by Denis Paul and G. E. M. Anscombe. New York and London: Harper & Row, 1972.
Wolk, Douglas. *Reading Comics: How Graphic Novels Work and What They Mean*. Cambridge: Da Capo Press, 2007.
Wright, Nicky. *The Classic Era of American Comics*. London: Prion Books, 2000.
Žižek, Slavoj. *Living in the End Times*. London: Verso, 2011. Kindle edition.

About the Contributors

David **Coughlan** is a lecturer in English at the School of Languages, Literature, Culture and Communication at the University of Limerick, Ireland. He has published on contemporary American fiction and graphic narrative in the journals *Derrida Today*, *College Literature*, *Critique* and *Modern Fiction Studies*, and in a number of edited collections.

Roy T. **Cook** is an associate professor of philosophy at the University of Minnesota, Twin Cities. He specializes in the philosophy of mathematics, the philosophy of logic, mathematical logic and the aesthetics of popular art (especially comics). He is the co-founder of the comics theory blog *Pencil, Panel, Page* (www.pencilpanelpage.wordpress.com).

Nicholas **Galante** recently completed an M.Phil in popular literature at Trinity College Dublin. He presented "Our Father, Who Art in Gotham" at Trinity's conference on Grant Morrison in September 2012. This is his first publication.

Darragh **Greene** lectures in Middle English literature at University College Dublin. He has published various essays on medieval English literature, including Chaucer, as well as later authors, such as Shakespeare. His research interests are wide-ranging, stretching from medieval studies to comics studies.

Schedel **Luitjen**, a Classicist and Latin translator, graduated from the University of Edinburgh with an M.A. in Latin and divinity and an M.Sc. in classics. He has contributed several Latin translations to Smith and Press (thelibraryconnection.net). His research focuses on late antique Latin literature and Renaissance Latin literature. He also maintains a superhero audio drama podcast, *The New Hero BLOB Adventures* (heroblob.wordpress.com).

Chris **Murray** is a senior lecturer in English and film studies and head of the department at the University of Dundee. He runs the UK's first comics studies M.Litt program and teaches several modules on comics at the undergraduate level. He is the author of a monograph on superhero comics and propaganda and researches the British superhero.

Emmet **O'Cuana**, a freelance writer and editor, contributes film reviews and articles to *Filmink* magazine, has had short fiction published by *Aurealis* magazine and has written comic scripts for Darren Close's cult comic *Killeroo*, the horror anthology *Decay, Outré* and *Home Brew Vampire Bullets*. He is the host of a podcast on Australian comics and creators called "Beardy and the Geek" and a regular guest on Joy 94.9's weekly "Sci-Fi and Squeam."

Muireann **O'Sullivan** is a Ph.D. candidate at Trinity College Dublin, where she studies the use of surrealism to combat authority in post-war British fiction. Her research interests include popular science fiction, fantasy and horror literature. She also has an interest in the use of comic books and video games in gifted and special education.

Clare **Pitkethly** is a Ph.D. candidate at the University of Melbourne, Australia, writing her dissertation on language in the work of Grant Morrison. She has published several articles on comics, in journals including *Animation: An Interdisciplinary Journal* and *the Journal of Graphic Novels and Comics* and in Angela Ndalianis's edited book, *The Contemporary Comic Book Superhero*.

Kate **Roddy** is an occasional lecturer at Trinity College Dublin and University College Dublin. She wrote her Ph.D. thesis on Tudor polemic 1528–1563 and has since published on Protestant martyrologies, Marian literature, and gender and sexuality in comic book fandom. Her article "Eternal Superteens and Mutant Spermatozoa: Grant Morrison and the Comic as Porneau" is forthcoming in a 2015 issue of the journal *ImageTexT*.

Keith **Scott** is a senior lecturer in English language at De Montfort University in Leicester, where is a member of the university's Centre for Cyber Security. He has worked in several disciplines, including foreign languages, American studies, English literature and English as a foreign language. His research interests lie at the intersection of language, culture and belief, with a particular interest in questions of rhetoric, persuasion and behavior modification.

Index

Numbers in **_bold italics_** indicate pages with photographs.

abjection 115–17, 119, 121, 123–7; see also Kristeva, Julia
Abraxas (comic) 27, **_29_**
Achilles 139
Action Comics 2, 4, 85, 216
aliens 27, 30, 47, 57, 139, 181, 206
All-Star Superman 5, 7, 12, 95, 131–3, 135–47, 186–93, 197, 202, 215–7
Amis, Kingsley 88
Animal Man (character) 4–5, 45–6, 48–51, 64, 66–73, 89, 91–2, 101–2
Animal Man (comic) 7, 11, 21, 23–24, 39–40, 45, 47–8, 50, 52–3, 55, 60, 64–72, 74–6, 78–9, 100–1
anti-climax 43–5, 48, 52–3, 57, 60; see also bathos
antihero 1, 3
Anti-Life Equation 90, 139, 164
Apollo 92
Apuleius 155–6, 164*n*27
archetypes 1, 7, 58, 131, 133–41, 144–5, 147, 155–6, 167, 190; see also Jung, Carl Gustav; Plato
Aristotle 143
Arkham Asylum 26, 166, 168–77, 179, 185–6, 189, 193–9, 201
Atlas, Charles 8, 88
Augustine, Saint 156–57, 164*n*29
authority 12, 58, 60–1, 65, 74–7, 86, 118, 122, 172, 183–202, 208, 215–9
authorship 8–11, 13, 17–18, 43, 60–1, 64–80, 80*n*6, 96, 102, 214–9
Azzarello, Brian 68

Badiou, Alain 210
Bainbridge, Jason 198
Baptist, John the 90
Barbelith 25, 39–41, 130*n*93
Barrie, J.M. 88
Barry, Sebastian 139
Barthes, Roland 65, 74–77, 81*n*29
Bartky, Sandra Lee 122
The Bat Whispers 197
bathos 43–61; see also anti-climax
Batman (character) 4–5, 7, 12, 48, 53, 71, 84, 88–9, 94, 96, 115, 150–64, 166–81, 185–6, 193–202, 206–7, 211–2, 214
Batman (comic) 7, 84, 100, 108, 150–1, 156–7, 159–60, 173–5
Batman and Robin (comic) 11, 84, 151–4, 168, 212
Batman and Robin (film) 159
Batman Begins (film) 160
Batman, Incorporated 7, 11, 150, 158, 160, 163, 178–81, 185–6, 195, 198–201, 205, 211–4, 218
Batman: The Return of Bruce Wayne 11, 150, 159, 162, 178–9, 181, 213
The Beano 83
Benjamin, Jessica 118
Bergman, Ingmar 39
Berlin, Isaiah 208
Bey, Hakim 87
Billion Dollar Batman 214
Bisley, Simon 69
Black Adam 75–76
Black Alice 27, **_29_**, 30
Blair, Tony 207–208
Blake, William 36–37, 83, 142
Boethius, Anicius Manlius Severus 131
Bolland, Brian 104
Bond, James 185
Borges, Jorge Luis 7
The Brave and the Bold 84
Bronze Age 2
the Brotherhood of Dada **_22_**, 23, 51, 55–7
Brown, Jeffrey A. 119–20
Bruno, Giordano 4, 6
Bukatman, Scott 116
Burnham, Chris 11
Burton, Tim 84
Busiek, Kurt 146
Butler, Judith 116–7, 120, 124
B'wana Beast 48, 55
Byrne, John 211

Callahan, Timothy 21, 43, 184, 187
capitalism 54, 58, 205, 208
Captain Marvel 5, 37, 88, 93–4, 211
Carroll, Lewis 36, 169
Case, Richard 11

Casey, Joe 211–2
Castiglione, Baldassare 5
The Catcher in the Rye 207
Chapman, Mark David 207
Chomsky, Noam 24–5
Chopra, Deepak 95
Christianity 168, 170–2, 190, 192
the CIA 151
Claremont, Chris 211
Clifford, Martin 92; *see also* Hamilton, Charles
Coe, Jonathan 56
the Cold War 12, 183–7, 189–90, 193–8, 201–2
Colden, Kevin 21
Comics Code Authority 2
Confessions (Augustine) 156–7, 165n30
Connor, Steve 122
continuity 4, 53, 65–72, 76–80, 81n25, 151, 154
Crafty Coyote 45, 61, 64, 67–72, 79, 81n22, 81n25
Crangle, Sara 54
Crazy Jane 49, 51
Cronos 88
Crowley, Aleister 169, 197

Dadaism 53–6, 60
Dalí, Salvador 63n61
The Dandy 83
Daniels, Les 190
Danny the Street 49–51
The Dark Knight Returns 3, 36, 94, 169, 173; *see also* Miller, Frank
Darkseid 139, 154–62, 165n49, 168, 173, 176–78
DC Comics (publisher) 2, 45, 52, 57, 61, 64, 84, 131, 155–6, 191, 205, 208, 212, 214
DC Comics universe 7, 45–6, 53, 115, 152, 155–6, 163, 176, 215
DC One Million 217
death 7, 12, 45, 48, 60, 77, 79–80, 89, 125, 131–2, 135–44, 146, 150, 154, 157, 159–60, 162, 166–9, 172, 174–8, 180, 188, 196, 200, 216–7
Delacourt, Sir Miles 90
Demian 138, 148n31
demiurge 45, 215
Dee, John 6
Dennett, Daniel 82
Derrida, Jacques 130n76
de Sade, Marquis 205, 219
Detective Comics 84, 213
the Devil 39, 45, 139, 150–5, 157, 160–61, 163, 170–2
Dick, Philip K. 82
Dickens, Gregory 94
The Discoverie of Witchcraft 151
Ditko, Steve 2

Doniger, Wendy 198
Doom Patrol (comic) 11, 21, **22**, 23, 26, 43–4, 48–53, 55–7, 60–1, 69, 100, 102
the Doom Patrol (team) 4, 49–52, 55–57
drugs 71, 110n23, 120, 206
dualism 41, 210, 219
Dwyer, Kieron 151
Dyer, Richard 115

Eagleton, Terry 135, 142–3
Eckert, Penelope 87
Eco, Umberto 47, 148n63
Edmundson, Mark 145
Eisenhower, Dwight D. 86
Eisner, Will 10, 85, 215
Eliot, T.S. 133
Ellis, Warren 18, 90; *see also* Planetary
Ellsworth, Whitney 214
Emerson, Ralph Waldo 129n74
Ennis, Garth 18
Erasmus, Desiderius 5

Feely, Greg 115–8, 120, 122–6, 127n15, 129n68, 217–8; *see also* Ned Slade
Ficino, Marsilio 4, 161
fiction suits 37–40
The Filth 11, 26, 39, 100, 108, 115–26, 128n61, 129n68, 129n74, 130n93, 215–8
Final Crisis 83, 90, 139, 150, 155, 157–9, 168, 176–7
Finger, Bill 214
Fitch, William Tecumseh Sherman 25
The Flash (character) 2, 37, 66, 191
The Flash (comic) 66
Flex Mentallo (character) 8, **38**, 39, 69, 84, 88, 94
Flex Mentallo (comic) 5, 21, 24–6, 37, **38**, 39–40, 93–4, 126, 187
The Fourth World 155–6, 158
Fox, Ruby, 33, 35
fractals 22
Fraction, Matt 206
Frazer, Sir James 167

Gaiman, Neil 184
Gawain and the Green Knight, Sir 139
The Gem 91
gender: fluidity 195; masculinity 8, 50–2, 115–6, 118–21, 123, 196
Genesis, The Book of 157
Genette, Gérard 19
genre conventions 35, 44, 47, 50, 53, 56, 198
Gillen, Kieron 206
God 6–7, 92, 94, 126, 131–33, 142, 153, 157–8, 161, 167, 170–1, 173
the Golden Age 2, 47, 66
The Golden Bough 167
Gotham City 84, 151, 166, 170, 176, 178, 180–1, 193–4, 196, 200, 212–3
Grant, Jamie 189

Index

Greenblatt, Stephen 6–7
Groensteen, Thierry 20, 23, 26, 30, 33, 35
Guevara, Che 209–10, 220n20

Hamilton, Charles 92
Harris, Jonathan Gill 123
Harvey, William 8
Hauser, Marc D. 25
Hayman, Ronald 133
Healy, Margaret 123
Hector 139
Hesiod 2
Hesse, Hermann 138
Hickman, Jonathan 206
Hinckley, John 207
Hinduism 168
Hine, Phil 89
Hofstadter, Douglas 18, 23, 41
Holinshed, Raphael 4
Holland, Catherine A. 123, 129n74
Homer 156
homophobia 195
Horace 133
horror 2, 86–88, 91, 218
Hughes, Rian 205, 208
Hughes, Spartacus 118, 120–2, 124, 217
humanism 7, 8
Humboldt, Wilhelm von 24
humor 44, 87, 94

Iamblichus 155
iconoclasm, 44, 54, 56, 60, 87
The Iliad 139
Incredible Hulk (comic) 3
The Invisibles (comic) 5–6, 11, 13, 22, 24–7, 39–41, 68, 84, 89–92, 95–6, 100, 103–4, *105*, 106–7, 109, 110n28, 111n34, 126, 185, 205–6, 208, 214–15, 218, 219n
The Invisibles (team) 206, 88, 89–91
Irving, Frazer 11

Jeffords, Susan 52, 194, 196
Jesus Christ, 40, 157, 165n46, 168–9, 170–2, 190, 218
Jimenez, Phil 11, 100, *105*
JLA (comic) 11, 131, 173, 177, 191, 215
JLA: Earth 2 53
The JLE 51
The Joker 154, 160, 170, 172, 176, 181, 194–8, 201
Jor-El 202, 142–4, 188
Jung, Carl Gustav 7, 11, 88, 131–147, 169, 193, 197, 200; *the Unconcious* 133–7, 139–41
The Justice League of America 51–3, 60, 155, 173, 179, 191, 213

Kal-El *see* Superman
Kane, Bob 84, 214
Karadžić, Radovan 210

Kathmandu 71, 79
Kent, Clark *see* Superman
Kent, Ma and Pa 138, 190
Key 17 24, 104
The Killing Joke 169, 173
King, Stephen 88
King Mob 8, 24, 39, 41, 68–9, 80n17, 106, 206, 214
Kirby, Jack 2, 58, 155–6, 158
Kristeva, Julia 116–7, 119, 121, 124–5
Kubrick, Stanley 124

Lacan, Jaques 100–9
Laius 88
Lane, Lois 137, 141–2, 190
Leary, Timothy 206, 219n5
Lee, Stan 2–3
Leonardo da Vinci 142
Lilo (character) 141, 191
Lincoln, Abraham 73, 93
Longinus 44, 54
Lovecraft, H.P. 83, 87, 161
Lucifer 154; *see also* the Devil
Ludlum, Robert 33
Luke, Gospel of 153
Luthor, Lex 53, 137–40, 142, 185, 188–90, 192–4, 217

Machiavelli, Niccolò 5
MacNeice, Louis 90
magic 5–6, 8, 11, 17, 24–5, 37, 39, 68, 83, 85, 89–90, 93–5, 152–53, 174, 206, 209, 220n17
The Magnet 91
Magneto 209–11
Magritte, René 55
Man of Steel (film) 216
Mandala (character) *see* St. John, Peter
Mandelbrot, Benoît 22
manga 33, 86, 160
Marvel Boy 209
Marvel Comics 2, 191, 205, 208
Marxism 208
Masterman 30, *32*, 35–6
The Matrix 40
Matthew, Gospel of 171
Maximan 30, *32*, 35
May, Elaine Tyler 195
McAfee, Noëlle 117
McCloud, Scott 10, 20, 25–6, 33, 111n37, 111n42
McGowan, Dane *see* Jack Frost
McKean, Dave 170, 172, 189, 193
McKenna, Terence 95
McMillan, Graeme 84
Meaney, Patrick 92, 219n5
metatextuality, 7, 35, 37, 39, 45, 52, 56, 58, 60, 64, 66, 78, 83, 177
Metropolis 80n19, 137, 216
Michael, St. Archangel, 170–1

Millar, Mark 18
Miller, Frank 1, 3, 18, 36, 47, 84, 94, 169
Miller, J. Hillis 124
Milligan, Peter 151–2
Miracleman 211–2
The Monster Raving Loony Party 56, 63n67
Moorcock, Michael 40
Moore, Alan 1, 3, 18, 22, 36, 47, 69, 80n19, 82, 143, 146, 169, 184, 211, 212
Morrison, Grant: authorial avatars 7–8, 21, 36, 45–9, 60, 64–80, 80n17, 81n21, 206; biography 6, 68, 71, 125, 183–4, 186–7, 189, 209, 215; career 4–10, 27, 41, 61, 82, 83, 101, 184–5, 204–7; on comics 3, 12, 17, 30–3, 35, 40, 47, 49, 66, 69, 92, 122, 125–6, 129n68, 131–2, 188–9, 191, 197, 201–2, 206, 213, 215–6; influences 21–4, 55, 66, 84, 89, 95, 150–64, 167–9, 174–5, 184, 197, 209
Müller, Friedrich Max 133
multiverse 7, 66, 84
myth 3, 5, 27, 83, 132–6, 139, 144–7, 155–6, 163, 166–9, 178, 188, 191, 215, 219

National Comics (publisher) 214; *see also* DC Comics
Near Myths 27, *28*, 40
Neoplatonism 4–5, 144, 155–6, 158, 161
The New Gods 155–6, 162
The New Statesman 205
The New Testament 171
New X-Men 100, 107, 111n38, 205, 209–11, 213–4, 218
Nicholls, Peter 54
Nixon, Richard 212
nostalgia 3, 47, 60, 146

Odin 169, 174
O'Donnell, Tony 27, *29*, 30
Odysseus 139
The Odyssey 139
Oedipus 88
Old Testament 172
On Free Choice of Will (Augustine) 157
O'Neill, Denny 84
Orwell, George 91
Ostrander, John 75–9, 81
Ovid 2

The Painting That Ate Paris *22*, 23, 51
Parker, Peter *see* Spider-Man
Payne, Dr. 36–7
Petrarch 5
Picabia, Francis 54
Pico della Mirandola, Giovanni 4, 6, 143–4, 161, 167
Planetary 90; *see also* Ellis, Warren
Plato 123, 131, 154–61
Platonism 154–60; *see also* Neoplatonism

Plotinus 155, 165n29
Politics 1, 11–12, 18, 55–6, 132–3, 135–5, 144, 146, 185, 207–9, 211, 218; body politic 122–5, 129n74
Polyphemus 139
Pope, Alexander 44–5, 53–4, 61
Porphyrius 155
Porter, Howard 11
Proclus 155
Pseudomonarchia Daemonum 151

Quintilian 5
Quintum, Leo 137–8, 140–1, 143, 186
Quitely, Frank 10, *21*, 37, *38*, 189

Rabinbach, Anson 118
Ragged Robin 39, 103, 106
Ratigan, Dylan 92
realism 3, 47, 61, 93
Rebis (character) 23, 43, 49–52
The Reformation 50
Renaissance 2–8, 11, 18–9, 94, 145, 161, 191
Revelation, Book of 170–1
revisionism 47, 146
Richards, Frank *see* Hamilton, Charles
Richards, Hilda *see* Hamilton, Charles
The Riddler 37
Ripley, George 6
Robertson, Robin 134, 137, 139–40
Rolling Stone 216
Rorschach test 194
Ryan, Marie-Laure 19

Sage, Wally 37, 39, 94
St. John, Peter 35–6
St. Swithin's Day 207–8
Salinger, J.D. 207
Satan 152–4, 160–1, 171; *see also* the Devil
Satire 44, 56–7, 61, 183–4, 195, 217
The Scarlatti Inheritance 33
Scivally, Bruce 214
Scot, Reginald 152
Seaguy 11
Sebastian O 11, 89
Segal, Lynne 120
Seuss, Dr. 96
The Seven Soldiers of Victory 11, 57–8, 59, 60–1, 100, 108–9, 139
The Seventh Seal 39
Shakespeare, William 4, 145
Shelley, Percy Bysshe 92
Shuster, Joe 95, 190, 214–6
Sidney, Sir Philip 5
Siegel, Jerry 95, 190, 214–6
Silver Age 2–4, 47, 49, 66, 84, 94, 146
Singer, Marc 9, 47, 58, 93, 111n35, 123, 129n68, 129n74, 135, 184–5, 208
Sixtus, St. 173
Sneddon, Laura 205
Snyder, Zack 216

Index

Spider-Man 2–3, 88
Stargrave, Gideon 27, 40
Steele, Cliff 43, 49–51, 55, 61
Stewart, Cameron 11
Streib, Heinz 90
The Sublime 44–5, 54, 132
Suicide Squad (comic) 65, 75–80
The Sun 207
Sunrise (Harrier Comics) 27
The Supercontext 40–1
Supergods 3, 92, 131–2, 167, 177, 187, 191, 201, 215, 218, 220n19
Superman 2, 4–5, 7–8, 12, 50–1, 53, 67, 70, 84, 86, 88, 90, 92–5, 115, 131–2, 135–47, 171, 181, 184–94, 197, 199–200, 202, 206, 214–8
surrealism 55, 169
Sutherland, Keston 43
Swamp Thing 3
symbolism 11, 12, 25, 145, 153, 166–7, 172, 175, 177, 180, 192, 193

Talking with Gods 82, 186, 188
Taylor, Sir Teddy 207
Thatcher, Margaret 207, 211–2
theology 156–7, 167, 190
Theweleit, Klaus 118, 121
Thomas, Calvin 117, 121, 126
Thoreau, Henry David 129n74
Thunderstone, Max 108, 115–6, 118–20, 122–3, 127n15
Trident Comics (publisher) 207
Truog, Chaz 11, 69–70, 81n22
Turner, E.S. 86
Tzara, Tristan 54–55; *see also* Dadaism

the Ultrasphinx 141–2
Utopianism 12, 122, 129n68, 129n74, 206, 209, 218

Vergil 156
Vesalius, Andreas 8

Vimanarama! 5, 110n28
violence 3, 45, 47–8, 53, 60, 87, 107, 115, 119–22, 169, 170, 173, 175–7, 180, 195, 206, 210–1, 216, 218
Voltage (character) *see* Fox, Ruby

the Wachowskis 40
Waid, Mark 146
Walton, Kendall 18, 65, 73
Ward, Stuart 183
Warhol, Andy 205
Watchmen 3, 36, 143, 146, 149n71, 211–2; *see also* Moore, Alan
Way, Gerard 206
Wayne, Bruce *see* Batman
Wayne, Martha 88
Wayne, Thomas 88
Weisinger, Otto 216
Weyer, Johan 152
Wildcats 211–2
Williams, J.H., III 58
Wittgenstein, Ludwig 134, 145
Wolk, Douglas 83, 85, 149n71, 197
Wonder Woman 53, 115, 171
World War I 54
World War II 30, 33, 184, 191, 220n19

X-Men (team) 2–3, 107–8; *see also* New X-Men

Yeowell, Steve 11, 30, *31–2*, 33, *34*, 35

Zatara, Zatanna 57–58, *59*, 60
Zenith (character) 7, 33, 35–7, 84
Zenith (comic) 11, 26, 30, *31–2*, 33, *34*, 35–7, 40, 83, 208
Zeus 88, 156
Žižek, Slavoj 210–11
Zur-En-Arrh, Batman of 159, 175–6

www.ingramcontent.com/pod-product-compliance
Ingram Content Group UK Ltd.
Pitfield, Milton Keynes, MK11 3LW, UK
UKHW041939140426
5217IPUK00014B/572